Pearl at a Great Price

Pearl at a Great Price

Theresa H. Raffael

Companion Press
P.O. Box 310
Shippensburg, PA 17257-0310

"Good Stewards of the
Manifold Grace of God"

ISBN 1-56043-559-3

For Worldwide Distribution
Printed in the U.S.A.

Dedication

Pearl at a Great Price is dedicated to Claire D. Stratford who was my therapist for over three years in the 1970's. Despite everything, she never once gave up on me. Many others had, and many Christians felt there was no help for me in God. I tried in vain to prove she was like everyone else I had met. I even went so far as to report her to the State Department of Mental Health and to Washington, D.C. What I did was lie to these agencies about her to prove she was like everyone else. Of course I did, after the fact, admit to these agencies I had lied. Through it all she hung in there, and after much prayer she has to be the person I dedicate this book to. Thank you, Claire, for caring and showing me that I could become a productive, useful, stable, God-centered person, so this book could go forth.

Acknowledgments

There are many people who have served as various instruments in my life. To name them all would require another book, so with God's guidance I will name a few. First and foremost I want to acknowledge my daughter Debi and my son-in-law Alan who gave me four beautiful grandchildren: Jennifer, Ryan, Shawn, and Jason Coombs. I have the opportunity to be to them what I could not be to my own children. Thanks also goes to Jeanne Conway, a public health nurse who with fear and trepidation brought me the good news of Jesus back in 1970; to Dorrene Russell, who God used in many ways to show me that the arm of flesh would eventually fail me and that I was to depend on Him; to Dr. Warren Litts who has been my doctor for 17 years and has blessed me in countless ways; to Nancy Alheim, Charles Russell, Kathy and Ron Keeney, my brother Freddy and his wife Pauline, Cecelia Monaco, and Kathy Yashencik.

Thanks and special remembrance goes to Julia Steyn and Josephine Lucas my recently deceased friends. Appreciation also goes to Dr. Arlene Knoblauch, Earl Wallace, and Elmire Figliuolo who I am privileged to have write my foreword. She spent countless hours correcting 951 pages of my manuscript. Thanks to Yvonne Porter who is a published writer and read some of my book. She told me the one reason this book would be published was because I was a *"survivor"* and she felt that should be the title. She doesn't know my Jesus yet but I am believing God to make Himself real to this kind and lovely lady. Please forgive me for inadvertently leaving out others but I thank God for each person who has ever prayed for me or said a kind word to help me press on, but most of all I give a great big thank you to my precious Daddy God.

The author can be reached at the following address:
P.O. Box 2391
Ballston Spa, NY 12020

Contents

Foreword

"Oh you know, when it comes to pearls, it's very seldom there isn't some shady story behind them."

The Photographer's Missus by Colette

Little did I know when I began reading Pearl Theresa Raffael's autobiography that I was going to learn many shady details about her life. I wondered why she was revealing the secret details of some of her life's worst periods, until it became clear that her book is about the formation of a pearl within the shell of her existence.

The unfortunate experiences of her young life seemed to be part of the plan to strengthen her soul, as preparation for the violent storms of her adult life. Although battered by the adversities of circumstances, hardships, illnesses, depression, and unjust and inhumane treatment, she overcame every hurdle.

When life becomes overwhelming, too frequently people choose to "opt out" by taking drugs, or by committing suicide. *Pearl at a Great Price* is a book of hope, or inspiration, and of strong belief in the reality of the ever-present God. It also demonstrates that the world has its supply of people who care and who are willing to help those who are struggling in the depths of their personal hells.

Pearl at a Great Price will lead the reader through the murky tunnels of the author's sometimes desperate existence, which finally bursts forth into the bright sunlight of truth. Perseverance and belief in the triumph of righteousness held Theresa together when all seemed very dismal.

Theresa has been able to weave throughout her life story the thread of the grace of a God who never forsook her, and who emerged triumphantly with her when she won her long-fought battle against the Veteran's Administration, a branch of the United States Government.

If life seems difficult, if even now the eye of the hurricane is upon you, in reading *Pearl at a Great Price* you will find a testimony to the survival of the human soul that has been placed in the hands of the Almighty.

And they overcame...by the blood of the Lamb, and by the word of their testimony; and they loved not their lives unto death (Revelation 12:11).

Elmire Figliuolo

Chapter 1

A Cry in the Wilderness

The Adirondack Mountains surrounding the obscure New York village of Tupper Lake must have echoed with my screams on the cold November morning of my birth in 1927. My mother was all alone and destitute, for my parents were separated. Turned away by the only hospital in the area because she couldn't pay, she made her way to a cousin's house and gave birth to me with the help of a midwife. I was a large baby, and my mother remained sick for some time after I was born.

According to my Aunt Rose, I was soon placed in a foster home because my mother was unable to pay for my care. I lived in approximately six foster homes by the time I turned two years old. Something terrible must have happened to me while in these homes; because by the time my Uncle Victor rescued me, I was so petrified of men that I screamed whenever any man came near me.

Later in my life Uncle Victor told me that I had probably been sexually molested by an elderly man in the last foster home I had lived in, and for weeks after returning home no man could come near me. I carried on so much that when he had come for me in a horse-drawn "cutter" sleigh over the snow he needed to put a burlap bag over my head to take me home.

I was the eighth of nine children. And in 1929, my mother gave birth to the youngest child, a daughter named Marie. A few years later, my mother took my sister Marie, Freddy (the youngest boy), and Billy (the oldest) to live with a man who owned a hotel in Tupper Lake. I was told she couldn't take the rest of us...I never believed it.

I stayed with Uncle Victor and Aunt Nanny, along with my oldest sister Aurora and my brothers Roger, Leonard, and Victor. Another brother lived with a great aunt on my mother's side. My given name was "Pearl Theresa," but I was always called "Theresa."

Uncle Victor took us in because he didn't want us to go into an orphanage, but Aunt Nanny made no bones about the fact that she didn't want any of us. She also didn't want to take us until we were toilet-trained, but my uncle insisted she take us in.

Aunt Nanny was a very sick woman. It was the worst thing anyone could have done was to place us in her care. She was convent-reared and sadistic. Although she lived in perpetual fear, she was quick to take advantage of fear in someone else. I was the youngest, and she purposely did a number on me with a "bogeyman" routine using masks and sheets. Only later did I discover that the night apparition plaguing my dreams was Nanny and not some strange visitor from outer space, but by then, the damage had been done. I don't know how many nights the little town of Riverview rang with my terrified screams as I was awakened in the night by ghostly sounds and terrible sights.

My terror actually thrilled Aunt Nanny. I can still hear the shrill cackling of her laughter. After nearly scaring me to death, she would leave and send one of the other kids, or shed her disguise and come herself to "comfort" me. Sometimes she would actually scold me for waking everybody with my "nightmare." I hated the nights more than anything, and most people thought I had nightmares because of the experiences in foster homes. Nanny was shrewd; she practiced her cruelty in secret so no one would know the truth.

Every time I wet the bed in my fear, she would drag me outside in my birthday suit and dunk me in the rain barrel. She would laugh shrilly as I screamed with fright. Years later, the neighbors told me that every time they watched her do this to me, they had wanted to shoot her.

My mother visited once in a while, and she seemed like an angel to me. I couldn't understand why she wouldn't take me with her, since I so desperately wanted and needed her love. One time she brought me a shiny new tricycle, but Nanny put it in the garage after she left. When my cousin, Madeline, visited, Aunt Nanny let her ride it, but not me. This broke my heart. At other times, she would force me to sit in a rocking chair for hours without getting up.

Several times we went to my mother's hotel in Tupper Lake. My sister Marie and I always had a grand time there, and each time I was sure my mother would love me and deliver me, but it wasn't to be.

I loved Nanny, even though I was so afraid of her. In my innocence I didn't know that she was the "bogey-man"—for to me, she was my security and I loved her. Sad to say, I thought she was the only stable force in my life. I screamed if she left me alone anywhere.

My Uncle Victor was a woodsman. Once he went with Aunt Nanny to Cobble Dam to check on a job, and he took along my brother Victor and me. I was dropped off in Springfield, Massachusetts, to stay with my Aunt Rose. She said that she had never seen a child like me. I stayed at the front door, sobbing for hours for Nanny to come back until I fell asleep. While I was in Springfield, my desperate hunger for love became exposed when Aunt Rose took me to a department store. I walked up to a woman I didn't know, put out my arms, and asked her to take me!

When I was five, I saw my father for the first time at Danemora State Prison. He scared me something fierce. My childish mind couldn't conceive how this bald-headed, bespectacled man could be my father, nor could I understand why he was in prison. It was so traumatic for me that I became hysterical and Uncle Victor had to take me to the car. I asked Uncle Victor if that place was really my father's home, and he said, "No." For what prison was ever a man's home?

In 1933, I started school in a one-room schoolhouse and loved it. I was curious, sensitive, and hyperactive; and I enjoyed learning new things. Aunt Nanny often put a damper on my emotions because she had never herself received love, and I believe she was incapable of giving it. Her mother had died when she was six weeks old, and she lost her only child at birth. (The doctor had inadvertently broken the baby's neck.)

The nicest thing Nanny ever did for me was to pack me a special lunch before school in 1933. I proudly carried it in a Karo syrup pail, as Victor took me to school on a sled because I had no rubbers. I was thrilled to open my lunch pail. I had a dill pickle, a peanut butter sandwich, and an apple. As I surveyed my treasure, my most prized possession was the dill pickle. I felt that I should share with my teacher, so I offered her my sandwich, and then my apple, but she declined. I had such a desire to make her happy that I reluctantly offered her my most prized possession. She declined with a smile, and I was happy because I felt she was pleased with my offering. Another time, this teacher put me in the corner on my knees. (See it didn't pay to be nice.) When Nanny came for me, she really told off that teacher. The lunch and the incident with the teacher are the only two memories I have to indicate that Nanny loved me. Today, I know that Nanny didn't know how to love, only to fear. Her fear came to control me too.

Aunt Nanny and Uncle Victor had a little candy store and a gas pump. We weren't allowed any candy, but my brother Victor would periodically snitch some for me. When I was seven, one of my molars was in bad shape. Our storekeeper pulled teeth with pliers, so I was sent to him. The more he pulled, the more I screamed and bit him. Finally, he let the tooth sink into my mouth. This reinforced the fear that had begun to dominate me.

In 1935, we moved to Hadley, New York. I attended my second and third years of school there. My sister Aurora, who was four years older than I, was in my class, and she never seemed to know any answers that the teacher asked her. I thought she was dumb. Once I threw my arithmetic book in the Hudson River and she told me she was going to tell Nanny. I told her I would tell Nanny how dumb she was and how the teacher always had to holler at her, so we had a "Mexican stand-off."

At the age of seven, I woke up one night with terrible chills and fever, and my lower lip was terribly swollen. I had an ugly cold sore at the swelling site, but no one knew what it was. A month later I recovered.

In 1937, we moved to Greenfield Center and lived in a Methodist parsonage. There I met Marilyn and Polly Claydon, who were about my age. They had a super mom who took good care of them. She was nice to me, but because they were very poor, she couldn't give me much to eat. I was always hungry because Nanny wouldn't give us much to eat.

Those were the depression years and we had WPA (Works Progress Administration) bloomers. Everyone laughed at me because I thought they were nice bloomers. When we had to move out of the parsonage, Uncle Victor bought a house on Grange Road. I slept in an attic that had three double beds. We also had a super collie named Sandy.

My brothers and sister didn't like school, but I loved it. When I was in the fifth grade, we put on the play "Old King Cole" to raise money for more library books. After hearing the lines so often at rehearsal, I memorized every one of them. I was in the choir and was to bring in the king's pipe and bowl, but just before the performance, one of the "pages" came down with the mumps. Everyone panicked. I told my teacher that I knew everybody's part. She told me I was going to "get it" if I was lying, but I proved to her that I knew all the parts. I dressed in boy's pants and saved the play.

Onto the Streets

In the summer of 1938, Nanny made Victor and I hit the streets of Saratoga to hustle for money. Saratoga was a gambling town, and August was the time to make money. We had strict orders to bring home a certain amount or not to bother to come home at all. We also sold magazines in Corinth, Palmer, and Greenfield, and we had a *Sunday Times Union* route.

We would awake at seven and walk through the woods to the main road to hitchhike to Saratoga. We bought our papers at Stroups

Newsroom and roamed the streets selling them. We sold racing forms when they came out, and during the races we would shine shoes. I believe I have knelt on every inch of Broadway in Saratoga. At 6:00 p.m., we got our pink sheets with the racing results. I can still remember our famous cry: "Extra, extra! Final extra—baseball and racing results!" We got home around 10:00 or 11:00 at night. In the summer, Sunday was our only day off.

My second summer on the streets, I met a lady who wanted to adopt me. She intended to send me to college, and I wanted to go with her (although I knew I would miss my beloved brother Victor). She took me to lunch at Lido's, combed my hair, and treated me like I had never been treated by a woman before. I loved her, but my mother wouldn't let her adopt me. I always hated my mother because she didn't want me but this woman did.

As I said goodbye to the woman, she embraced me. Tears rolled down both of our cheeks. After she left, I asked Victor, "Why wouldn't they let me go with her? She really wanted me. They don't want us. They just want to use us." He turned to me and said, "At least, Theresa, you were wanted. That's more than I can say."

Once I went in the Worden Bar and Grill and recited the whole play, "Old King Cole" and I made $47. By this time Victor and I had "wised up," and we stashed some of the cash for a rainy day.

Bigger kids would try to stop me from selling my papers. That's how I got my first "sucker punch" from a girl, but that time I plowed into the barroom in spite of the pain and threats. I actually sold even more papers with my head bloodied but unbowed. When my brother Freddy joined us, we had a newsstand. We would buy two bars of candy for a nickel and sell them for a nickel apiece. We had all the local papers on the stand, and we took turns selling them.

I continued to suffer with toothaches. One time I had to leave the streets early because of the pain from an exposed nerve, and Nanny was furious. She asked me where it hurt, and I pointed to my mouth. Suddenly I saw stars; because she hauled off and hit me right where I had the toothache. She said, "That was to remind you that you are never to come home until all the money is made." After that,

I sat in the back of Millet's Bar and Grill whenever I had a bad toothache. I was on the streets for two years until the welfare system stepped in.

In 1939, my mother went bankrupt and went into the woods to work as a cook. Freddy, Marie, and Billy moved in with us; and Marie and I didn't get along very well. She lied about me, and I always paid her back. Victor and I ate only junk in those years. One day I stole a pound of candy and slipped it into my paper bag at the old A & P store on Broadway in Saratoga. They caught me red-handed and threatened to put me in jail. I was scared to death. I decided then and there that I would never be a thief.

Occasionally my uncle would take a truckload of logs to North Creek, and Victor liked to go with him. That meant that I had to carry on the street selling alone. I did not like to hitchhike, but one day in 1939, Victor left for North Creek with my uncle, so I had to hitchhike alone. I had just purchased some things for July Fourth, so I was glad when the owner of a garage in Corinth stopped for me. I became scared when he turned onto a side road. Then when we passed another dirt road, he grabbed me and tried to molest me. I managed to get a metal cap pistol from my bag and hit him in the temple. I escaped and ran all the way to the main road.

My brother Leonard told Nanny he had seen me on a dirt road with a man. She gave me hell and told me never to ride with strangers. I was in shock over what had happened to me, and there was Nanny was giving me hell for riding with someone. I had been doing this for two years. I couldn't tell anyone about the horrible thing that almost happened to me, so I remained silent.

Nanny would have made a terrific psychologist. She told us in 1939 that she would take us to the World's Fair if we made a lot of money. We did make a lot of money, but we never saw the World's Fair. We rode into Corinth every Saturday with a man from the Salvation Army and hitchhiked back. Through the day we sold *Collier's, Ladies' Home Companion,* and *The American.* One time a man named Mr. Densmore bought the very expensive *American* for a quarter, and asked me if I wanted to see some flowers. I agreed and he took me into a room filled with beautiful flowers. I was basking in their beauty when I suddenly saw a shriveled-up old lady lying down. When the man told me she was dead, I let out a scream and ran. Today I know that I was one child in the world that this shouldn't have happened to.

Mr. Pitkin used to give me lunch every Saturday, and I would look forward to this event with joyful anticipation. This kind elderly gentleman was just plain super to me and I loved him. One Saturday, I ran to his real estate office door and found it draped with black, but I had no idea why. I began to become panicky anyway because no one was there, but when I was told Mr. Pitkin was dead, I became hysterical. I pictured him laid out like that old lady, and it was too much for me. For some time after that, I went to pieces every time I heard about someone dying. The day I was told that a man had dropped dead at the paper mill, I was so petrified that I was useless. Victor had to do all of the selling that day.

There was one old man who never touched me, but he would tell me how he loved me. I reminded him of his youth and his girlfriend who had been killed in a dynamite explosion. I was afraid that he wanted to kill me because I reminded him of her. One Saturday, I again had to take the route to Corinth alone. The night before, I told my sister this old man was going to kill me when he saw my brother was not with me. I even told her where they would be able to find my body the next day.

Nanny had ordered Victor and I not to call Uncle Victor for a ride, but once we had to disobey. We became caught in a terrible sleet and snow storm as we were walking out of Corinth. I had a big hole in my shoe, and when Victor stopped at a house on the outskirts of Corinth to ask for a piece of cardboard for my shoe, a man ran him off. We managed to get a ride as far as South Corinth and my brother called Uncle Victor. By the time he came for us, my foot was in bad shape, and Uncle Victor gave Nanny holy hell for not seeing to it that I had boots.

The Welfare department finally told my aunt that she could be arrested for allowing me on the streets, and thus ended my street career in the 1940's. Unfortunately, at about the same time, a man we called "Old Frank" was living with us in Greenfield. He had built a room on the garage and he ate with us. He was a dirty old man, and whenever I was sent to give him a message or something he would try to violate me. I always managed to get away, but I also made myself scarce because he knew it would have been useless for me to say anything to Nanny. He died when I was 13, and I was glad.

Periodically I got to visit Aunt Vina and Uncle Frank at their farm in Riverview. I loved Uncle Frank because he liked me. He defended me if Aunt Vina hollered at me, and he let me drive the team of horses, pitch hay, and help with the milking. They were very poor, but we always had enough to eat. His daughter Madeline and I were only six weeks apart in age. Aunt Vina had nine kids (plus a twin girl who died when she was 11 months old). I thought those kids were lucky to have a mother that really cared for them. She was my mother's sister, and she kept all of her kids. I wondered, *Why couldn't my mother keep me?*

I still remember the taste of fresh-made bread and delicious salt pork and gravy. I also remember the love that was in that place as a result of one woman—Aunt Vina. She had a rough road to travel, but she was willing to take up her cross and follow Jesus. As a result, today her children are fairly good examples of what she sowed.

Periodically I would suffer from that facial affliction that started with cold sores. My uncle took me to a doctor in Corinth, and he asked me if I chewed straw. I told him no. He gave me some sweet stuff to put on my mouth that didn't help at all. I also suffered from more toothaches. One time Uncle Victor took me to a dentist at Lake Luzerne who would give me laughing gas to overcome my ungodly fear. Uncle Victor was on one of his frequent drinking binges, and we stopped at many a wayside tavern. To top it all off, the dentist pulled the wrong tooth while I was under the influence of the gas!

Nanny didn't want to be disturbed for anything. I suffered in silence through many a long night with a toothache, afraid to wake her. I just had to lay in bed crying and wait for the rooster to crow. When I was suffering from the facial affliction, my sister Aurora would try to keep me warm by doubling up her blankets.

Aunt Rose, my mother's other sister, had gotten married by this time. I liked her because she was so smart. I once told Bill Wing, a man I worked for in Greenfield, that I wanted to take after my Aunt Rose, and he responded, "You may take after her, but you will never catch her." It was a pun, of course, but it left an indelible mark on me. Aunt Rose and her husband lived in Mount Arab in the Adirondacks, and I loved to go there. One time, while my mother was living with them, my oldest brother Billy, took Aunt Nanny and me up to Tupper Lake to see them. We were in an accident on Blue Mountain Lake Hill. My aunt was hurt, and my jaw was injured. I will never forgot what my mother asked when she heard about the accident; she said, "How is the car?"

Eventually, my mother met a man named Walter. He was a lumberjack and project supervisor. He made a lot of money, and he even paid the travel expenses for my mother and Aunt Rose to go to Reno so my mother could get a divorce from my father and marry him.

Walter was super, and I learned to love him. At Aunt Rose's request, I went into the woods and became a chore girl at Walter's lumber camp for two weeks. It was hard work, but I loved it because my Aunt Rose encouraged me and because I was with my mother, who was part-time cook, bookkeeper, keeper of the little store, and also the boss's wife. We got up at 4:00 a.m. and stoked the fire to feed the lumber jacks. Those men ate like kings. I had never seen so much food in all my born days, and I loved it there. At night I would whittle wood with the men and talk about life and nature. It hurt me when I found out that these men would go to Tupper Lake after they finished a job and spend most of their hard-earned money on wine, women, and song.

I come from a long line of Canadian Frenchmen and Roman Catholics. I didn't know what it was like to have grandparents, but Aunt Rose told me stories about my maternal grandfather. I could almost see him in my mind, and I learned to love this man who died at the age of 38 shortly after being crushed by a log. I referred to him the rest of my life as my "Giant Woodsman." I was told that my mother's life would have been different had my Giant Woodsman lived, for she was only 11 when he died. My grandmother died the year before I was born.

I received my first Holy Communion at the age of seven or eight in Palmer, New York. Kneeling all alone at the altar in a pink dress, I thought it was very strange that I had to "stick my tongue out at Jesus."

I was confirmed at St. Joseph's Roman Catholic Church in Greenfield, and I thought it very odd when the bishop hit me on the cheek so that I could receive the Holy Ghost. I thought God couldn't be very gentle if He went around hitting people. We went to church every Sunday, but I learned to fear God, not love Him. Aunt Nanny's faithful attendance didn't seem to make her any better, so I equated God the Father with my aunt, and the bogeyman. (I didn't realize this until recently, when the Holy Spirit showed me how I had fed a schism between the Father and Son in my mind.)

I loved the Blessed Virgin because she was supposed to love me—no matter what (something I had never experienced). When I was told that she was a mother to me, I started revering Mary above all others because now I knew I had a mother. The priests were gods to me. One time, a snake crawled over my torn moccasin as I returned from picking berries. I ran in terror all the way to the house of the Catholic priest and begged him to save me. I thought that since a snake had touched my foot that I was going to die. Another time, after I was caught wearing smuggled nail polish on my nails, the priest told me that it didn't look good on little girls, so I removed it. After all, wasn't the priest God?

I was allowed to join the juvenile grange and I liked it. I still liked school too, but since my teacher, Mrs. Northrop, didn't like my brothers, I decided I did not like her. Aurora and I gave her "stink pots"—and did we get it. Once she accused Victor of starting her car, and she hit him on the back with a wooden pointer, leaving permanent marks. I wasn't there when it happened, but that incident was to alter the course of my life.

When Uncle Victor saw welts on my brother's back, he went to the school board and demanded that we be allowed to ride the bus to a Catholic school, and he won. As a result, Aurora and I entered the seventh grade at St. Peter's Academy. Victor went to school #1 on Division Street in Saratoga, and Freddy and Marie went back to live with my mother in the woods.

I was 11 and Aurora was 15. Aurora told our teacher, Sister St. Pierre, that she was only 13. About two months later, when she was really 16, Aurora quit school, and I was left with the task of telling the nun that my sister had lied about her age. That really bothered me because Sister St. Pierre was nice. I wrote a story about the farm and homemade bread, and when I read it aloud in class, Sister St. Pierre really appreciated it. She even told me she could taste the bread! I was on the debating team, but the other kids were snobs. Compared to them, I had nothing. The girls wore nice plaid skirts and solid-colored sweaters, with nice shoes and bobby socks. I had long, ugly granny dresses, and I didn't even own a comb. I stuck out like a sore thumb. Most of them ignored me, and a few made snide remarks.

I had to walk from my home to the country store to get the school bus. I got off at the corner of Division and Broadway and walked to St. Peter's—no matter what the weather. It made for a long day and I loved school, but I desperately wanted to be accepted for myself.

Chapter 2

Life With Aunt Nanny

I was extremely hyperactive, and I craved love and acceptance. However during my years with Aunt Nanny, I received neither. My aunt took me along, more than the others, when she visited relatives, but she wasn't really nice or fair at home. Besides the torment she gave me at night, she hated to listen to me talk about school or anything that happened to me.

Aunt Nanny was nice to my brothers, especially to Billy, the oldest, who drove her all around, and Leonard, who could get away with murder. But Roger used to defy her when she called him in to say the rosary. She seemed to be afraid of the boys. My beloved brother Victor was the only one, in my opinion, who didn't take advantage of her.

Whenever I tried to say something, I was told to shut up, and this angered me. I was becoming immune to beatings, so I talked all the more. Finally my aunt ordered me to the cellar. At first I was petrified of that dark dungeon; I screamed for over an hour. However, the more I hollered, the less afraid I was (and the longer I had to stay down there). This won me a reputation for having temper tantrums.

Aunt Nanny was such a kleptomaniac and pack rat that she used to hide food. Whenever she made doughnuts, she would give each of us only one, and then she would hoard the rest. Our diet in those days consisted of bread and coffee for breakfast, oatmeal for lunch, and pork and beans (sometimes with meat) for supper. I was always hungry. My mother had made arrangements for Nanny and Uncle Victor to buy groceries at the local store, but Nanny kept everything for herself. At times, we lived completely off of Social Services money. Uncle Victor was never home (I know why, now), and that's why so many bad things happened to me. I know he would not have condoned some of Nanny's actions.

Nanny kept a lot of the change we made on the streets in a chest of drawers. One month, I used this money to eat royally until I got caught. I got a terrible beating for reminding her that my brother and I had earned this money.

My mother came a couple of times when we were in Greenfield. I loved her, but it hurt when she left and didn't take me with her. I knew Aunt Nanny hated my mother, because she told me terrible things about her. She said my mother cursed me on the day I was born, and I believed her. It was hard for my mother to come to see us, knowing how my aunt felt.

Nanny hated it when Uncle Victor was gone. One night, she sent Marie and me to a bar room to secretly confiscate Uncle Victor's car keys. He was furious. He smashed a huge pan that was on the stove, and Nanny told us to get the neighbor. We learned to never again take my uncle's keys. This was the first and last time I ever truly feared my uncle, even though he once made Marie and I smoke a whole cigar after catching us smoking corn silk.

My sister Aurora had to do all the inside work, and I worked outside while my brothers worked in the woods. I cleaned the backhouse, cared for the chickens and hens, deloused the henhouse, took care of the garden, carried potatoes to cellar (a long way away), filled the cellar with wood for winter, milked the cow, and took care of the goat. I also had to ride my uncle's work horse, Popeye, for miles to where my uncle needed him. I hated this job because Popeye spooked easily (once he headed right for a car!). It was only the power of God that saved me.

In the fall of 1941, I entered eighth grade at St. Peter's school. I had an incredibly mean nun as my teacher. One time, I got a cold sore and became very sick. (I remember this attack well—even Nanny was fairly nice to me.) When I went back to school, the cold sore was still on my mouth, and the num refused to touch any assignment paper that I had touched. She announced to the whole class that she didn't want to be "contaminated." Finally Nanny sent me to Doctor Harrington who gave me a paper stating that I couldn't contaminate the teacher.

I prayed fervently to the Virgin Mary to deliver me from this wicked nun and from all of the stuck-up kids. Once the Mother Superior found me lingering by the seventh grade room and asked me why I was there. I tearfully asked her to let me go back to seventh grade because I hated eighth grade. She gently escorted me back to the eighth grade and the ugliness of that nun.

Two things also happened that year that deeply affected me. My aunt was a movie buff, and oddly, she always took me with her when she went to the community theater in Saratoga. We were on our way there on December 7, 1941, when I heard a newsboy cry, "Extra, extra! Final extra—Japs attack Pearl Harbor." Shortly afterward, my brothers, Roger, Leonard, Billy, and Stanley (he lived with Aunt Emma) entered the service, and the following year, Victor entered the armed forces too.

When we moved to Greenfield, in 1941, I also met Marilyn Claydon. Now Marilyn was Protestant, and that was bad. I knew that I belonged to the one true religion and that my best friend, Marilyn, was well on her way to hell because she was a Protestant and I told her so. I told her she would be lost if she didn't venerate Mary. I managed to get her to go and talk to a priest by agreeing to go to Protestant services with her. I kept my side of the bargain and even partook of communion at a Methodist church, but I suffered the conscience of the damned. I went to confession and confessed that I had taken communion at a heathen altar, and I promised not to go back. Marilyn couldn't become a Catholic, either. We decided to remain together as friends anyway—at least in this life.

I started high school in 1942, at the age of 14, and I loved my language teacher, Sister Anna Roberta. She gave me a reason for living because she consistently cared for me. That was the first prolonged period of my life that I knew someone actually cared for me, Theresa Gagnon. Only God could tell how much I truly loved this nun and what happiness she brought me. Now I could take the lack of love and understanding and meanness in the home because, miracle of miracles, *someone cared.*

When Mother Superior, who was also my history and civics teacher, told us that four people were to talk about current events every week, I saw my chance to show everybody what I was made of. It was at that time that Leonard came home on leave after Marine basic training. He took us to Saratoga and bought us ice cream, and he talked about why he was fighting. He said that he didn't think he was going to come back. His words inspired me to write a theme called "What I am Fighting For." Night after night I recited my speech as I milked the cow—why not, no one else at my house would listen to me.

Finally the day came, and I stood in front of those kids who were sure they were better than me. As I talked, the room became strangely quiet. Then it happened—I knew I must have surprised those kids out of their wits; they were sure that a poor, unkept country bumpkin like me couldn't do anything that would please the Mother Superior. Yet when I was through, the Mother Superior stood up and said words to this effect, "I have never heard anyone speak like this, come with me." Then she took me to the senior class, where I recited the speech in front of them. From that day until I graduated, I heard no more snide remarks from my schoolmates.

Later, I was given a major part in a Christmas play directed by Sister Anna Roberta. It was called "Christmas Bride." We performed this play several times, and years later, people still came to me and remarked about my role in that play. I also had two of my poems published in the Catholic newspaper *The Evangelist.* Boy, was I riding high!

That Christmas, Sister Anna Roberta also got permission to use me in a Christmas program (separate from the play), in which I recited the poem, "I Heard the Bells on Christmas Day." Marilyn Claydon's sister, Polly, actually allowed me to borrow a gray skirt and a yellow sweater, and I felt ten feet tall that day. Someone gave me 50 cents in appreciation of my recitation, and I gave it to my beloved Sister Anna Roberta because she had made it all possible. On another occasion I stood in front of an auditorium full of kids and recited "In Flanders Fields" and received a standing ovation.

A New Home

My mother and stepfather bought a mansion on Ballston Avenue during this time, and Mother wanted me to come live with her! Walter, my stepfather, was really interested in me; because my insatiable desire to learn had won his heart. He had come from the Ukraine and knew how important an education was, and he admired me for caring about school. So when I was 15, Aurora and I went to live with Mother. I had all I wanted to eat. A jelly doughnut every morning blew my mind! My cup was running over!

I was truly happy, and for the first time in my life, everything seemed to be going my way. I now knew that my mother didn't hate me (although I knew she didn't really love me either—we didn't really know each other). I had no more nightmares, and I was delivered from Nanny's tyranny. Except for the going away of my brother Victor, I was the happiest 15 year old in the world. My mother was kind, and she bought me new clothes. Wonder of wonders, the kids wanted me to be a cheerleader and I accepted! Once, my mother let the kids come over to our three-story mansion to practice cheers and she made us refreshments. I was so proud of my mother. What she did for me could never be measured except in terms of eternity. "Oh God," I cried, "Thank You. You really do love me."

Nanny's Fateful Phone Call

One fateful Saturday, Aurora answered the phone while I was sleeping. She woke me up to tell me that Nanny wanted to talk to me. When we had left Nanny, my great uncle and aunt were living with her, but they couldn't take her sadistic trends and were moving out. Nanny was afraid to live alone (what about Uncle Victor?), and she asked me to come back and live with her. She promised to buy me a new bicycle and new clothes, and she promised to be good to me. I actually felt sorry for this woman. I certainly knew what it was like to be afraid, but I didn't want to leave my new life to to live with a fear-ridden woman.

I told her I would call her back to let her know what I would do. I felt that I couldn't let Nanny down. Although I feared and hated her, I also pitied and loved her. So I went to my mother and told her that I was going back to Greenfield to live with Nanny. Before I could explain, she called me ungrateful, and she warned me that if I went back to Nanny, she would never do anything for me again. She was convinced in her mind that I was choosing Nanny over her. I tearfully packed my things and returned to Greenfield Center. My youngest brother also joined the Marines, which broke my mother's heart further. She now had six sons in World War II.

I hated life with Nanny. All the old fears came rushing back. Whenever there was an electrical storm, Nanny made me follow her as she paced nervously about the house, reciting the rosary and burning holy oil. Nanny treated me better this time, but I was scared to death of her; and she was scared of everything else.

On Sundays, I listened to the radio broadcasts of Fulton Sheen, Jack Armstrong, and the Shadow. My favorite was Fulton Sheen, who used to send shivers up and down my spine, for I really liked the things of the Lord.

Then a new family moved to Greenfield, and Jeannette O'Malley went to school on the bus with me and became my friend. It was nice to have someone to talk with, and I ran interference for her at school so she wouldn't be snubbed. One Sunday in May, Jeannette's father was plowing, when the horses spooked and literally dragged him to death. Jeannette begged me to stop at the funeral parlor in Saratoga after school. It was the first corpse I'd seen since my initial experience in Corinth. Mr. O'Malley looked horrible. The undertaker had done a terrible job on his face. I tried to steady myself while at the same time holding onto Jeannette and trying to comfort her.

I felt myself sinking fast when strong hands took me and led me away from the casket. My friend's dead father looked like some of my night apparitions. I was too afraid to go home, so I walked back to St. Joseph's convent with some of the nuns. Finally, Uncle Victor came to the convent and got me, and boy, did I get scolded. That night all I could see was that dead man's face.

I hated summer because I knew I would have to wait until school started again to see Sister Anna Roberta. I was lonely without her, but I met a boy from Saratoga who would travel to Greenfield to see me. He showed me how to drive, and we used to lie on the ground and talk. I loved Tony and I felt my first strong sexual stirrings at that time, but never went all the way.

In my fifteenth year, I started my menstrual period, and Aurora told me what it was. I often heard Uncle Victor tell my aunt not to worry about me getting pregnant; he said it was Aurora they had to worry about. This made me more determined to never get pregnant unless I was married. I knew that if I had relations with a boy I could get pregnant, so even though Tony turned me on, we never went all the way (but we wanted to). Tony was so possessive that it later caused us to break up.

My best friend, Marilyn, got me my first job that summer as kitchen helper at a Campfire Girls camp. The kids were super to me. Some of the campers even went to the counselor and asked if I could move in with them and offered to pay my way. I loved being wanted and accepted, and besides, the job paid fifteen dollars a week!

The second week I was there, Nanny sent me a message that she wanted to see me after church on Sunday. I was rather apprehensive over this message but I dared not disobey. When I went to the house that Sunday, my aunt and uncle seemed glad to see me, and they asked me how I liked my job. I told them I loved it, but I felt the uneasiness in the air. The tension continued until about three o'clock when I asked Uncle Victor to take me back to the camp. The silence that followed seemed unending. My heart began to palpitate wildly and I felt shaky. Then Uncle Victor said, "You are not going back. You know how your aunt is afraid to be alone because of storms and things. She needs you here."

Yes, I know! I thought to myself, *She needs me to walk behind her during every electrical storm so that another radio can blow up in my face.*

She needs me because she is a parasite that feeds on me! I looked at my uncle and thought, *Aren't you supposed to stay with her?*

Then I said, "I am going back, and you two are not going to stop me! You have never loved me, you only used me. Now I have a job that I love, and I am loved there. I am going back, and don't try to stop me, for you can't. Is this what I get for leaving my mother to come back to you? You are both heartless. No, sir, I am not going to stay here!"

My voice by this time had reached a fever pitch and tears were streaming down my cheeks. I don't remember everything I said, but I know I shocked them. They heard Theresa, for the first time in her life, raving outside the confines of a dark cellar; and they were totally unprepared for the words of condemnation and hate that spewed forth at them. My uncle was the first to reply: "You ungrateful thing, here I kept you out of an orphanage, and this is the thanks I get."

I shouted back, "I wanted to go in an orphanage, so don't think you did me any favors. I had a chance to be adopted on the streets, so I am sure someone would have wanted me in an orphanage. Besides, I have earned my way! When we were on the streets, you were getting help from Welfare for us! My mother told me that it was us kids who did you two a favor!"

Uncle Victor was livid with anger, and started to come toward me, so I said, "Go ahead—beat me. It's not going to change anything I said about your life." He sat back down, stunned. The quiet and the shock of silence hit us all. This was real life drama. Much had been said, and all of us had been cut, but most of all my uncle.

My uncle went outside, and I got ready to return to the camp. I knew I had won, because I had told the truth. Then my aunt came in and said, "Please Theresa, we'll get you a bike. Please stay with me, I need you." But for the first time in my life, I told her no. I assured her that I would return at the end of the summer. She called my uncle and put on a grand crying act, saying she couldn't reach me, and what was she going to do....

It was then that Uncle Victor talked to me with ice in his veins. His very calmness scared me. He told me he didn't relish taking me away from a job that I liked, but he insisted that I not go back. He said that under the law, he was responsible for me, and I had to legally obey him. I couldn't believe it. In a final effort, I told him that I would walk back and he need not do anything for me. It was then I knew that he would go to any measure to keep me here as company for this woman whom he could in no way handle. I said, "Oh no, you wouldn't forcibly bring me back, would you?" He didn't have to answer me—now it was my turn to take a walk.

They had won. It was as simple as that. But they had again toyed with a young woman's mind, a young woman who was searching for an identity apart from her aunt. *O cruel fate! How dare you give me a taste of life and then wrench it from the very core of my heart?* Was I never to be allowed to drink fully from the cup of happiness?

I returned to the house and asked Uncle Victor to take me back to the camp that night to get my belongings and offer my resignation. I couldn't bear to say goodbye. Uncle Victor simply told them that I was needed at home. The girls hugged and kissed me. Some broke down and cried, but they thought they would see me again—I knew differently.

That summer, my aunt had a new respect for me, but I could not go anywhere unless my uncle was at home. I often sat under a big elm or oak to write poetry. All that summer, I was sustained by my hope of seeing Sister Anna Roberta again when school started. Then my world fell apart; I heard that Sister Anna Roberta was to be transferred to Syracuse. I fell on my knees in a field and cried out to God to not take her away. I prayed to Mary to please go to Jesus and tell Him that He mustn't remove my all and everything that existed in the person of this sister.

When I returned to school in the fall of 1943, she was gone. The first day I met her replacement, I politely told her that she could never take Sister Anna Roberta's place, and that I was angry at her for trying. In spite of my behavior, Sister X was very nice to me. My stepfather, who was still determined to send me to college, gave me 20 dollars around Christmas time. I was allowed to take a train and go to Syracuse to visit Sister Anna Roberta, and that was exactly what I was living for.

By 1943, five of my brothers were in the service and in January of 1944 my sixth brother went in. That winter, Uncle Victor rented an apartment in Saratoga at 63 Ballston Avenue, just a stone's throw away from school. I hadn't had a bad nightmare for a while, and that was good.

Prior to this, my mother went to live in the woods to work with Walter, and Marie was placed in a private school. Aurora had met a man and wanted to marry. When the family said no, she had a baby out of wedlock.

In the summer of 1944, Leonard was killed on Saipan. Two short months later, my world again crumbled when Victor was killed in France. At first he was declared missing in action. I refused to accept his death, and for years I was convinced that he had amnesia and would someday return to me. I lashed out, crying that I wanted all my other brothers dead and Victor alive.

After the war, my mother brought the two boys' coffins home. The wakes were at my mother's house, and it was a terrible experience for me. I will never forget the bugles playing taps. And although we never opened the coffins, I was plagued by nightmares of opening Victor's casket only to find stones and bones. The terror overwhelmed me.

At times like these, I seemed to talk to my maternal grandfather, my "Giant Woodsman," who had been crushed to death by a log at the age of 38. I loved and respected him because I had been given a glimpse of what this powerful man was like and what he would have done for me had he lived. I whispered to him silently, "O, Giant Woodsman, arise from your grave." As I stood at the cemetery, I told my Giant Woodsman that it was all right for him to take Leonard, but not Victor; Victor was all I had really ever had. I counted on him to protect me. I was convinced that it was all a fraud, that my beloved brother was alive, and that he would someday come back to America to take care of me.

In 1945, we moved to Saratoga, and Nanny suddenly informed me that I had to quit school or pay her room and board. I couldn't believe that this woman wanted me to give up school. I got a job at a diner and gave my aunt ten dollars each week, eating most of my meals at the diner. During my first two years of high school, I had been on the honor roll but everything suffered those last two years.

Aurora was back again. She fell in love with a guy who wasn't too swift and married him. Johnny was about to beat her up when she was eight months pregnant, but I jumped in before he could land the first blow. I maneuvered him out of the door and told Aurora to run. She ran and left the hall door open. I was able to grab a piece of firewood and hit him with it. I got him off balance and practically threw him down the stairs, but I ended up with a scar to show for it. My sister left him and boarded the baby out in Ballston Spa. One morning, when the baby was around six months old, we received a phone call. The baby had been suffering from whooping cough and had choked to death. No one mourned for the poor little fellow, for we all felt he would have had a terrible life had he lived. Johnny paid for the funeral and even got him a headstone.

I entered my senior year in September of 1945. My stepfather still adamantly declared that he was going to finance my way through college, despite the way my mother felt. I worked at Harry's Diner from 4:00 p.m. to midnight, and Harry was wonderful to me. I didn't tell him that I was living with my aunt because I didn't want him to know how rough I had it with my family.

Walter got cancer that year and went to Memorial Hospital in New York. He was terminal, so I gave up hope for college and Columbia University too. Once again, someone I truly loved was about to be taken from me. I went to the Mother Superior and told her that I was quitting school, and she had a long talk with me. I had no idea that she had known so much about me. She said things would work out and asked me to stay, so I did.

I saved diligently so I could buy my class ring and a gown for a public speaking contest. I picked a very dynamic speech based on human interest, and I expected to have everyone in that auditorium crying, and I did. However, I was informed through the grapevine that Father Burns didn't want me to win the $15.00 award (which to me was a huge amount of money) because I was not one of the elite at St.

Peter's. Afterward, Father Curley told me that he had only heard one other person speak as well as I had, and that person had been a missionary. That was the ultimate compliment, coming from a priest.

I wanted to go to the prom, but I didn't have a boyfriend. The boys I admired would never have asked me to go to the prom, but my brothers got a friend of theirs to take me. My mother reworked a dress of hers to provide me with a lovely pink gown. The awe and glamour of it all was too much for me, and although I appreciated someone caring enough to see that I went, I knew I was out of my element. I was one of the most insecure people there. It was a pretend night. I didn't fool the young man who took me, and I knew he had a lousy time.

In June of 1946, at an 11 o'clock Mass, I graduated from high school. Not one member of my family came. My mother would have come, but she was in New York City with my stepfather Walter, who was dying with incurable throat cancer. On graduation day, as I looked up at the crucified Christ, I sadly wondered why all my plans seemed to fail.

"Why," I asked God, "is my hope for college being extinguished as my compassionate stepfather nears death? Why are You taking the people who really care about me and leaving those who don't care whether I live or die?" I saw the crown of thorns on His head and He seemed to say, "Look what they did to Me. Can you ask for better treatment?"

At that time, I felt like an outcast. Today, I know that Jesus was there all the time. When all was dark, the light was shining on me even though I didn't recognize it. Some of the kids invited me to their graduation parties that day, but I declined. In the final analysis, on graduation day I came to grips with the fact that I was a nobody. Something was wrong with me: Everyone else had someone, but I had no one. It was simple, but it was a horrible burden for an 18 year old to bear.

Of the nine children in my family, only two graduated from high school: the first and the eighth, my brother the prince, and me the pauper. He had received a princely ceremony. My ceremony consisted of Uncle Victor handing me five dollars in front of the house, saying he was sorry he couldn't do more. (I appreciated what he did do.) Inside the house, my aunt sat alone, lost in her own ugly world. I celebrated the day with a girlfriend, getting so drunk that I got sick. The next morning I knelt before the sacred heart picture in its old tattered frame, and I told Jesus that I was sorry. I felt His love, but I couldn't understand why He allowed me to be born. I had no direction, no apparent destiny, and, above all, no love.

My Best Friend

In the spring of my eighteenth year, Marilyn Claydon and I often went for walks together in the country, but Marilyn was not well. Marilyn was employed with Tracey Purcell's band as a pianist on the weekends at Joyce's Log Cabin in Mechanicsville. Sometimes I went to see her since the bar did not close until three o'clock in the morning. During her breaks she would come to my table, and we would have a Coke or two. She talked about the behavior of people she knew at this job and how they acted under the influence of alcohol. People fascinated her, and she had a rare ability to say just the right thing, no matter who drew her into conversation. She had empathy for all who crossed her path.

Marilyn developed a rash on her face, and her hands were swollen. After a grave discussion, we decided to stay optimistic. The rash, we agreed, was from nerves due to fatigue, and we felt her hands were swollen because of her piano playing. We knew we were not doctors, but we decided that our conclusions made as much sense as those of professionals. We convinced ourselves that with some rest, Marilyn would once again bounce back.

Dr. Vincent R. Kelleher (who himself had an incurable disease, and a heart as big as all outdoors) finally diagnosed Marilyn's disease as a rare ailment called "Lupus Erthymatosus," and its prognosis was certain death. It caused scaly patches to erupt over the skin, excessive weight loss, and nearly complete loss of hair. Marilyn had beautiful thick, brown hair, but toward the end it fell out by the handful. She suffered unspeakable pain and torment. It was agony for her to be touched by anyone. By June, all her activities had stopped and she grew steadily worse. She was hospitalized for a time, but when medical science bowed out, the family took her home to die.

I would not "buy" it. No way was Marilyn to be taken from me. Hadn't I lost the brother I idolized? I was told that God doesn't send any more than one can bear. Since I couldn't bear the loss of this friend, I just knew that Marilyn would not die. Jesus and Mary wouldn't let her.

I was one of the few people outside of the family who was allowed to see Marilyn in her semi-comatose state, and until the very end I had hope. Finally, with tear-filled eyes, I had to say like Caesar, "The die is cast." On the night of August 22, 1946, Marilyn Claydon entered the portals of Heaven singing "How Great Thou Art." That night the Lord gave me a glimpse of what her passage into Heaven may have been like for my friend:

I believe Marilyn glimpsed a beauteous throne in what appeared to be the far-off distance. As she blithely began approaching it, the lights became brighter. They were of every shade and hue she knew and some she had never seen before. Oh, the awesome wonder of it all! I'm certain it was such a scene like she could never have imagined in her wildest dreams.

Marilyn would have thought that very soon she would awake and this dream-to-end-all-dreams would vanish. Her mother and her nurse would be there to minister to her aching body, and she wouldn't even have the strength to thank them. She thought that as soon as she became better she would express her sincere gratitude to everyone...

Yes, just as soon as she was better..., but when would that be, Sweet Jesus? And as she said, "Sweet Jesus," she was transcended— but she didn't know how—to the very feet of her beloved. A feeling came over her like she had never before known: there just wasn't anything that she could compare to this peace, serenity, and joy.

She slowly lifted her eyes, and there in a garb of pure white stood the most indescribably beautiful face she had ever beheld. (Such beauty was not for the natural eye.) She stood entranced as she bathed in the light that came forth from this face. And then she knew, yes she knew, that she had crossed the great gulf between here and Glory. She then clasped the feet of the Savior and said, "My Lord and My God." The heavens reverberated with hallelujahs, the echoes of which can still be heard on a clear night (by all who believe).

The next morning, a phone call confirmed my vision that the Lord had claimed His own. I was sad because I didn't want to be separated from my loved one. We all knew she would probably die, but, "Everyone can master a grief, but he that hath it" (Shakespeare).

Marilyn's mother asked me to write a eulogy for her funeral and to recite it in the church. I asked Marilyn's mother to have someone else do it, but she said Marilyn would want me to write it. With God's help, I managed to write some words about my dearest and best friend, but whether or not I would be able to say them was another matter. If I knew then what I know today, I could have expressed myself in different ways.

The day of Marilyn's funeral started out as very drab, but by the time her bier was brought into the church, the sun had come out in all its magnificent glory. The church was full to overflowing and it seemed as though Marilyn were saying to me, "Theresa, you were never afraid to speak in front of me, please don't be afraid to speak for me. It will help my Mom." Still thinking of Marilyn, I took a deep breath and began:

> "Friend! How much that word implies for all of us who have known the friendship of Marilyn. She laughed and talked with us. She carried out to the highest degree the meaning of friendship. On earth she was an angel—what, my friends, Must she be in Heaven?
>
> "Now she has the greatest Friend of all, a Friend who will not allow her to suffer. A Friend who will shower upon her numerous gifts. A Friend who will love her as she as loved Him. That Friend is God...."

I continued on until my words were gone, and when the service was over, we went to the cemetery. I watched in amazement as they lowered Marilyn's coffin into the hole below. All I could think of then was what the priest said to me every Ash Wednesday, "Remember, Man, that thou art dust and unto dust thou shalt return." I also thought of my maternal grandfather, my "Giant Woodsman" who I had never really known; they had done this very thing to him. I wasn't there at his burial, but I felt, at that moment, very close to him. (It would be but a short time after this when I would attend the funerals of two of the "Giant Woodsman's" grandsons—my brothers, Leonard and Victor when their bodies would be returned to thte States.)

I bid my friend goodbye, but somehow I knew she was looking down on us in her spirit form, fully realizing that we should mourn for ourselves while we lived amid this vale of tears, for until we are called to our heavenly mansion, we will not know paradise. I may put it into words today, but I couldn't then. So, "Farewell, Marilyn, we shall meet again." I have never stopped believing this, and I feel sorry for anyone who has.

As I walked away from my dearest friend's gravesite, I felt a great closeness to my "Giant Woodsman," and I said with tears in my eyes: "Are you proud of your granddaughter who in church and at the cemetery fainted not, despite her terrible fears?" Did you look down on me with the Master at your side and whisper to Him, 'Help her. You see she needs it because she is a child of fear'? Did He not answer you thus, "Someday she will have little fear of earth and people and she will become My child of love…"?

Chapter 3

From the Convent to the Army

At the end of that terrible summer in 1946, I applied for admission to Plattsburgh Teachers College. It wasn't my first choice, but I had to plan on being admitted to this tuition-free college and find a job to pay room and board. I was determined to finish college, work for a few years, and then go to Columbia University to earn a degree in journalism.

I roomed with my first cousin Madeline, who was in her sophomore year at Plattsburgh. We had to each pay $5.00 a week, and we made about $10.00 a week at a college dorm serving meals. We never missed Mass on Sunday. I loved college because I loved to learn. During my second semester I took a job at Parson's Diner from 4:00 p.m to midnight, earning more money and tips. I was a good waitress, and I rarely, if ever, lost my temper in front of a client, but the hours were long. On the nights before exams, Madeline and I would take "No Doz," guzzle coffee all night, and really cram. Since I was the writer, I did her term paper that year.

I saw Aurora at that time, and she said Nanny had asked her to tell me that I was mistaken "if I thought she was going to help me with money." I hadn't asked her for a dime, but this was typical of Nanny. I told Aurora to tell her not to worry; she would be the last one I would ask for anything.

I wrote lyrics for the college class song and someone else wrote music for it. I felt I had a little taste of heaven when I heard the whole class sing the words I had conceived. I was making it. I was proving to myself that I could make something of myself. I had a goal I was determined to obtain. I was going strong when my world suddenly caved in. I went to bed one night in April awoke with violent chills and fever—my weird facial malady was back again! The cold sore, the massive edema, the whole ugly and heartbreaking scene was upon me. What was I to do?

I couldn't work or go to school, so I took the train back to Saratoga—and Uncle Victor and Nanny. As mentioned before, even Nanny seemed to have compassion for me during these episodes. When I went to Dr. Kelleher, he took one look at me and ordered me into the hospital. I spent my first night in a hospital on April 12, 1947 of my nineteenth year, only days after my stepfather died. I was unable to attend his funeral due to my sickness. I was in despair. What could I do now? School would be over and I would have no job when I recovered. No one could help me financially.

I received penicillin treatments and was discharged on April 16th. Dr. Kelleher thought my teeth were causing the problem. I suffered repeatedly from pyorrhea and trench mouth. I decided to have my teeth extracted immediately. (I only had 13 teeth left at this time.) There was no way for me to go back to college this year. Maybe next year....

I had landed a job at King's in Saratoga, which was a real swanky place, but I had to quit my job to have my teeth extracted. I went into the hospital and was administered laughing gas. As I was going under, I heard everyone in the room laughing with me. But the gas made me violent. Heavy blankets covered my bed rails to keep me from hurting myself.

I was discharged at 4:00 in the afternoon and went home to recuperate. It wasn't pleasant. My brother Stanley stopped by and asked me if I wanted a steak, and I felt like chopping him up. I had to work to pay for my new dental bills, so within ten days I had my dentures and had resumed waitressing, this time at Howard Johnson's. My dentures bothered me, so I used to take my bottom dentures out and put them in my waitress pocket.

I began going with a guy named Herbie who took me horseback riding, bowling, and out to fancy places. One night, a horse spooked on me and did everything possible to throw me. The animal went absolutely crazy. (I realized only recently that it was the power of God that sustained me—I should have been killed.) I brought the horse back to the stable and told the owner to kill the S.O.B. When I went back to ride later that week, I heard that the same horse had killed someone. I knew it could have been me, and for many years I was afraid to ride.

A black man named Louie used to join us, and one day Louie handed me a package at work. I opened it in front of the other girls and found a pair of nylons, a box of candy, a bottle of gin, and a card that read "To a friend." The girls started chanting, "Louie is in love with Terry." I told them they were nuts. I also told Louie that I could not accept his gifts, but I explained that my friendship was free and no one had to buy it. He told me that I was always polite and kind, unlike some of the others who considered him nothing but a "nigger."

From the end of September 1947 until March of 1948, I was a paper sorter at the International Paper Company. At this time of my life I was enjoying the effects of intoxicating beverages and meeting new people. I met Dot who was to become my best girlfriend and Bud with whom I was to have a long and stormy relationship. I also met Hugh Kelly and Mary, who was the huge woman in charge of the girls at the mill. I didn't like her, and I knew she tried to cause trouble for me.

I liked to dance, play darts, and listen to music. Bud was really serious about our relationship, and for a time we got along very well. He lived with his aunt and uncle, and one night I went there for dinner. I discovered that they were Christian Scientists. They hated my religious persuasion and forbade Bud to see me. Bud was afraid of their wrath but he was unable to give me up. He went so far as to buy me a 1948 Studebaker, but he kept it in his name. Every time I got angry with him I gave him back the car. We had some good times, and the one thing that was in his favor was that my Uncle Victor liked him.

The Secret Passion of Sister X

I found another mentor in Sister X, a nun whom I became fond of and respected (but she was not Sister Anna Roberta). I would visit her at the convent, and she was kind, understanding, and loving toward me. When things piled up, I went to her knowing I would get good direction. This helped me to stay on the straight and narrow path. Then she started to caress me and speak sweet things to me. At first I liked it because I equated it to a mother physically comforting her child.

One night, however, she turned the lights out and took off the white frontpiece of her habit. She was breathing heavily, and she pressed her body close to mine and fondled me. I was really confused because sexual feelings were aroused in me, feelings like I had when Bud and I were necking. She often tried to put my hand on her breast, but I would always shoot it right back to my side and stand there like a zombie or mechanical toy. Every time she tried to put my hand somewhere I felt it should not be—down it would go by my side. How could I, a mere mortal, touch this holy bride of Christ? As weird as it may seem, I didn't understand her motives and needs. Years later, I learned the truth about what she was, and I hated myself for being so ignorant. I also hated her for trying to violate me.

In March of 1948, I was laid off at the paper mill, and I got a job as a nurse's aid at the Homestead Sanitarium for tuberculosis where my sister Marie and mother worked. We had to wear masks and gowns while caring for the patients, but I didn't like wearing the masks. I felt much closer to the patients without the mask.

One morning, Arabella Mackey was brought to us from the Saratoga Hospital. She was 27 years old, afflicted with heart trouble, living on one-third of a lung, and recuperating from a bout of pneumonia. Her head had to be elevated at all times, and she was unable to get out of her bed. She wrote poetry, so we had something in common. I became her self-appointed guardian. One day, I noticed that Mrs. Mackey's chart indicated that she was not expected to live. A wave of sickness flooded over me and I choked up. I went to my room and cried out to God, "Why her?" I asked her doctor, "Can you stop her from dying? I can't bear to stay and watch this…" He responded, "No Theresa, I can't. I wish I could, but I am only human and her life is in the hands of a far greater Power. I just wish you could accept this and reconsider staying." I knew I couldn't stay.

I went into her room in my street clothes, with no mask or gown, and I told her I was leaving the job because I never got to see any of my friends anymore. I told her that if she ever wanted anything, she should let my mother know and I would come to her. I told her that knowing her was one of the highlights of my life and that I would always love her. She thanked me for everything and told me she loved me too. Then I did something that very few people would have dared to do—I gently kissed her on the lips. I saw the tears in her eyes as I turned quickly and said, "God bless you until we meet again." Within two weeks she fell into a coma and died in the night. I often wonder if she met Marilyn in Heaven. I don't see how they could possible miss each other.

I got a job as a waitress at a Jewish hotel and was assigned to care for a certain number of guests. I knew absolutely nothing of the kosher Jewish diet, and once I abbreviated an order for four hamburgers by shouting "four hams" to the cook. This faux pas earned me some odd stares. I soon found out that Jewish people did not eat ham. Another night, while our guests were eating, we all went to Brown's across the street and got ice cream cones. We were sitting on the back steps of this Jewish hotel enjoying them when a couple of rabbis walked by and chewed us out. I am sure they thought we were going to hell.

In November of 1948, Uncle Victor had Nanny admitted to the Royal Victorian Hospital in Montreal because of her fear that something was wrong with her throat. Since I was unemployed at the time, he had me accompany Nanny on the train to Canada (she was afraid to go alone). I planned to stay at a rooming house overnight and return to Saratoga the next day. In Montreal, I got a room, and then I took Nanny to the hospital. I could feel a cold sore forming, and this was bad news. I know I would probably end up with that miserable facial affliction.

I asked a nurse at the hospital to put something on my mouth with a cotton swab, so she put alcohol on my lip. When I left Nanny, I went back to the rooming house where I fell asleep in my room. I awoke in the middle of the night with violent chills and fever. It was a bad attack. I cried out, "Help me! Please someone help me," but only the echoes of my cries met my ears. There was no one to help me. Then I cried out to God to help me as I shook violently with chills. This had to have been a foretaste of hell.

I had always taken aspirin at the onset of these attacks to break the fever, but I had no aspirin in this foreign city and no way to get any. I was desperate and dejected as I cried out to God. Then, miraculously, the fever broke by itself—without any medication. It was the first and last time it did so. The chills abated, but I was still warm and my mouth remained swollen to massive proportions. On the train ride back to Saratoga even the conductor felt sorry for me. When Dr. Kelleher saw me at home, he ordered me into the hospital. He now knew that my teeth were not causing this affliction.

I was again given penicillin, but this time I got worse. All medication was stopped without a word from anyone. I just knew that I was going to die with some weird disease. I was really afraid. I didn't know why someone didn't come to me and tell me the truth and comfort me? Why didn't they call a priest so I could receive the last rites? I thought the staff was cruel to let a person die without at least some spiritual comfort. Around 10:30 that night I started crying, and a nurse asked me what was wrong. I told her that I knew I was dying, and I wanted my bed to be put in the hall.

I was hysterical, and nothing the nurses said could convince me differently. Then Dr. Kelleher arrived and assured me I wasn't going to die. When he asked me what made me think I was dying, I told him that it was because all medicine had been stopped. He explained that the penicillin had made me worse because I had become allergic to it. They were waiting 24 hours before starting me on a new medicine. Then he apologized for not telling me. He had gotten out of bed to come to the hospital to comfort and reassure me. He ordered a sedative for me and waited until it took effect. This doctor was kind to me, for he knew my family circumstances. He never cared if I had a dime, and never once did he bill me. What a crown of glory he must have received from the Almighty! Truly Dr. Kelleher gave me ever so much more than the biblical drink of water.

I was discharged the latter part of November. Jobs were scarce but I kept on looking, and because of Bud, I never went without. During Lent of 1949, I quit smoking and spent a lot of time in church. I visited Sister X, but I was lonely most of the time because of her strange way of caring for me, and because of my mixed feelings about her. I had met a man who was involved with the so called "jet set" in Saratoga and I went with him to some ritzy social affairs. Yet it seemed there was something lacking in the lives of the affluent as well as the poor. Without alcohol, it seemed that people were basically emotionally crippled. What was it I was looking for and where could I find it?

On Good Friday, in 1949, I returned from St. Peter's Church to find Nanny sitting in her chair and Uncle Victor standing by the bedroom door as white as a sheet. Aurora was living in their house with her second husband, George, and their five-year-old son. (George was the father of Aurora's first child, who had been born out of wedlock.) I knew something bad had happened. I told Uncle Victor to lie down because he had a very bad heart. When Nanny told me that George had violently beat up his little boy, Stewart, my blood began to boil. Stewart was the apple of my eye. What maniac would beat up a little child?

I wanted to kill George, but I knew I had to control my emotions. Stewart had evidently set fire to the wastebasket in the parlor and George went berserk. He locked the door and beat up Stewart with his fists. I asked Nanny why they didn't take the crow bar and break the door down, and she said that she couldn't think, she just screamed. As I look back now, I am glad I wasn't there. I knew George's history, and he had done time in Dannemora. I know I wouldn't have called the police. I would have busted the door down and attempted to kill him for what he had done to my nephew. George was a very sick man, mentally and physically.

I carried Stewart downstairs and made him as comfortable as possible by applying compresses to his bruised face. I gave him an aspirin and started telling him make-believe stories like he loved, and finally things seemed to settle down. Then I suggested we say the rosary, but we suddenly heard a blood-curdling scream—it was my sister upstairs! I looked at Uncle Victor and told him not to move. I was determined to handle whatever was wrong. I also told Stewart to stay put.

I ran upstairs and found my sister screaming by the open door of a room. I brushed past her and saw George lying in a pool of his own blood. He had slashed his wrists and had done a real gory job of it. I called an ambulance, and then asked a priest to meet me at the hospital. So off I went in the ambulance with this blood soaked man who truly wanted to die. George was administered the last rites in the hospital, but he managed to live due to blood transfusions. My sister took him back and had another child by him. He stayed until he did something violent again. Then he left for good. A few years later he died in the Utica State Hospital.

My Search For "Absolution"

I was always seeking absolution from God's chosen ones—the Catholic priests, who were my only mediators, my only way to remain in the good graces of God. At this time in my life, sex was the worst sin imaginable. Every sexual desire I felt led me to the confines of the secret box called the confessional. I had never "indulged" in this great sin, but at times I wanted to.

I had been told if I attended Mass and received Holy Communion for 15 straight Saturdays, I would be assured of a ticket to Heaven. In April of 1949, I initiated this rite of passage. I stopped smoking and drinking, and I basked in His presence in church. I felt His presence and had love feasts with Jesus and Mary. I had great adoration for Mary, for she was the only mother I ever had. She loved me no matter how much of a waif I was. I felt she really understood the depths of my loneliness and despair. She knew Jesus personally, and I believed she had told Him I, too, was her daughter like He was her Son.

One day while alone in St. Peter's Church, I laid down in the middle of the aisle and looked up at the crucifix. I couldn't talk. I was speechless with awe and amazement. The crucified Christ was emitting rays of brilliant light. It was real. He was sending out rays of love to me, the most unworthy one of the graduating class of 1946. Tears were streaming down my face and when I opened my mouth it was to tell Him how sorry I was I had ever sinned against Him. For many years, satan tried to convince me that this experience had not been real and that God didn't really love me. It was at this point that I decided to follow the crucified Christ. Never in my quest for real, pure love had I ever felt such love as I did that day in 1949. It was then I resolved to become a nun, in the hope that I would possess the constant joy and peace I had seen written on the face of Sister Anna Roberta.

When I told the family of my plans, they didn't even phase Nanny, as usual. She could have cared less what I did. Uncle Victor, though, was very happy. I couldn't be accepted by the local Sisters of St. Joseph because of my background (my parent's divorce and the life styles of my brothers). I heard of the Sisters of the Presentation at Watervilet, New York, an order that took care of love-starved children from broken homes. I thought that would be right up my alley, so I applied for admission to that order and was accepted. Then their Mother Superior told me to obtain a letter of recommendation from my pastor, which was their standard procedure before anyone could formally enter their order.

So I went to Father Burns, who I knew would judge my family harshly. I so wanted to be a Bride of Christ that I was willing to be humiliated by him if I needed to be. I told him what I needed and why. He wrote a letter relating how faithful Catholics Nanny and Uncle Victor were and stated that I was intelligent, did well in school, and was a regular communicant of St. Peter's.

On the other hand, he also said I wouldn't be a good risk because my mother and father and some of my brothers and sisters were living in sin. Bringing this letter to the Watervilet convent broke my heart, and I was scrutinized closely by the Superior.

Sister X came to visit me there, and she consoled me by holding me and stroking my hair. She aroused sexual desires in me, but no matter how hard she tried to manipulate my hands, I did not in any way desire to touch her in a sexual manner. These feelings bothered me because I couldn't understand how she could arouse me sexually like a boy could. Today, I understand that I was aroused because of the erogenous zones that she stimulated by her fondling. I really needed her caring, but I had never heard of a woman liking another woman sexually. Unfortunately, she was my sole confidant. I had no one but her to go to and question about our puzzling relationship.

Each person in a convent lives in a room called a cell with a bed, a dresser, and a closet, but you never call anything yours—it was always ours. I was called Sister Mary, and I wore a black dress, a veil, and black shoes. Postulants looked like nuns, except they didn't have to cut and conceal their hair. Each morning we left our cells to go to chapel for morning meditations. Later we would have Mass and Communion. After Mass, we went to the refectory for breakfast. Then we had chores to do. After another chapel session, we had lunch, then vespers, then the night meal. At about 7:00 in the evening, we would have a general recreation time when we could sew, knit, or talk. At 9:00 at night began "The Great Silence," when we were not allowed to talk to anyone unless there was a dire emergency. That was a general day for a postulant.

Sometimes we watched over the orphan children, and I soon found out that not all the children were treated equally. Children from broken homes were looked down on and treated like they didn't matter. It was hard to believe that nuns, brides of Christ, could be so unfair. The children the court had placed there were actually treated like criminals sometimes. There was no justice at this home. I don't think the majority of those nuns ever knew Christ said, "Suffer the little children to come unto Me...for of such is the kingdom of heaven" (Mk. 10:14).

Mother Superior was making it increasingly difficult for me to accept her open hatred and disgust for me. I began to hate her as much as she hated me. I became very moody and sick, and I knew I would have to leave or be kicked out. After four months of diabolical persecution, I knew for certain that Mother Superior would do all in her power to stop me from becoming a novice. She had declared I wasn't worthy, and by this time, I realized that I could not be associated with the elite of the Catholic church because of my background.

When I came back to Church Street in Saratoga Springs in September of 1949, I was very despondent and depressed. I still believed the Catholic Church was the one true church and I still wanted to be a Bride of Christ, but how could I be? I had to try another convent, because I had to have Jesus morning, noon, and night. I started working at Kaye's Newsroom on Church Street and was still trying to figure out how I could be a nun. In November of 1949 I developed severe pains and I was put in the hospital where my appendix was removed.

Nanny had a good friend who was a Sister of the Holy Cross in Montreal, Canada. I asked Nanny to write to her, and then I applied to that order. They required a letter from my first convent, but since I had not done anything wrong, per se, at St. Coleman's, the letter they sent did not damage my chances at the Canadian convent. (I did not know until recently that Father Burn's letter followed me to Canada.) Nonetheless, in February of 1950, I was off to Montreal, Canada, to be a nun—again. This was a fresh start in life in another country where I wouldn't be judged by my past—or so I thought.

St. Laurent's was different from St. Coleman's. I went to classes every day and I enjoyed them. There was a girl there from Massachusetts named Elaine, and we really liked each other, but every time we got to talking we were reprimanded and told to keep quiet. There were about 600 nuns there, and when the whole community ate together, postulants had to take turns kneeling down while the nuns walked into dinner. This was supposed to be a lesson in humility, and when my turn came to do this I obeyed. We were also required to eat our dinner kneeling down.

Now I truly wanted to serve the One who died on the cross for me. If He wanted me to eat all my meals in the kneeling position because of what He did for me, I would certainly do it. But in my mind,

I knew we were kneeling before a bunch of humans. I felt like laughing right out loud because I thought it ridiculous, but I kept my laughter to myself.

We slept in a dormitory-style room with curtains around the individual beds. I would go in the bathroom late at night and look at the lights of the city of Montreal and pray for all the people who were trapped by their sins out there in the messed-up world. Yet, through it all, I hadn't found the peace that I so longed for. I got a boil on my face, and it really hurt and looked gross, and it didn't ever seem to want to come to a head, and when it finally did, it had several heads. Sister Mistress was very kind and she broke the boil and took care of it for me. I thought it was nice of her and thanked her sincerely from the depths of my heart for I was not used to someone ministering to me like she did. However, she said something that shocked me. She told me that the boil breaking was the devil coming out of me and I really believed it.

I began to wonder if I had had a devil in me all along. I went to bed that night and told Jesus I was sorry for having the devil in me. Little did I know what was going to happen to me.

That morning, I was on my way to breakfast when Sister Mistress told me I was not to go to breakfast. I was to go to the lab to have a blood test. I sat in the lab, puzzled by this turn of events. When the sister went to prepare the needle to draw my blood, I glanced at the paper on her desk. I slowly digested the fact that I was having a Wasserman—I was being given a blood test to determine whether I had *syphilis*! I was so hurt that I wanted to cry, but no tears would fall. My thoughts went rampant: *These nuns aren't the Brides of my crucified Christ; they're the Brides of Dracula!* Although they thought my blood was diseased, in reality, it was their minds that were diseased.

Things came to a head in study hall when a postulant told Sister Mistress that Elaine and I were talking about her. I told Sister Mistress right out loud that the postulant was a liar and a troublemaker. When I was invited into Sister Mistress's study, "the fur hit the fan," and I unleashed all my fury on her. I told her what I thought about the nuns in general and her in particular, and she told me to take the next train home. I told Sister Mistress that I knew all about the Wasserman test and that when she died, she would be sorry for judging me according to my past. By this time I was crying and she was livid with anger. Several weeks after I returned home, I wrote to her an apology.

I sank into a pit of despair and aimlessness. I got a job at a dry cleaning establishment where I met Ed, although I still went with Bud most of all. I would not allow Bud to go all the way, but I continually went to confession because I knew it was a sin to gratify myself sexually in any way outside of marriage. Then I would be miserable to Bud for tempting me. Boy, was I messed up in the head.

I went out with Ed a few times, but wasn't interested in him as a lover. I knew that he had a drinking problem and that he was a divorced man. Back at Nanny's, I occupied the little room where my brother-in-law had tried to commit suicide. On the wall I had a large framed picture of Jesus. It was an old picture, but I had many a rap session with the lonely image that looked down from that tattered frame.

One night I was at Dunham's and this guy, whom I will call Tom, offered me a ride home. I knew him a little, so I accepted, and he took me for a long ride in the "boondocks." He unexpectedly parked his car and the wrestling match began. I told him that I would never give in, and he said I had better give in if I wanted to go home. If it hadn't been so damp and cold it would have been funny. Like Napoleon, this dark and handsome man had met his Waterloo.

In the spring of 1950, I met Bob at Dunham's, and it was love at first sight. He was a fair-skinned soldier with beautiful, blue eyes. We hit it off right from the start. He was on leave, and we had some good times together. I broke things off with Bud because Bob became my all, but Bud remained persistent about our getting married.

Bob got his orders from the Army and came home for a 15-day leave early that summer. He came to Saratoga on the early morning bus and would go back at one o'clock in the morning. I spent every spare minute with him. We went bike riding and ran through fields. We laughed with the laughter of young love. Neither of us had much money to waste, but my days with Bob were the happiest days of my life. We went to Paramount Pete's at night to drink Coke and dance. It was beautiful to be in Bob's arms and glide slowly over the dance floor. Every night we would neck in the hall, but we didn't allow ourselves to go too far.

Neither of us wanted to part, but we often said goodbye hastily. I would flee to the sanctuary of my living room when temptation seemed so unbearable. This had to be love because I had never felt like this about any other boy. I was walking on air most of the time and truly had stars in my eyes. When the stars in Bob's eyes met mine, we didn't have to say a word, but we would just drink in one another's love.

We wanted to get married in the Catholic church but we didn't have the time or the money. We were sure that marriage was for us and decided that we would wait until he came back from Korea. I told him that I planned to go into the service too. I could get my college education on the GI bill, and we could marry and have children later, for we both would get out around the same time. At first Bob didn't want me to go into the service. I told him I would go crazy waiting in Saratoga for him. He knew how I felt about college, so I finally got his approval. I brought him to Sister X, and we told her how much we loved each other. She seemingly was happy for both of us. We met Sister X at St. Peter's Church the morning before Bob was to leave for Korea. She gave Bob a rosary then we went to Mass and Holy Communion together. As we held hands while kneeling at the altar, it seemed like we were already married. We both cried, and I promised him I would not marry Bud or anyone else for I loved him too much to even consider anyone else.

I saw him off the next morning, and then an overwhelming sense of loneliness engulfed me. I went to my room and cried and cried, and then I cried some more. I traveled to Albany to enlist in the Marines, passing their tests with flying colors. Then I had a preliminary physical exam. When it was discovered that I had dentures, I was rejected, so I enlisted in the Women's Army Corp. I was told that I had to lose 15 pounds and would probably receive my orders in March or April of 1951.

It was November of 1950, so I decided to go to Tupper Lake and seek employment there and live in with my Aunt Rose and Uncle Arthur. I was hired to work in the diet kitchen at Mercy General Hospital—the very hospital that had turned away my mother when she was ready to deliver me. It was while I was working there that I had sharp pains in my side, and on November 8, 1950, I had a partial ovarian cyst operation.

I was back in Saratoga in January, 1951, and Uncle Victor took me to visit Aunt Rose and Uncle Arthur. This would be a first for us—going without Nanny and really enjoying each other's company. We were a pinochle-playing family, and every night found us playing the game. Uncle Victor and I laughed a lot because Aunt Rose and Uncle Arthur chewed each other out so much. They were partners, but you would have thought we were playing for mega-bucks. We left there as pinochle champs, and I had never seen my uncle so relaxed. I loved him more and more as I saw him in this different light. Now I could recognize the fact that he was my dear Giant Woodsman's son.

One day a call came from the Salvation Army in Buffalo, New York. My natural father had been struck by a hit-and-run driver and was in critical condition. He died a few days later. My father had been working and living at their headquarters mission in Buffalo. He had stopped drinking and gambling, and the staff had really liked him.

My two brothers told me that Simone's Funeral Parlor would bury him and we would pay later (this was typical of my family's "pay later" ploys). I could now relate to my earthly father. I had seen him only three times in my life, but one day he had turned to me and said, "Theresa, don't blame your mother; it was my fault more than hers." This statement won my heart, for this man didn't try to lay all the blame on my mother. When his body arrived, I was nominated to identify his body, and I elected Aurora to go with me. The mere glimpse of my father lying on that slab sent me running like a bat out of hell. My father was buried next to my two brothers who were killed in World War II. I couldn't help but feel that my beloved brother, Victor, would welcome his errant father. Since I was still waiting for my orders from the army, I borrowed money from the bank, Nanny co-signed, and I paid my share for the funeral expenses. Some years later, I learned that Simone had never been fully paid, and I was absolutely furious. I vowed to pay the whole bill myself. It took me ten years, but I paid everyone's share. After I paid him, Pat Simone declared that I was the only one of the Gagnon's worth the powder to blow to hell with.

At that time, I began to feel very close to Uncle Victor. One night in particular, we had a super time talking, especially about my deceased brothers, whom he truly loved. He had never really gotten over their deaths. He went in his bedroom and brought out a belt that had belonged to my brother Victor and gave it to me. How this touched me! I knew my uncle enjoyed conversing with me, and I made a mental note to spend more time with him. He asked me if I would go to early Mass with him, and I told him I would. Around midnight, I joyfully bade good night to Uncle Victor, and as I walked to bed, I remarked that I had spent a very pleasant evening with him.

It seemed that I had just gotten to sleep when I heard a banging on my door. Nanny said Uncle Victor had suffered another heart attack! I ran down the stairs just in time to meet the litter, and I jumped in the back of an ambulance with him. This dreadful scene was written so indelibly on my mind that I was to fear a heart attack for 28 years. After a false hope that Uncle Victor would make it, he died at the hospital.

When I arrived home after Uncle Victor's funeral, my orders from the army were in the mail. I was to leave Albany by train for basic training at Fort Lee, in Virginia, on March 30. I had already made my commitment so the die was cast. Madeline was going to stay with Nanny so she wouldn't be alone. A day or two prior to my leaving, Madeline walked in and announced, "Can you take another shock? Uncle Arthur passed away this morning."

Those that could went to Uncle Arthur's funeral. But the day Uncle Arthur was buried, I was on a train. Just before leaving, *I was informed that Bob was missing in action in Korea.* I was launching out on a new life—that might be without Bob.

Chapter 4

I Join the WACS

The Pullman car rocked from side to side, but I didn't notice much of anything during that long train ride from New York to Virginia. It was March 30, 1951. I carried the induction papers that would place my life in the hands of the Commanding Officer at Fort Lee. I was so worried about Bob that I hardly cared.

When I arrived at the station with two other female recruits, no one was there to meet us. Finally, we saw an army vehicle approach the station and sighed with relief. The driver checked our identification and told us to "climb in."

We received a small allowance to buy undergarments the first week, but in everything else, we stepped into the high fashion of "government issue" uniforms, including GI trench coats (we sent our civilian clothes back home). We looked comical in our trench coats, but we didn't have the luxury of laughing at each other while in formation. We couldn't buy cigarettes or other personal items unless the whole company and/or platoon was marched to the Post Exchange (which wasn't decided by us). The only place we were allowed to go without a group was to church.

We were issued two sheets the first week, and one sheet each week thereafter. (We took the bottom sheet and put it on top and used the clean sheet for the bottom.) At 5:00 a.m., the bell rang for us to "rise and shine." Every morning we had to stand inspection by our beds, and we went to a lot of "GI parties," where we got out buckets, brushes, cloths, soap—and you name it—and started scrubbing the barracks or whatever. Even during our rare free times, a corporal or sergeant might come along and say, "I need five volunteers," and immediately start pointing to certain ones and say: "You, you, and you!" (That's what we called "volunteering in basic.")

Basic training lasted eight weeks. The first week and most of the second was spent "getting it all together," and from then on we had school, marching, physical training, a week of "KP" (kitchen police), and a week of bivouac. Mail call was our greatest (and sometimes, our only) highlight. My main supporters through the mail were Bud, my girlfriend Dot, and Sister X. I heard nothing from Bob and everyone presumed him to be dead. The letters from Nanny were downright discouraging, but I was so busy and determined to do my very best that I wouldn't allow her depression to fall on me.

One day everyone got a typhoid shot. Afterward, we all went to our Atomic Energy class. I became very sick, running alternately hot and cold, and I could barely lift my head. I heard the instructor say we had to have a certain number hours in to pass basic, and I wasn't going to take the chance of staying back—no matter how sick I was. When the class was dismissed I made it to the bathroom and to my bed. Other girls were prostrate on their beds both upstairs and down (eight of us in all).

The corporal came in to have us all stand for a retreat. I knew that nothing short of a miracle could get me up from my bed. Then the corporal came by my bed and simply touched my head and walked away. I had seen my miracle. Later, she came in with the company lieutenant and said, "You can fry an egg on Gagnon's forehead." In the end, they decided to see me through until my fever broke. Most of the time I was delirious with a fever of 104 degrees, and they took turns giving me alcohol baths and cold compresses. They told me I talked a lot and kept asking for my six-year-old nephew, Stewart. Everyone wanted to know about him when I recovered. I was admitted to the base hospital for two days, and the doctor told me if I actually had gotten typhoid fever I would have died, because my system had no antibodies to fight it.

During the last week of basic training, we took a battery of tests to see what we were best suited for. I received orders to clerk-typist school at Fort Dix, New Jersey, and was given a ten-day leave to go home before reporting to my new post. So in June, 1951, I proudly wore my uniform back home. Bud got a three day pass when I arrived in Saratoga. We had a good time, but I reminded him I still would not believe that Bob was dead. After that forgettable leave, I reported to my new assignment and met a new friend from New Hampshire, Peachy.

While at Fort Dix we were encouraged to donate blood as a part of our duty (it also earned us a half day off from school). With this incentive, off I marched to give my pint of blood. When I returned to my barracks, I was dizzy to say the least. As the day progressed, so did my dizziness. Eventually I went on sick call, and the doctor decided that my sickness was more "emotional" than "physical"! For the first time in my life, I was admitted to a psychiatric unit for observation for a few days. This experience wasn't traumatic, but my dizziness was diagnosed as a "conversion reaction" and I was discharged as fit for duty.

The corporal in my barracks was one of the sorriest excuses for a WAC I had ever seen. She was just plain sloppy, and I began to notice something strange going on. A certain girl was frequently visiting her room for long periods of time. Finally I had to ask some of the other girls what was going on. Some laughed, and others were convinced I knew the score. I was dead serious, and I told them so. I had a sense of humor, but I also had a French temper, and they soon saw it in operation. It didn't seem right for this corporal to bring this girl into her room so much. Some of the girls were as anxious to learn the truth as I was, but nobody was willing to speak up.

Finally, I went to my friend and said, "Peachy, you're going to tell me or I'll wring your neck." Right then and there we had a wrestling match. She hadn't been brought up in the rough-and-tumble way I had been, so I ended it by making her give in. We were both a mess, so we went to the bathroom to clean up. "Now Peachy tell me—out with it—what goes on in that room?" Then she told me the corporal was making love to the girl, and gave her extra favors for being her "sweetheart." Wow, this was some news! So some girls really loved girls?

This really threw me a curve, because my mind flashed back to Sister X and her attempts to manipulate my hands. I recalled all those weird feelings I had, and all the guilt and anguish I felt. I went for a walk alone and tried to absorb the shock of my new-found knowledge. A well of hate rose up in me for this nun. She was a phony, and she had tried to use my body to satisfy her sexual needs. I wanted to vomit. Years later I talked to her on the phone and confirmed that she was as guilty as sin. She evaded all my questions and avoided me like the bubonic plague.

Except for my new-found knowledge about girls loving girls sexually, I had a ball at Fort Dix. I completed my classes and received orders to report to Fort Meyer, Virginia, where I was to work in the Pentagon in Top Secret work. I was now a Pvt. E-2, a rank everyone gets after four months of service. Before long I was promoted to a Private First Class (PFC). I was one of the few military personnel who worked with all civilians. Of course, my boss was a military officer. He was super and got me corporal's stripes shortly after my PFC promotion . He told me he was putting me up for sergeant because of the quality of my work. Boy was I happy!

There is an Officer's Club in the Pentagon that is reserved for enlisted commissioned officers only. Enlisted non-commissioned personnel were not allowed to fraternize with officers, but some of the women I worked with bowled there, and they asked me to join their bowling league on Monday night. I declined, but they convinced me that no one would know and that if anyone found out nothing would happen to me. So every Monday night I sneaked out to bowl and enjoyed every minute of it.

I went out with a married colonel for a while, but I felt I had to tell him I was an enlisted WAC. That didn't deter his pursuit of me, and I was giddy with my popularity. I literally threw all caution to the wind, so I managed to arouse the curiosity and jealousy of a few in the barracks. One night I was followed and reported.

When I was called to the Orderly room I thought sure I was going to be court-martialed, but so many people pleaded my case for me I was admonished not to return to bowl at the Pentagon. My bubble had burst! When I found out who reported me, I had enough buddies to take care of her without personally becoming a suspect. The whole experience, like my whole life, was a tremendous learning experience. I knew I was fortunate to come out of it so well.

I found it easy to make friends, but my special friend was a girl named Ginny. Something seemed to draw us together. Then one night, Ginny and I went to a movie on the post, and she took my hand and held it. This hit me like a ton of bricks. What was this electricity that shot through me? Those feelings that were supposed to come only with a boy—I was so shocked that I immediately pulled my hand away. I wondered to myself, *What kind of freak am I?* I tried to laugh it off and told her she must have forgotten who she was with—but I knew differently.

Now I knew these feelings were very real. I really liked Ginny, but I didn't want to have these feelings. Did she want to make love to me like that corporal at Dix was making love to that girl? I know this couldn't be right because any kind of sex outside of marriage was a mortal sin. I decided to put this all on the back burner as though it had never happened. I still liked Ginny, but I avoided getting close to her from then on.

I had a long talk with the Catholic chaplain regarding Bob. The chaplain had been to Korea, and he honestly felt that my hope was fruitless. It had been nearly a year since I had last heard from Bob. Finally I told Bud we would make plans to be married. Why not marry him? He was crazy over me and I felt, in many ways, that he would make a good husband. I was planning to put in for a leave for my birthday, and we were going to make our plans. We decided to wait to have a family because he knew how much school meant to me. Since I was doing so well in the service, we both decided we would finish our time and go on from there.

I was still with Mary and Jesus, and I went to church faithfully and said my rosary. I was well liked, had a super job, and I would be getting my sergeant's stripes any time now. Except for my concealed and mixed feelings for Ginny, I was sitting on top of the world—and I hadn't been in the service a year yet.

I was flying high until the morning of November 8, 1951, when I felt the tingling sensation in my lip. I knew what was going to happen. Dr. Kelleher had told me to get Benadryl from the military if I ever had another attack, and he had given me a statement detailing my allergy to penicillin. I feared that this attack could change my whole life.

I was feverish but managed to get washed and dressed. Why had this mysterious affliction ruined my life through the years? I went to sick call, and told the doctor, Captain Kaplan (I will take this doctor's name with me to my grave), about my condition and the Benadryl. Then I showed him a copy of the statement Dr. Kelleher had given me. Amazingly, Captain Kaplan told me, "I'll tell you what you do: You go back to the barracks and let it swell up."

I was so stunned that I asked him if he really had said what I thought I had heard. He answered yes, and asked me what was so big about having a cold sore? Then he said: "You don't like your job, and you just want to get out of work. I can see right through you."

This guy was unbelievable. I told him that I didn't care what he thought, but at least he should give me some Benadryl. I told him that if he didn't, I'd be back to show him what massive edema was like. He laughed disgustingly and said: "Take a day's rest and then get back to work!" I wondered if this was the way they treated all the women.

The next morning, November 9, 1951, I had a full blown attack of my mysterious affliction and all Captain Kaplan had to do was look at me to see I had not lied. Yet, he was still very hostile. He wasn't man enough to admit he had treated me shoddily, so he sent me to Fort Belvoir Hospital about twenty miles away. As I was lying in the ambulance, I peeked at my medical papers and saw his handwritten note: "Am sending patient to see if she is a fit candidate for a 368." (A 368 is an undesirable discharge!) I had taken some abuse for having these attacks, but nothing was as bad as this.

When I arrived at the hospital, I was shown my bed and given a pair of PJ's, a bathrobe and slippers, and a regular meal, which I could not eat. I could only sip liquids through a straw, but they didn't give me liquids for a couple of days. Doctors began to come to my bed and ask, "You ate something so this would happen, didn't you? You want out of the service don't you?" I tried to answer them through my swollen mouth by mumbling they were wrong. I had done nothing wrong, but they chose to ignore my muffled words. Every time this disease struck, it triggered sharp pains that would travel up the right side of my face. One night I asked the nurse for something to numb the pain. The next day I found out she wrote on my chart—"Patient asked for pain medication because she was hearing noises in her head." You guessed it—next I had my second official visit with a *psychiatrist*. I told him I never said I had noises in my head, and he said nothing. I was deeply offended at having to see him when there was absolutely no legitimate reason for it.

As soon as my weird disease abated, I developed pains in my lower abdomen! I told the doctors the symptoms were like those I had experienced before my ovarian cyst operation, but they told me there was nothing wrong with me except that I was a goof off. They gave me a ten-day convalescent leave and sent me home with pain in mind and body on November 30, 1951. It was no thrill for me to return to Saratoga. No one there really cared about me. Bud managed to come to see me on the week-end, but we really didn't enjoy ourselves. I was in a pensive mood, and I was unable to tell anyone about the pain I'd received under the "care" of the medical staff at Fort Belvoir. Bud kept asking me what was wrong, and I assured him it had nothing to do with him, that I just didn't feel well yet. He obviously suspected something because he said: "Please Terry, I want you to share everything with me—even your pain."

I returned to work at the Pentagon in the middle of December, but the nagging pains on my right side were getting worse. I found myself right back at Fort Belvoir for my first "Army Christmas." The doctors told me there was no reason for my alleged pain and that it was all in my head. I argued right back. I told them that just because they couldn't find anything wrong didn't make it any less real. In January, a doctor told me he had ulcers, and that I had to learn to live with pain. We had a big argument over that.

I returned to the barracks and talked to my Company Commander, who promptly sent me to the North Post Dispensary thinking that maybe the doctors there would be able to help me. I saw two doctors who, I do believe, were actually sadists. After making snide remarks about my so-called pain, they said that maybe I was sick, and said they would send me to Walter Reed Hospital.

Wow, I thought, *what a change-about!* Maybe I had misjudged them, Walter Reed was an elite hospital. They called for a staff car, and it took me to Walter Reed. I was sitting in the hospital for some time waiting to be admitted when I spotted a sign that said, "Neuro-Psychiatric Wards," with one arrow pointing to 42 East, and another pointing to 42 West. I wanted to die. I was trapped and at their mercy. I wasn't going to the gyn ward like they told me I was. They came to get me and *put me on 42 East!*

The attendant unlocked the door to let me in the ward, and then he locked it after me. I was spellbound. It was a large dormitory with a lot of women of different ages. Many of them were doing weird things, others just stared. Some sat on the floor in a fetal position, and many of them were just talking loudly to themselves. Every now and then a scream was heard. "Please," I cried, "Please, let me out of here. Honest I'm all right. It's just my side and that doesn't hurt anymore, I want to go back to the barracks! Please, oh please, nurse, let me out."

A nurse made me undress and put me in the first bed to the right. I was running a temperature, and they knew I had something wrong with me. I was given Demerol for pain, and that helped ease my body pain and mental anguish. I was scared to death. If I had known then what my future held for me, I would have, somehow, saved my sleeping pills and ended it all right then. One woman jumped on my bed and I screamed. It was as though I had gone to sleep and was trapped in a long, never-ending nightmare!

Finally, a psychiatrist came and talked to me for over an hour. I told him what had happened, and how the weird affliction had periodically struck me since I was a child. I told him how afraid I was, and about the pains on my right side. The next day, a gynecologist examined me and said I had an inflamed pelvis, and that a number of small cysts would have to be cauterized. I told him about my allergy to penicillin, and he promised to get me a bed on the gyn ward as soon as possible. When he left, I thanked God that at last I would be helped, but for now I had to return to 42 East.

The psychiatrist came and told me he had given me full mental clearance, and I told him what the gyn doctor had said. He then said: "You know Theresa, it's hard to get into this hospital, so you will have to stay here until you can get a bed on Ward 7. You're to stay in bed and you have Demerol ordered for pain and let's hope you go down to Ward 7 soon—it's really too bad what happened to you." The tears welled up in my eyes because he was so sincere and had empathy for me. His kindness was like a drop of water after being in the desert.

Finally, after what seemed to be an eternity of suspended hell, I was transferred to Ward 7, to be treated for pelvic inflammatory disease through a cauterization procedure. The doctors ignored my warning and gave me penicillin anyway. The day I got back to the barracks my face and lips swelled up to massive proportions with the "affliction," and I was taken via ambulance to the hellhole of Fort Belvoir hospital. They treated it like leprosy—still convinced it was all mental despite the outward manifestations. They sent me to a "specialist" who was actually another psychiatrist. He was just as baffled over my condition as every other doctor had been, but he wasn't nasty to me.

I listened to everything and kept notes on the time and days of every incident I observed on that ward. Finally, Walter Reed Hospital had me transferred to the North Post WAC detachment so I could take hot sitz baths and have diathermy. I did not return to South Post or to my job in the Pentagon.

Prior to my encounter with Captain Kaplan over my "affliction" on November 9, I had gone on sick call twice. But my experiences after that left me an emotional wreck. I continually found myself going on sick call from every reason from stomach pains to head aches. I began to live the life they created for me with their words. Over a period of years, the mold solidified, and only the power of the risen Christ could break it.

In March, I had another attack of pelvic inflammatory disease and landed back at Belvoir for a short period. I now had many emotional scars and I was definitely going to expose the treatment afforded me and other WACS at Fort Belvoir, Hospital, Virginia. I also met Larry Higgins at the non-com club, and he seemingly fell in love with me. The feeling wasn't mutual, and I told him I was engaged (in a way), but that I really wasn't sure about marriage. I liked him, and he seemed nice. When he got orders to go to Korea, he left me his new Buick to use until he came back. He also sent me money every month for its upkeep.

I wrote and told Bud all about Larry. I told him I didn't know what I wanted and asked him to let time be the answer. When Bud got orders for overseas, he said he was also planning on leaving his car to me. How ironic!

In the meantime, I had kept a written record of all that happened to me at Fort Belvoir Hospital, and I was in constant touch with Lieutenant Helen Continho, the female doctor I'd met. She supported my telling about the goings on at Belvoir, but she also warned me that if I submitted the information to the Inspector General (IG), that my enemies would somehow get me. I didn't believe her because I knew I wasn't going to do anything wrong. Unfortunately, I was naive enough to believe that Washington would really want to right the wrongs. I was now working as a dental receptionist on South Post. I continued preparing my document and submitted it to the Inspector General in May of 1952.

On Memorial Day weekend, I went with three friends to the beach at Georgetown. We rented a row boat for five dollars. We rowed for a while, then we switched to a canoe. We were told that our seat cushions were life preservers (I could not swim). It was fun until my friend reached for her cigarettes and tipped over the canoe. It all happened so fast that the cushion got away from me. The canoe was turning over and over and I couldn't get a grip on it. Mackey was treading water and screaming: "I don't want to die." I went down again and my whole life flashed before me.

When I came back to the surface the second time, I heard screams from the distant shore, and the Harbor Patrol was on its way to rescue us. I went down for the third time saying the Act of Contrition. I fought one last time to reach the surface again, and when I did the canoe was on its side. I grabbed it and pulled my legs up in the water until the Harbor Patrol rescued us. The next day, the incident made the front page of the Washington paper.

Marie was the company clerk, and she was a confirmed lesbian who was determined to woo me into the gay life. I was curious, but not that curious. She always let me know about anything that was going on in the company. She'd often save a place at the table for me, and sometimes I would sit with her. Other times I'd say, "Sorry this is my week for men." If we went to the non-com club with friends, she'd play the song: "I'm yours" and come to my table and whisper in my ear: "That song is for you."

Early in June 1952, I was assigned to bathroom duty at the barracks with another girl, and we completed our work. Then I went back to my area to get my cap. Sgt. Oldfield said, "Gagnon, do your detail." I said: "I did it." The girl who worked with me backed me up too, but the sergeant insisted that I hadn't. Other witnesses told her they had seen me mopping the latrine floor too, but she still maintained I had not done it. I said, "Look, Oldfield, get off my back. I did my detail and now I'm going to work." Then I left. On my way to work I thought: *Is this the way they are going to get me for the report I sent to the Inspector General?*

No one really liked Oldfield, but I never had any trouble with her. We were both non-coms, but she had one more stripe so she was my senior. She had charge of seeing to it that the barracks were clean and she made out the duty rosters. Otherwise there was no relationship between us. I had always performed my detail, so why, out of the blue, would she be doing this—unless she was told to frame me?

I went on to work, and when I returned for lunch Marie was waiting for me: "Terry, they are going to court-martial you and it's a setup." I asked: "What for?" She answered, "Failure to obey an order and insubordination—and Lt. Weir has to do it. She wants to see you." (Marie knew the whole story, and she was keeping her eyes and ears open for me.)

Lt. Weir approached the matter in a very official manner and told me that I had failed to obey Sgt. Oldfield and had been insubordinate to her that morning. I told her I had not failed to obey an order because I had completed my work, and the other girls backed me up. "Barnette and I did the detail together. While she cleaned the sinks, I mopped the floor." Lt. Weir said: "According to Oldfield, you said, 'Just because you have one more stripe than I have, you think you can boss me around. Well you can't.'" This was not true, but the die was cast. I phoned Dr. Continho that night and told her what happened, and promised to keep her posted.

In the service there are three court-martials: Summary, Special, and General. I was to get a Summary court-martial, where one person hears the evidence and decides the outcome. Let me tell you right here and now—a court-martial is cut and dried before it is harvested. I still believed that justice would prevail so I requested a Special court-martial, where a panel of five officers would hear the case. I was going for safety in numbers. I was restricted to the post, and of course, I was allowed to go to work everyday on South post.

I wanted to make sure that when my court-martial came up I would be guilty of only one thing—trying to see if something could be done about the unequal medical treatment for WAC's at Belvoir. If they were going to rake me over the coals for that, I'd just have to take it. I got the best defense lawyer the Army had. His record of wins was close to 100 percent. If he didn't win, then one knew for sure that something was rotten in Denmark. The court-martial was set for the latter part of June 1952, so I had to wait nearly a month before I knew what was going to happen to me.

In June, Bud sent me another letter from overseas, and he still wanted to marry me. I thought a lot of Bud but I just wouldn't tell him by mail. There was no one to write to back home who would really understand. So I kept my own counsel. Larry, who was also in Korea, was having fits because I hadn't written to him. I didn't actually feel guilty because I had not told either of them that I loved them. Since Bob was supposed to be dead, I knew if I married Bud, at least

I would be marrying someone who would be good to me. What a mess! (I never saw Bud again and have been unable to trace him.)

Meanwhile, Ginny was waiting for orders to go overseas. I wished her the best in Japan, and she expressed her concern for me regarding the court-martial. She made me promise I wouldn't let it get me down and left to visit her family. On June 24, 1952, I had my so-called day in court. First I had my say, and then Sgt. Oldfield testified. My defense attorney was excellent. Eight girls testified under oath that I had done my detail and Oldfield had no right to accuse me differently. (Today, I know if 800 had testified for me the outcome would have been the same.) It all came down to Sgt. Oldfield's testimony and nine others who refuted her allegations. I knew no one in their right mind could find me guilty, but Dr. Continho's words were ringing in my ears. I stood before the five officers as they found me not guilty of not doing my detail but guilty of insubordination.

Two-thirds of my pay was taken away for three months and my rank was reduced to a Pvt. E-2. I had already served 52 days of restriction. They had really raked me over the coals. All the girls were waiting for me, and I told them in a soft choking way that it wasn't good. There was still a glimmer of hope that the review board would overturn the decision.

We gave Ginny a farewell party and I danced with her. She said, "I never thought you would ask me to dance. Terry, you know I love you. If only I had the time to make you love me." Then I told her, "I don't think it would be too hard for you to do." Now I was saying good-bye to Ginny whom I loved and with whom I shared mind intimacy. If there was sexual gratification between women, she is the one who could have initiated me, but remember I also liked men. Ginny left and I never saw her again.

Dr. Continho retained a civilian lawyer to initiate an appeal, and my mother went to her Congressman in Messena, NY. I wasn't finished yet, or so we thought until we learned that with the kind of court-martial I had was not appealable.

While all this was going on, Marie was constantly trying to get me to have sexual relations with her. After two Army doctors called me in and tried to give me a mental discharge, I had to blow off steam. They actually told me that the government would pay for me the rest of my life if I took the discharge! I left there to have a few drinks and ended up having more than a few. When I got back to the barracks Marie was there to console me, and that's when I said to her, "They took my soul, now you can have my body." She took me into her room. And even though I was inebriated, I found out at last what women did with women. She was real good at it, and the first thing I said afterward was, "It's a sin. I have to go to confession." So that is how I got initiated into what gay life was all about.

I was ordered to report to Fort Jackson, South Carolina on the August 29, 1952, for reassignment in the Third Army area. I went home on leave, and Dot, my best girlfriend and I had some good times. My leave was a conglomeration of a little bit of everything but soon it was over and I was headed to Washington. I picked up a WAC friend named Ruth who wanted to ride to South Carolina with me to see her brother. I picked her up on August 27. She wrote to warn me "I have just been given reasons for more concern on your part. It probably seems I am writing in circles, but you can read between the lines—I've been talking to Mac, you can gather the rest."

When I read this I knew what had happened. Mac had opened up her big mouth about Marie and I because most of the company considered us lovers. They didn't know I had not, by a long shot, bought into the gay life. It was good that when I received this letter I had a week to cool off before I went to Washington. I was angry enough to get into a fight with Mac, and this time they could court-martial me for something I did do.

I went back a day early in order to spend some time with Marie. Today, I know that part of my sexual ambivalence stemmed from the time I was a victim of date rape. One afternoon in my teens, I was sitting in a truck with a casual boyfriend, and he grabbed me. He started to penetrate me and I let out a blood-curdling scream. He did not ejaculate in me, but immediately he let me go and said: "Oh, my God, I didn't know you were a virgin." I was hysterical. I told him that

I never wanted to have sex with him, for I wanted to be a virgin when I got married. However he had violated me.

Now, I was confused about my sexual orientation. Marie had satisfied me, and this boy had done something horrible and painful to me. I had sexual feelings for boys as strong if not stronger than the ones Marie initiated. Although I had more than one encounter with Marie, I had to be fairly well inebriated. Even though I had never read the Bible, I knew it was wrong. Marie told me she would be getting out of the service soon, and we said our goodbyes.

I was at Fort Jackson for less than two weeks when I received orders to report to the WAC Detachment, 3420 ASU (Army Service Unit) at Fort Bragg, North Carolina. I hated everything about the service by this time. I worked in Personnel with about five others, and the Sgt. Major in the office didn't seem to know what to do half the time. I had no difficulty in learning my new position, but my attitude was rotten to the core. The Lord must have watched over me because I didn't get into any trouble.

I quickly found out our first sergeant and mess sergeant were gay and so was about 80 percent of the company. I affiliated with the straight girls, but I was liked by a lot of the girls. Twice in the middle of the night I was awakened by a girl in my bed—this was much too much and I told them so.

One time I was riding in a car with the first sergeant's "sweetheart" and she tried to "rape" me just like a man, and she weighed over 200 lbs. I kicked her and pulled her hair and called her all kinds of names. Really this was the limit! What more could happen? I was promoted to Private First Class (again). Marie wrote to me all the time pledging her undying love for me, and promising she was someday going to buy a home and get a good job and care for me, but she still wanted to come back to Fort Bragg to be near me.

Larry's mother was dying at this time, and Larry flew home to be with her. After the funeral, he came to Fort Bragg and begged me to marry him—right away. I told him it was too soon after his mother's death, but he assured me he was too much in love with me to wait.

Now, I really did not love this man but I really wanted out of the service—Fort Bragg was a breeding place for gays. I told Larry, "Let's get married by a justice of the peace." This way I knew if it didn't work I could get a divorce, while a Catholic marriage would not allow this. I explicitly told Larry that I did not love him and was marrying him to get out of the service. I had enlisted for 3 years, but if you've served a year—not counting school—you could get an honorable discharge by marrying, and that's what I did.

Larry purchased my dress and other accessories, and many of the girls helped me prepare for the wedding scheduled for December 20, 1952 at the Fort Bragg chapel. After rehearsal, Larry and I went out for a while, and when he brought me back to my barracks and parked the car, he tried to "make me"! He was such a good Catholic, and we had gone to confession that night. I reminded him that you couldn't go to Holy Communion if you committed a mortal sin, and he said: "What the heck, we'll be married in less than fifteen hours." Now right there, if my mind hadn't been so mixed up, I would have dropped it all. I should have seen that if he was not honest with God, how could he be honest with me or himself? Unfortunately, it went over my head that night, but I still refused to have sex with him.

The next morning we married at a nuptial mass, and we had a double ring ceremony. I wasn't the least bit thrilled. This was my escape from the service and all the gays. I did not want to go to a hotel in Fayetteville with this man, I didn't want him to do anything to me. Well, we got to the hotel and this was it. I had a beautiful blue negligee that matched my eyes. I pulled the covers down and got into bed, and my new husband got in beside me and started kissing and fondling me. I was getting sexual feelings…and suddenly he stopped and went into the bathroom. What in the world was this? He just started warming me up and went into the bathroom? I learned that night that Larry suffered from premature ejaculation, a problem that was to plague him all of our married life. It was to be hell living with a man who satisfied himself and refused to get help to satisfy his wife.

In April I began making plans for my discharge. I bid everyone good-bye and took a train to Chicago to meet Larry and move to his newest Army assignment. I was leaving the service with many invisible scars.

Chapter 5

Marriage and Children

I looked out of the train window and wondered, "Where are the mountains?" (I thought the whole world had mountains like the Adirondacks.) When I reached Chicago and saw my new husband approach me so placidly, I could not believe I had trapped myself so cruelly. Larry responded to my effervescent greeting with a dull and disinterested look. I looked intently at him and thought, I don't belong with him—what have I done?

Larry was a robot devoid of any feelings. Before we married, he told me he would make me love him. He was doing such a good job that I was actually *sorry I ever met him*. Every night Larry would ask me to have sexual relations, but it was always the same—his pleasure in "two shakes of a lamb's tail," and me left next to him, unsatisfied. I thought sexual satisfaction was one of the fringe benefits of marriage—but dissatisfaction was my lot. When I went to confession and told my priest I was contemplating finding a real man, he told me to masturbate after my husband ejaculated! (But at any other time, this was a mortal sin?) Right then I should have put together the incongruities of the Roman Catholic church, but this came later.

I discussed the problem with the post psychiatrist, and Larry wasn't too pleased. Still I insisted that he come too if he wanted me to continue our marriage. He told Larry that he would have to undergo therapy if he wanted our marriage to work. Larry just said, "That's the way I'm made and nothing can be done about it." When the doctor said his actions were inhumane to me, Larry said, "Then give her help."

I went through hell sitting across from Larry every morning, while he ate and slurped like an animal. After two weeks, I grabbed my coffee and cigarettes and went to the living room. When he asked me what was wrong, I told him he was nothing but an animal and I couldn't take it any longer. Then he stalked out.

Around this time, I received a letter from Bob dated December 4, 1952 (I married Larry on December 20, 1952.) Nanny had kept this letter from me all this time, and when I read it, I knew Bob was alive. I cursed Larry and told him how I hated him. I also called Nanny. She was sorry, but nothing else had come from Bob since December. Now I believed he was not dead.

Marie also wrote to express her love for me and her disappointment that I didn't give the gay life a try like I had promised. My unhappy marriage gave me second thoughts about it sometimes, but I told Marie to never bother me again. I continued to live in my haven of hell where Larry would work every week night packing beer at the PX. Meanwhile, my friend Irene and I would sit and drink more dollars worth of beer than he would make.

One time, my brother, Roger, asked me if I wanted to visit Saratoga with him. Any escape would be better than my prison, so that night, I told Larry I wanted to go to Saratoga with Roger. He began to rant and rave, then he packed his bags, tore up all our wedding pictures, and flushed his wedding ring down the toilet.

Irene and I huddled together, afraid of what he might do next. I told Irene that if Larry stopped me physically then she was to call the MP's. When I picked up the phone, Larry forcefully took it out of my hand, so Irene called the MP's, who escorted him out.

Larry's commanding officer called that morning asking if he and the Catholic chaplain could come over. I left the place just like Larry left it, with the wedding pictures all over the floor. They brought

Larry, and I told them what happened and showed them the beds and torn pictures. Then the commander asked Larry why he was working at the PX every night instead of working on his marriage and why he hadn't saved any money after being in the service for ten years. Larry was very uncomfortable, but dared not answer back. The chaplain told me, "Mrs. Higgins, I advise you to leave this man or you will never have another moment's happiness. Now since you are a Catholic, you know you can never marry again?"

After they left, I went to a bar called the "Saratoga" and nursed a few highballs. Larry and my brother came to see me, and Larry begged me for another chance. With tears in his eyes (the first and last time), he promised to quit his night job and try to be different. I didn't ever want to live with him again, but I had never seen him humble himself. Inwardly, I was crying out to this man to love me. He really tried, but it was all in vain. I even asked Dr. Arnold to hypnotize me, but he said my will was too strong.

I was put on phenobarbital to calm my screaming nerves, and one day I threatened to kill Larry with a paring knife. My brother wrestled the knife from me and they took me to a psychiatrist at Great Lakes Naval Hospital. He advised me to go to the Downey Veteran's Administration Hospital right away or be "carried in" within a month.

On June 23, 1953, I was admitted to Downey Hospital and placed on a ward for semi-catatonic patients (mostly uncommunicative patients with no suicidal or homicidal tendencies). One girl washed her hands at least two dozen times a day and never said a sane word. It was a locked ward with female attendants, student nurses, and a charge nurse. Ward "D," upstairs, was for the seriously disturbed homicidal and suicidal individuals. It was practically bare of furniture. Many a night I heard blood-curdling screams coming from the second floor. This ward appeared to be devoid of all light. Later, I was to witness two women growling and foaming at the mouth in that ward, strapped to 100-pound chairs cemented into the floor.

I wouldn't conform to anything, and turned many of the staff members against me. I didn't even like myself. Today I can understand my diagnosis of Paranoid Schizophrenia—I had become two different people. Dr. Chelnek was the head doctor, and I refused to have anything to do with him. It infuriated him that I would not condescend to him. He told me there were ways to make people like me condescend to their superiors. I told him I couldn't stand being in the same room with him.

Downey truly initiated me to the "escape" offered by drugs. I was given round-the-clock doses of chloral hydrate and phenobarbital. There was a gigantic night attendant named Abdullah whom I hated as much as Dr. Chelnek. She weighed over 300 pounds, and she was six feet, three inches high. When I got up, she would have her troops take me to the second floor, undress me, and wrap me in two ice-cold sheets like a mummy, with only my head exposed for 2-1/2 hours. She helped Dr. Chelnek justify the treatment by reporting that I was "out of control."

She knew how I hated this cruel and inhumane punishment. Dr. Chelnek just smirked and said, "Don't you know sedative packs are good for you?" I threatened three different times to sign myself out against medical advice (but I was too afraid to face my demons outside). Dr. Chelnek pressed Larry to sign commitment papers, but he refused.

In August, a young resident named Dr. Wasserman came to Downey, and I liked him. I was one of six people he selected to receive insulin shock coma treatment. When I found out I had to stay on ward "C" with mostly lobotomy cases during the day, I refused them. Dr. Wasserman fixed it so I had a little alcove outside the insulin room.

I had completed ten insulin shocks and was doing great but then my bubble burst. On Labor Day of 1953, I went to the dining room for lunch and saw some of the staff from the 1st floor. I quipped, "Why the storm troops? Are you expecting a prison break?" This went over like a lead balloon. After lunch, I was told to go with a student nurse to Ward "C" until something was settled (I was locked up and told not to ask questions). Finally, one of the student nurses asked me if I had planned to break out! I laughed and told her I did not have to break out—I was not committed! My husband could take me out at any time.

She told me that Mary (a girl in seclusion) told someone that she and I had planned to hit one of the attendants over the head, steal the keys and escape. I couldn't believe they could believe the words of a lunatic while ignoring the obvious fact that I could walk out legally! Dr. Chelnek came to investigate, and I called him a liar. He ordered me back to "C" to be locked up, and they put me in "hydro" (the cold, wet sheet treatment). I continually cursed them for 2-1/2 hours. They wrapped me again for another 2-1/2 hours, and I again raved on. After five hours, they didn't dare to keep me in hydro any longer, but by then I was physically and mentally drained. I was determined to find out who Chelnek used to create this lie.

The next morning I asked the nurse to let me be the last one to receive insulin—I was timing the elevator facing the insulin room. I sat in a chair waiting for it to open while a nurse gave me insulin. They told me to go to bed just as the attendant who lied about me came out of the elevator. I was weak from the previous day and the insulin shot, but I lunged at her with super human strength and spit at her and hit her across the face while screaming "Liar!" Several orderlies pulled me off and were ready to put me back in hydro when the nurse said, "My God! Let her go. She's had a shot of insulin. Let's get her in bed fast."

Later Dr. Chelnek said, "I hope you're having fun. I am going to take you off of insulin for one week and put you in daily hydro—you need to be broken." I told him my husband was coming today and he would have to find someone else to torment. He just smiled and said he would convince Larry that it would be dangerous for him to remove me from the safety of his hospital. I cursed him and he called his troops to put me back in lock up.

My husband signed me out, but on our way out, Chelnek stopped him and pressed his case, "She's a very sick person, very sick." Well he had me convinced I was crazy. When we left the hospital I was sold on the fact I was a real incurable psycho of the worse kind. Once you leave a VA hospital against medical advice, you can't go back for 90 days unless you are an emergency. That only made my fears worse. Then I lost my memory. Larry took me to the base hospital. They sent me back to Downey, and when I was refused admittance, Larry took me to the Cook County Psychiatric Hospital.

I woke up the next morning and wondered where I was, and they contacted Dr. Chelnek. On the strength of his report, I lost all my rights, was declared incompetent by the Circuit Court of Cook County, and committed to Manteno State Hospital. On the bus to Manteno State Hospital, despair consumed me. We were herded like cattle into the admitting room, but we were well treated.

The examining doctor put a thermometer in my mouth, and after reading it she told an attendant to call an ambulance. The next morning a medical doctor examined me and put me in isolation with an acute and contagious throat infection. I received excellent care, but they were perplexed as to why I was committed, for they could see nothing wrong with my mental behavior. When you are committed you have to stay at least 60 days, and there is little chance to get out—especially under a court order. (I later discovered that if the court had used the term *mentally ill person* instead of "a person in need of mental help," I could never have left that institution!)

At Manteno, I did what I was told and no one harassed me. I can see my true self was unveiled there more than at any other mental institution before or after. I got along with the help and all the patients. Best of all, I wasn't given any mind-altering drugs. I felt like a human being for the first time in many months. A social worker told me I had done so well that no one could understand why I was committed there. They gave me an Absolute Discharge with the diagnosis of "Anxiety Reaction." *They were practically saying the judge had made an error.*

I left Manteno on October 12, 1953, feeling like a new creature. But my new-found joy was soon to diminish with the help of my husband and other events. Larry had believed I would never leave Manteno so he gave up our apartment, put our furniture in storage, and had my allotment checks sent to his uncle in Chicago. He even sent all my belongings to my brother—the same Roger who left his apartments in the middle of the night because when he couldn't pay his rent due to his compulsive gambling. I had lost everything again, and I had no VA money. I had no place to live, so Larry got a leave and took me to Saratoga.

In Saratoga, he met Nanny and my oldest sister, Aurora. She and her husband invited us to go to a bar, and we were sitting at a table when Aurora suddenly said, "Theresa, do you see who's standing at the bar?" I felt like someone had poured an ice-cold bucket of water on my head when she said, "It's Bob." I was so shocked that it seemed like Aurora had called someone forth from the dead! I saw Bob, and remorse filled my soul. What a cruel trick of fate! Bob was alive and I was married to a man whom I despised.

I left the table and softly whispered a hello to Bob. He turned and looked at me with those beautiful blue eyes of his and his charming smile. My heart melted like butter just to be near him. I told him I was married, and he asked me why I didn't wait for him. I told him I had waited for two-and-a-half years and I thought he was dead. He said he had been a prisoner of war, and that was why I hadn't heard from him. We knew we still loved each other, and we planned to meet each other the next night at Dunhams.

With tear-dimmed eyes, I walked back to the table and the man I had married, determined to stick it out. I was resigned to a loveless marriage. Larry condemned me for still loving Bob. He took the car the next morning and drove back to Illinois alone. The next day, I wrestled with my conscience. Should I meet Bob or not? Whatever made me discontinue my relationship with Marie also refused to let me see Bob. I called my girlfriend Dot and we went to a movie, although my heart was breaking because I wanted to see Bob. I left the movie and drowned my sorrows, but I never did go to Dunhams that night.

My husband phoned several times and asked me to start all over. I had no choice. We rented a furnished one-bedroom apartment two miles from the base. My one prayer was that when I was stoned enough to have sex with him, I would at least become pregnant and have a baby girl. But I then discovered that Larry had a weak sperm count due to a severe bout of the mumps in childhood. If he married me fraudulently, could I get an annulment?

In December, Larry went to his uncle's to pick up my allotment check to pay our rent, and I waited for him at Toby's bar where we were having a party. He returned and joined in, and when the check was lost, he blamed me. In bed that night, he slapped me across the face without provocation. I immediately called the police and they put him in jail for the night. I wasn't about to be abused again. I couldn't pay the rent, and the VA was dragging its feet for some reason about the money I had accrued. They told me to go to the Red Cross, and they would pay everything back to them, so I got myself a room with a widowed lady with two children.

The VA also thought I was at Manteno for life. Since I was in Saratoga, they made me get an exam in Albany. The doctors said I was still 100 percent disabled. So what were they waiting for? The letter from Manteno told them, "Patient was not found to be psychotic during her stay here and was not found to be incompetent. She had ground privileges and did excellent work as a typist in our X-ray technicians' office."

I spent most of my time shilling for Toby's bar, but I never went out with any of the men. One of Larry's friends warned me not to go back with Larry—he had a venereal disease and had to be relieved of his cooking duties for awhile! (The sergeant he was living with liked his drink, and he and Larry would indulge in wine, women, and song.)

In March, my brother Roger secretly went to the VA and told them I was incompetent to handle my funds. He suggested they be placed in the Exchange National Bank of Chicago (the vice president was his friend). The VA declared me *non-compes-mentes* and named this bank as conservator. (I did not know until years later that my brother was a con-artist and gambler.) Manteno had exonerated me of this label, but they were putting it on me again.

On April 2, 1954, I stood before a judge again, thanks to the VA's handywork. I was to receive $80.00 twice a month, my rent was paid, and my account was brought up to date with the Red Cross, but I didn't get an account of what was going on or how much money I had until 1956. My brother stuck his fingers into the pie and got away with it.

I was trying to destroy myself with alcohol but I never thought of suicide. I was only a shell of a person. One night I hit a guy over the head with a bottle, and was taken to the local hospital where I met Dr. Black. He said I had Psychoneurosis Hysteria, and kept me for two days. They suggested Downey, but I wouldn't go there.

Late in June of 1954, I hit a stop sign, and the police took me to Downey. I ran away, but the guards caught me. I was admitted and put to bed around 3:00 in the morning. There I met a WAC I had known at Belvoir—the same one the doctors had told to go to bed with a man and she would be fine. All my old fears came rushing over me. I demanded medication, and I sure wasn't all there mentally. The uncanny mixture of sanity and insanity I displayed at this time was something they could not grasp—they called me crazy, and yet treated me as though I was sane, and they took offense at my actions.

I figured I had gone too far, and now I was in for some "hydro" treatments. They told me to get dressed, and so I decided to play their game. I thought I was headed for a new form of hydrotherapy where you were fully clothed, but instead they led me to the main entrance of the building! The door bell rang and two burly policemen entered and told me I had to come with them!

I told them I had been admitted the previous night and someone was fooling around when they called them—it was all a mistake. They assured me it wasn't a mistake. They were to remove me from the premises and I could go with them quietly or not, but go with them I would. When they came close, stark terror came over me and I begged them not to hurt me. By this time I was a blubbering idiot.

The officers placed me in the front seat of their car and drove me to a large, looming building in Waukegan, Illinois. They told me I would have to go with them while they wrote up their report, then they would drive me home. When they got me inside (I quickly learned it was the local jail), they dragged me up some stairs, unlocked a door and shoved me inside a chasm of hell. I screamed to them not to do this, but my screams fell on deaf ears. My life had been a series of nightmares but this was the granddaddy of them all. I am firmly convinced I went insane that night, yet I retained everything. I screamed and cried, and then screamed and cried some more—I was once again in the cellar of my childhood, shouting, "It's unfair, all so unfair!" The more fearful I got, the louder I fumed and exploded into tirades. In torment I cried out to God and the Blessed Virgin and all the Saints to deliver me out of this abyss and quagmire of darkness.

I realized I was not the only person in this penal colony. I saw, crouched in a corner by a barred window, another lost, unsalvageable, wounded animal. She was so placid that I thought maybe she was my alter ego. Was she real or just a twisted, tangled part of me? When I fixed my eyes on her in the dimly lit dungeon, she said, "It's not bad in here. You'll get used to it. I have 15 days to stay." I said, "Why are you here?" She told me she was a prostitute, and I mused: *She sold her body and God sold my soul.* I was sure God was paying me back for all the bad I had done and for not being a nun.

Somehow the night passed, and without warning I heard keys opening the door. Two men walked in saying they had to fingerprint me. I broke out with a stream of curses and demanded to know why. I reminded them I was taken against my will from the confines of a mental institution—what law did I break? They slowly backed up to the door and one unlocked it while the other guarded me with his eyes.

Around 4:00 in the afternoon, they released me and said someone wanted to talk to me on the phone. It was the head of the regional VA office in Chicago. He apologized and told me a horrible mistake had been made, and asked me to please return to Downey. First, I was totally stunned, then I hysterically told this man the VA had gotten their revenge. Only a skeleton of Theresa walked out of jail that day. I was a sorry excuse for a human being, and I loathed all authority figures. Most of all I detested Dr. Chelnek, the Frankenstein of them all.

I lost myself in booze and drugs during the most harrowing two months of my life. I had only a glimmer of hope. I would drink to oblivion then pop a few pills to assure sleeping the sleep of the damned.

Out of desperation, I went back to Downey on August 25, 1954, but I was determined not to agitate anyone. I discovered (joyfully) that Dr. Chelnek had nothing to do with me. My past records were, as usual, used against me, and at times I was defensive for being judged too rashly. (I didn't know until 1963 that my records were filled with lies and innuendos. Anyone reading them could easily think I was the lowest form of being to enter the portals of Downey.)

Neither Abdullah nor Dr. Wasserman were there either. I did a lot of number paintings and made frames and stained them and gave two of them to the Downey chaplains. I was indirectly trying to make my peace with God by making a peace offering to His servants. I cooperated and was seemingly getting it all together mentally and physically, but I was still given too much sedation. My husband visited me regularly, and he was well on his way of establishing a pattern of being overly nice to me while I was in the hospital (even though when I got out, we could not relate to each other).

It was during this period that secret plans were formulated to sever my VA compensation. Although the plans involved the signature of Dr. Chelnek, I never saw him during that time, and I never even met some of the people who signed a statement certifying they had examined me.

I was discharged on October 22, 1954, but I still would not live with Larry. One night, Larry and I went out to a bar and began talking to this man who asked me how many children I had. I told him none, and he started to rant that I was too afraid and lazy to have children. He bragged that he had four, and he couldn't stand people who had none. We moved away from him, but when he left, Larry followed him.

Larry caught the man outside and began to viciously beat him. He had him on the ground and was kicking him in the face. I screamed at him and tugged at him to let him go. He finally did, but the man was really in bad shape. This was one side of Larry I had never seen before, and I didn't like it. Larry never said a word to this man in the bar. He just waited calmly until he could get him alone to beat him up.

I received a letter from the VA telling me I was no longer service-connected, and as of March 1955, I would no longer receive compensation. I asked the American Legion to help me find out why, but they could only confirm that my diagnosis had been changed. I received no money from the bank when they closed out my account.

In May, I went to Saratoga with my sister to see my nephew, Stewart, who was in a home for undisciplined children. He was at the same place I had entered to be a nun—St. Colman's Home. I took him a lot of goodies and visited a few nuns I knew. I also bought a Chihuahua and named him "Buddy Boy the XIV."

I gave Larry another chance and we rented an apartment. Two weeks later we went to a bar, and Buddy Boy was with us. Larry was really drunk, so I told him I was going home. Then I realized I had forgotten Buddy Boy, so I went back. Larry was belligerent about me taking the dog, but I wouldn't leave without him. I came home with the dog and fixed something to eat. Larry came in and told me he was going back to the barracks. He asked me to get his barracks bag, and when I went into a large walk-in closet to empty the bag, Larry went berserk. He punched and kicked me from one wall to another. I knew he was going to kill me.

I tried to shield my face, but blood was gushing all over me. Just as quickly as it started, the brutal beating stopped! Larry looked at me and said, "Who did this to you? I'll kill the S.O.B.!" He gently took me to the bathroom and started to wash off the blood, but I knew I was with a mad man. He had what is termed a "brain storm," but what was I do to if he were to go back to the other personality? I remained cool and said, "Larry, I feel weak and dizzy, may I please go and sit on the steps outside?" and he nodded.

There were about fifteen steps and I was in a printed green pair of blood-soaked PJ's, but I slid cautiously on my behind to the bottom step. Then the adrenaline kicked in and I ran about a block to an all-night cab office. They took me to the hospital, and the police took Larry to jail for assault and battery.

Doctors managed to control the bleeding and pain with medication, but I was bruised all over the arms, breast, face, and legs. I cried for Buddy Boy, and a nurse called a friend of mine asked her to get Buddy Boy for me. I was transferred to Downey, for I had no insurance—and I was considered a schizophrenic. But on June 11,

1955, I left there against medical advice to make sure Larry didn't get away with what he had done.

Larry was put on one year probation—his active Army status kept him from serving jail time. I went to Waukegan and got a room with an elderly couple named Mr. and Mrs. Walker. I got a job as a waitress at a restaurant, and I got along great with Pete, my boss. I worked from 4:00 p.m. to 2:00 a.m., and Pete would drive me home. He was a good family man and was honorable in all his relations with me. Mr. and Mrs. Walker were super. She would do my laundry and even feed me on my days off. I loved this couple, and I told them everything that happened concerning Larry.

Around Labor Day, Larry and I went to an after-hours gambling joint. Afterward we came back to my room and had intercourse. The next morning, Mrs. Walker met him. She told me later that she did not like him and asked me not to let him come anymore. One morning while eating breakfast, I got real sick and Mrs. Walker said, "You are pregnant." Great Lakes Hospital confirmed my pregnancy, and I spent eight days there with another attack of my facial problem. I had a job at Fansteel, and now I was pregnant and afraid to live with Larry, but Mr. and Mrs. Walker seemed more than willing to stand by me during and after my pregnancy. I told them how much I wanted a girl and she told me it was going to be a girl.

Larry kept after me to live with him but I wouldn't. Then he got orders to ship out for Korea. This gave me food for thought, and we decided I had better go back to New York during the pregnancy. I cried when I left Mr. and Mrs. Walker. If they had they been younger, I would have stayed with them. Christmas 1955 found me and Larry at my mother's place. Larry left to go to Korea via Washington State after New Years. I was living with my mother, who never wanted me—what a twist of irony. I found out she had access to numerous barbiturates that she overindulged in. Also, two of my brothers were constantly after her for gambling money, and she never could say no.

The atmosphere there was so chaotic that I went to Nanny's and rented a room from her brother and sister-in-law for $10.00 a week. I had kitchen privileges, and it was peaceful and tranquil there. Nanny suggested she and I buy a car together, so we got a brand-new red Ford. I took her to church and other places and enjoyed the car myself. I didn't drink any alcoholic beverages, but I did smoke and occasionally had one of Nanny's sleeping pills. Aside from that, I was taking good care of myself.

In mid-February, I developed cystitis, but sulfur drugs cleared it up in a few days. I had fixed up a baby room with a bassinet, a bathinette, a crib, a bottle sterilizer, a layette, diapers, and everything needed for a newborn. Larry and I had agreed we would call the baby Deborah Jean if it was a girl. If it was a boy, we decided to call him Ricky James.

My "water broke" in the hospital on May 24, 1956, and I screamed, thinking it was blood. Several nurses came and nonchantly said that it was only water. Around 9:00 p.m., I went into labor. One minute the nurses would say "don't push," and then "push." They said I had hours to go, but I told them the baby was ready to be born. They looked down and called a stretcher to rush me to the delivery room—my doctor was nowhere in sight. They gave me ether, and when I came to, the doctor was there, but I am still convinced the nurses delivered my baby.

I had a six-pound six-ounce baby girl, and I was thrilled. With the nurses' help, I fed and changed Debi (I had never been around a baby before). Sunday, I was writing to her father when I suddenly burst out crying. The nurse told me not to worry, that this often happens after childbirth. I was depressed despite the elation I felt over my bundle of joy. On May 29, I brought little Debi back home, not knowing I would be unable to perform the duties of a mother. I had no hint of the nightmare to follow, or how long I would wait to be with my baby.

I arrived at Nanny's place with no one to turn to. Nanny was a closet alcoholic who mixed wine with barbiturates, and at night she was completely out. She knew as much about babies as I did, which was nothing. I was afraid something was going to happen to Debi. Dr. Gilbert my obstetrician came to my home and administered a sedative so I would sleep. He thought I had a bad case of post-partum depression.

I went from a whirlpool of madness at Downey to having this beautiful little infant at my mercy. I had no confidence in my ability to do anything right with this baby, so Aurora agreed to help watch Debi. I woke up at 5:00 a.m. and discovered that Debi had vomited. I screamed to Aurora to hurry up; Debi was sick. She cleaned her up while I watched, wondering why in the name of God couldn't I do anything for Debi? I never thought of hurting my daughter, but I was consumed with the fear that my very presence was doing her harm. I was told I needed to be relieved of the care of the baby. I felt like a guitar string that was ready to break. My little baby was placed in foster care while I underwent therapy for this condition.

Social Services made it possible for me to see my daughter for a little each weekday, so I could gain confidence in myself. My doctor hoped I would be able to care for Debi and get over my depression. Finally, I was able to give her a bath and relax when I gave her bottle to her, and I had shades of hope. One day I was feeding Debi applesauce when she started choking and turned blue. She was rushed to the nearest hospital, and I was crushed beyond comprehension. I ran into the woods and let out a blood-curdling scream to God. I vowed to serve Him the rest of my life if He would save my baby. Then I was told my baby was going to be fine. They found out she was tongue-tied and kept her one night at the hospital. This was an answer to my prayer, but I still blamed myself.

My mother was good to me and the baby, and very supportive in our time of need. I began to have back pain and went to a doctor in Ballston. She said I had kidney problems and admitted me to the VA Hospital in Albany. My mother kept Debi, and I left the car at her disposal to use for any of Debi's needs. I gave her my whole allotment for the three months I was at the hospital.

I didn't know that all my records from Downey were already in the possession of the hosital in Albany. I had consistently asked the VA to send my folder to Albany, but they kept giving excuses why they couldn't. The things Dr. Chelnek said about me were very damaging. As a result, even though I had been admitted for treatment of a kidney problem, *they treated me like a mental patient.* They gave me a lot of medication and addicted me to Demerol.

When my mother came to see me, my eyes were all sunken in and hollow, and she raised cain with the administration. So for one solid week, except for meal times, they kept me in a twilight zone of existence by saturating my system with Thorazine. I was a zombie, but it did the trick. I got over being addicted to Demerol.

One night, a nurse kept asking me what brother lived near my baby. I told her Freddy and his family lived in the garage apartment behind the big house. The staff always kept me in their sight, and I thought, "There they go, thinking I'm crazy." I went into my room and closed the door, and a nurse came rushing to see if everything was all right. At bedtime, a the nurse came in with a hypo—even though I had just withdrawn from Demerol. In addition to the injection, she gave me two sleeping pills, saying I needed to have a good night's sleep. It was really weird.

Thanks to the medication, I had a vision of two men in military uniforms coming to my bedside. I thought they were my two brothers who were killed in service. They told me there was a fire and that that was *how my brother died.* It was like a nightmare because I knew they were lying. My brothers (if this were they) were killed in battle, yet I was to discover this was not an empty dream.

The next morning, the nurse asked me if I was prepared to go home. I said, "No, why?" Then she told me *my brother Stanley had burned to death* the day before and I was to go to his funeral. They had been watching me closely because they feared I would hear the news on my bedside radio.

My daughter was four months old the day Stanley was buried in a closed-casket ceremony. My mother had given him a shot of Demerol the night of his death, and he had been waiting for admission in a VA Hospital for treatment of serious sinus trouble. Either a cigarette or a heating pad caused the fire. He stayed upstairs alone. His wife, his mother-in-law, and the three girls slept downstairs. He called for help and his wife Mary, who wasn't too swift, got dressed and walked several blocks to my mother's house. My mother had no phone, so she had her husband pull the fire alarm, and she had to wake up the neighbors to call for help. When they found Stanley, he was lying over the bathtub around 6:00 a.m. He died twelve hours later. The last thing he said was, "I don't want to die." This was the third tragic death in our family.

I returned to my mother's to reestablish my relationship with my daughter, and we were doing just great. Then I started having severe pains in the lower right side of my abdomen. The VA examined me and said it was all in my head. Dr. Rockwell in Saratoga however, confirmed that I did have female trouble. He hospitalized me on December 3, 1956, for chronic salpingitis. I was discharged on December 15, but once again, was again addicted to pain killers. On December 29, I went to the mental ward in Albany Medical to get my system cleaned of drugs, and was discharged on January 7, Significantly, they diagnosed me with the personality disorder–Passive Aggressive Personality.

I returned to my mother's home to find that my car had been ruined by Roger. It burned oil so badly you couldn't go 20 miles without it needing more. I told my mother that I appreciated the good things she had done but that it wasn't fair of her to let anyone use my car but her husband and herself.

On January 9, 1957 I was able to take my baby back to Nanny's and care for her without any uncontrollable panic or fear. It was breathtaking to hold the apple of my eye and know that now I could attend to her. I adored my gorgeous bouncy baby, and it was like Heaven for me to have her at long last. In April, Nanny, Debi, and I went up to Aunt Rose's in a new Chevy Nanny had purchased to replace the ruined Ford. Aunt Rose enjoyed holding Debi and giving her a bottle. Nanny also liked to feed her the bottle, and there was a tinge of jealousy between them but not enough to spoil our nice vacation in the majestic scenery of the mountains. It was glorious for me. I slept with my baby. And God was on His Throne, and all was right with the world. Larry was due to come back to the States in May when Debi would be a year old.

Larry seemed to like his daughter, but he was a man who displayed little emotion. He was somewhat skittish in handling her, even though she was walking around holding onto things. Two days after he saw Debi, she started to run a high fever. Dr. Mintzer told me she had Roseola (infant's measles). He said it was going around and not to worry. I managed to get her fever down and prepared her bottle for Nanny. Larry and I were going out for awhile, and Nanny was going to watch her. I was waiting in the living room when I heard a loud and frightened scream. When I ran to where Nanny was, I saw my daughter in the throes of a grand mal seizure.

Larry and I ran to the car with Debi and headed for the hospital, less than a mile away. When we reached a railroad crossing, the red lights were on but the gates were just coming down. I screamed at Larry to gun the car. Onlookers claimed we made it by inches.

I jumped out of the car, ran into the hospital, and gave Debi to the supervising nurse, begging, "Save my baby!" She immediately took Debi into the emergency room. I can still see her there in her little yellow print PJ's as Dr. Mintzer went right into the room. I knelt on the floor and cried out to God not to let my baby die. Within a few seconds, which then seemed like years, I heard the most marvelous sound ever—the cry of my baby girl. Dr. Mintzer told me that sometimes a baby will convulse with Roseola, but the percentages were low.

Since Debi was fine, Larry and I decided to go out before he returned to duty. I ended up having sex with him two times while he was home on leave. Thinking I only had one tube and ovary—I thought I could not get pregnant. Both times I was three sheets to the wind, since we were by no means in love. This particular night, it didn't take much alcohol for me to feel my oats. I wasn't exactly happy being with Larry, and when we came back to the house that night, he was the first in bed.

I was sitting in Nanny's big chair when I suddenly had a flashback of the time Larry viciously beat me. I took a large pair of scissors and told him if he moved an inch I would kill him. "Come on, now is your chance to try again. This time I'm not in a closet." I stayed there for an hour and I'm glad he didn't move an inch, for if he had, I might have spent the rest of my life in prison. When Larry returned to his base, he wrote me and said he was not sending me any extra money because I had threatened to kill him.

I needed to earn extra income, so I took a job at Dewey's Taxi as a dispatcher where I worked until midnight. I liked the job, and the money came in handy. I met a man named Howard who was just super. He was 27 years older than me, but that made no difference. He had been married once but had no children. One morning he left a new dress and a pair of baby shoes in my car for Debi.

At the end of July I found out I was pregnant and I wasn't at all happy about it. Larry had come home, got me pregnant and left as usual. And here I had thought I couldn't get pregnant. In August, my cousin told me Nanny was scaring Debi at night like she used to do to me. I was furious. I quit my job, told her off, and moved out. Howard stuck by me in my move and loved my baby. In September and October of 1957, I was again hospitalized with pregnancy-related kidney problems.

Howard lived with his sister, his brother-in-law, and a niece. When I was in the hospital, he and his sister cared for Debi, and I knew she was in excellent hands. When I was discharged, Howard picked me up and we went to my apartment. For the first time, I had sexual relations with him, and he took me to the heights of ecstasy. At last I knew I was a woman. But the sin factor entered into our relations, and many times I denied myself his love because of it.

I told Larry that I was pregnant and when the baby was due. He wrote back and said he was going to get a leave during that time, which was February 18, 1958. I told Larry about Howard and how much he meant to me, and I asked for a divorce (Larry knew too well that I did not love him). Being a Catholic he would not consider it.

I told Larry I had no objections to him coming to see Debi and his new baby, but I made it clear to him that Howard would be around because I needed him with me when the new baby was born. I told him if he didn't like these conditions he didn't have to bother to come. I reminded Larry that I met Howard only after he decided not to send me and Debi anything extra to live on, so I had to seek employment. Howard never let Debi and I go without anything. It was like Heaven for me to have someone who was looking after me and who really cared.

Kidney problems put me back in the hospital in December, but I was still happy. Debi was just a joy. She was walking and really getting into trouble. One day she smeared her feces all over the wall, and I think she thought she had made a masterpiece. We had a pleasant Christmas. I visited Nanny and took her a gift. She really missed Debi, but I couldn't allow her to do the bogeyman routine with my baby. She promised she wouldn't do it again if we would come back, and I told her I'd have to think it over.

Larry came home on leave, and Howard continued to care for Debi at night. He would bring her to my apartment and put her to bed in her own crib. She was now 20-months old and was a little ball of fire. It was such a comfort for me to have someone like Howard to count on. He was so reliable, and he never really let me or my child down. Larry picked me up and drove me home. When he met Howard, he was cordial to him, for he knew I meant what I said.

On February 13, I was having breakfast and a sharp pain shot through me. I was admitted to the hospital at 11:00, and by 1:06 p.m. Ricky James was born, weighing 6 pounds and 12 ounces. We brought him home with 24-hour colic and watched him in shifts. Larry had to go back to his base, and he knew I couldn't care for Ricky so he offered to pay Mrs. Claydon to care for the baby until I got on my feet.

I went to Greenfield to see my son several times a week, and I was very run-down. In mid-May, I was back in the hospital, and I wasn't even home for my daughter's second birthday. Again, Howard and his family gave her a royal party. Howard visited me every day to make sure I wanted for nothing. Mrs. Claydon wrote to Larry telling him she could no longer care for Ricky. I got out of the hospital on May 28, and Larry came home on an emergency leave and told me I had to take care of Ricky "because the Army was his life."

I told him I wasn't able to care for the baby yet, and that instead of beating me up, he could have been a father to our children. I asked him, "If it wasn't for Howard, where would I be?" Larry had never really wanted to assume any responsibility; the Army was his wife, mother, and children. He left, and a few days later I went to visit my friend Mary. She was making a pot of coffee when the telephone rang. It was Larry. I wanted nothing to do with him, but Mary said, "Let's invite him up for coffee and maybe we can talk things over." I told her it was all right with me: "Larry Higgins isn't a man you can reason with, but I'll give it a try."

Mary told him to come up, and he did—*with a process server!* I was handed a summons to appear in Family Court on June 21, 1958, because Larry told the Child Welfare Department that I didn't want my son. What a cruel and terrible lie. Mary felt bad, but I told her that it would have happened anyway when I got back home. I needed to get someone fast to care for Ricky, and Mary knew just the person—Mrs. Drum lived in a mobile home park and she cared for kids. She was willing to take Ricky until I got on my feet, so I went right up to Mrs. Clayton's house and took my son. She knew I wasn't too happy with her. As always, Howard was watching over us.

I went to Family Court in June and told the judge that neither he nor anyone else was going to take my son away. As I was talking, I felt something running down my legs—it was blood! I was rushed to the hospital and treated, then I went back home with Debi. Larry returned to his beloved Army.

I met with Rose, another one of Mary's friends, and I really liked her. She wasn't the type to panic if my baby cried. I rested for the month of July, then told my landlady that I was leaving. She and her husband were my son's godparents. I thanked them for the beautiful christening dinner and for the gifts they had given me. I kept in touch with them for some time.

August 1, 1958, found me at Rose's home with my two children. The last two weeks of August, I tended bar in the daytime to help financially, and Rose took care of the children. In October, I moved back to Church Street. Nanny promised she would not play her bogeyman routines. She still knocked herself out at night, but it no longer bothered me. I felt secure in my ability to handle my children and any emergencies that might come up. I decided to go back to work and got Ethel Tragni to stay with the children. Howard spent the nights there until I got home when he wasn't driving cab. I felt I had all the bases covered. Although Howard didn't let us go without, I wanted to increase my income for the kids' sake and for my own self-esteem.

One morning while Debi and I were eating, I wondered why my son wasn't awake. Then Debi said: "Mommy, I gave little brother a pill because he was sick." Then she showed me how she climbed up and got the medicine bottle. Thank God, I knew it had only one sleeping pill in it. I rushed my son to the hospital. They said he would be okay but he would be dizzy for some time. I thanked God for protecting him.

On May 5, 1959, I sprained my ankle on railroad tracks that were being torn up. I spent a night in the hospital and it was a while before I could put weight on it. I initiated a neglect suit against the railroad with an attorney.

When I got better, we all went to see Aunt Rose in Tupper Lake and had a good time as usual. From there I went to Ogdensburgh to meet my father's sister, Aunt Minnie. She told me about the family. The Gagnons were a very respected family in Ogdensburg, and most of them were well off, with the exception of my father, the black sheep of the family. I found her to be very interesting, and I felt badly that I never met my grand parents on my father's side.

In 1959, my favorite nephew, Stewart, was placed in a reform school. This broke my heart, but there was nothing I could do. I knew his home life was chaotic and that he never got along with his stepfather. My brother Roger was always after Nanny for money. He would even send his wife down to plead for him. He talked my aunt into mortgaging her home for cash after he got an insurance policy and named her beneficiary. No one knew this, but we couldn't have stopped her. Roger was too much of a con-artist.

I suffered regular bouts of diarrhea and pain, along with the rare facial affliction. I still loved Howard, but most of the time I would deny him sex because I suffered too much for the pleasure it afforded me. It was hard to resist him, for I longed for him to bring me to heights of ecstasy. I did resist him for long periods of time: *I was proving to God that I wanted to be good.* I had asked Larry for a divorce so I could marry Howard. Of course Larry refused and my hands were tied, for I couldn't initiate divorce proceedings while he was in the military.

I was hospitalized 37 different times in 11 different hospitals from Illinois to New York in the 1950's. I spent a total of 427 days in these hospitals. On New Year's Eve in 1959, I knew I had to return to the VA to determine the cause of my diarrhea. Life was bleak, and I felt I was of no use to anyone. In my desperation and need, I turned to the mature man I loved and whispered to him, "Take me and love me." Afterward, I suffered pangs of guilt that drove me to confession. I encouraged myself by saying: "Nothing can be as bad as the 50's."

Chapter 6

The Sixties

By January 6, 1960, I was back in the Albany VA Hospital for persistent diarrhea and unexplained weight gain. I should have been losing weight, but I now tipped the scales at 196. After a series of tests, Dr. Yunich told me I had an irritable colon. He assured me I didn't have cancer, and he compared X-rays of a normal colon with mine. The extensive bouts of diarrhea I had after my son was born had weakened my bowels to a degree that they became susceptible to this disorder.

This was a tremendous ego booster for me, because this doctor didn't treat me like a crazy person. I never saw him again, but he won my undying gratitude. I was put on a bland, low-residue diet, and remained hospitalized several weeks to give the bowel a chance to recuperate.

I felt bad that I was unable to be home for my son's second birthday—my children's birthdays and Christmas meant a lot to me. Many years later my son told me, "Mom, no matter how bad things were, you always gave us a nice birthday and Christmas." I knew that Howard, Joe, Susie, and Nanny would give him a nice party, but I would have liked to have been present.

In June I received a $1,000 settlement check for injuries suffered in a fall on the railroad track. I asked Pat Simone at the funeral home how much was still owed for my father's funeral years ago, and paid the debt in full. It was also about this time that Aunt Rose told me that she wanted to leave me some things in her will.

I continually pressed to get my VA claims folder forwarded from the Chicago Regional VA Office, and I wrote a strong letter to officials there. (It didn't do any good.) I also applied for Social Security disability and was sent to their doctor in Glens Falls, New York for an examination. They told me it would take them time to evaluate my eligibility.

In the fall of 1960, Aurora and her three children were destitute because her husband was an alcoholic. I started World War III with the Welfare Office to get them help. Aurora was out of everything—her rent was due, the electric bill was due, and she didn't have a quarter to give to her children for their school lunches. When she ran out of fuel oil, she called Arthur Armstrong at the Saratoga Welfare Department. He told her to call Ballston Spa, which she did.

Mrs. Lohnes at that office told her that a case worker named Mrs. Summers would come to her home that day. No one showed up. The second day, I also talked to Mrs. Lohnes, and she told me that my sister "would just have to wait" until Mrs. Summers came to see her. I pressed the issue and she told me that Mrs. Summers would *definitely* come and see her that day.

At 4:45 p.m., Aurora called me—no one had come. She was crying and in a real depressed state. I called Mr. Gemetti, the Commissioner Of Public Welfare in Saratoga County, and was told he was in New York City. I called Mr. Armstrong, and he said he couldn't do anything until the next day. I reminded him that he had promised this woman help for two days, but nothing had been done—now they were without heat. He bluntly told me he "wasn't going to take the children into his home." Then I called Bertha Callahan, and she said I would have to talk to Mrs. Lohnes. When I asked for her telephone number, she told me to "look it up in the phone book."

I did just that and contacted Mrs. Lohnes, who was downright sarcastic. She told me she didn't want to be bothered at her home. I then asked her if those children had to freeze because of her laxity, and she said; "*If they freeze, they will just have to freeze.*" I said: "So, it's all right for those kids to freeze?" and she said: "Right!" and banged down the receiver. Three adults were in my living room and heard my side of this conversation.

The next afternoon, my sister found out through Mr. Armstrong that a check had been left at the Grand Union for her. I drove her to the Grand Union and we were told the check had been left *the previous day*—but no one had informed her.

We then went to Ballston Spa, and I went up to Mrs. Lohnes and told her that it was a pretty sorry thing when a person in her position did not care if children were cold and hungry! She hastily called the Commissioner and went into his office when she hung up her phone. I waited for her to come out, and when she did, I politely walked right into the Commissioner's office. He told me he would not tolerate anything from me, and threatened to call the police if I made any derogatory remarks about the Welfare System. I told him to call the police if he wished, but I intended to say what I had to say.

I told him Mrs. Lohnes was "an ancient relic in the guise of a humane welfare worker," and that he had done little, if anything, to improve the predicament of the poor in Saratoga County. Then he called the police. I used no profanity and made no statements that I was not able to substantiate.

I stood my ground in front of the police and the Commissioner. I was not arrested, but I got my message across. I relayed all of these details to Gov. Rockefeller in my letter. The Commissioner and I even had a battle in the *Saratogian* newspaper. The Commissioner actually accused me of political aspirations.

Howard worked at the harness track taking care of horses, and he would be going south in January. I worried about him, for he had suffered two coronaries. He would return in late April or early May. He called me and the kids often. He wrote and sent them money. He really didn't want to leave, but he had to if he wanted to hold down his job.

My kids had a nice Christmas and were both very healthy and thriving. They missed Howard, who was like a father to them. We knew we loved each other, but would I ever be free? Larry was writing, but I didn't answer many of his letters. I just kept him informed about his children and how I really wanted a divorce.

I ran into Bob again in 1961, and we had some good times. I still cared for him, but my young love had diminished. He too had many emotional scars. He was in the fast lane and had gotten in trouble with the law several times. He was finding it difficult to adjust, and like me, he lacked emotional stability in many areas of his life.

It was then that I realized that Howard was everything constant and stable I needed . Despite our age difference, his love bridged the years. Bob was my young love of the early twenties. My love in my early thirties was very different.

Bob met my children and they liked him. We were birds of a feather. I delighted to be in his arms and to feel his heart beat next to mine. I wasn't going to let fate cheat me again, but circumstances and events did. It was not to be. For the first few weeks, we had a whirlwind romance devoid of sex. Something was missing. Bob wanted us to go back to the way it was, but we were unable to turn back the hands of time. I haven't seen Bob since 1961. In 1988 I contacted him about my VA case. He wrote a letter about our former relationship and helped to dispel false allegations by the Veteran's Administration. He became a barber, married, and had seven children. I'm glad that Bob got his life straightened out. We still talk to each other, occasionally, on the phone to this day.

On April 19, 1961, I entered the Mosher Memorial Psychiatric Unit at Albany Medical Center. I had a lot of colitis and cramps, and I was given my first shot of morphine. All pain left and I was in heaven—no problems. This all-around euphoric feeling was so dynamic that I would not allow myself the luxury of falling asleep. It was the first time in my life I felt that "all was right and no one but no one could hurt me." But, all too soon, I awoke only to face the darkness of this world and of the soul within me.

It was during this four-and-a-half day hospital stay that a *resident anesthesiologist*—notice that again—a *resident anesthesiologist*—diagnosed me as a "sociopath addicted to alcohol." Before coming to Albany

Medical Center, I had gone to the Albany VA. They accused me of being drunk, and I had not even been drinking. This hospital stay, and the idiotic diagnosis made by an inexperienced physician outside of his specialty area plays an important role in the VA's allegations, lies, and nefarious deeds.

At this time, I told Howard I really loved him, but I could not suffer the conscience of the damned every time I tasted of the forbidden fruit (sex). I told him I would fight him tooth and nail if he tried to tempt me. I wanted him around me for he gave me a sense of well-being, but I knew I was weak in regard to his advances; one can't be taken to the heights of ecstasy without wanting to be taken there again.

Around this time, I discussed my weird facial condition with Dr. Lionel Truscott, the Chief of Neurology at the Albany VA. He did not think I was crazy—he was genuinely interested in my strange malady. Finally, after more than 12 years, someone diagnosed it properly. Dr. Truscott acted like a little kid when he found out what I had, and so did I! Finally, there was a medical name for my affliction: "Melkerrsdon's Rosenthal's Syndrome, Lingua Plicata." This malady caused paralysis of the right side of my face during the attacks.

I got home in time to celebrate Debi's sixth birthday. At this time I also contacted Congressman Samuel Stratton and asked him to help me get my VA claims folder sent to the Albany Regional Office. I renewed my friendship with the priest who used to visit so often. I had many doubts about the validity of the Catholic Church, and I thought that he could answer some of my questions. He told me to write down everything and come to the rectory some evening so we could discuss everything.

One night I went to the rectory with my notebook, and he suggested we go for a ride. We went out of town to a bar room where he continued to drink (he was an alcoholic who finally left the church). Sure enough, we tasted the *forbidden fruit*. I suffered terrible pangs of guilt. Although my "absolution" was sitting right next to me, I felt dirty all over. I sure hadn't planned this night, and God knew I did not want sexual relations with one of His "chosen vessels." As we started back to town I told him he had to hear my confession right then. He told me he couldn't because he, too, had to go to confession to another priest! I was stunned. He couldn't even forgive my transgression, far less his. A couple of weeks later he came to Church street and asked me to go out. I gave him an emphatic no. That was the last time I saw him. It was very traumatic—first I encounter a lesbian nun, and now I was seduced by a priest. Who could one trust? Some time later, I was to find the answer—God.

In November, my claim for compensation was again denied by the Regional VA Office in Albany. My claims folder had finally been transferred to Albany VA. I discussed my case with John McMahon, my lawyer, and he promised to go to the regional office, look at the records, and try to overturn their decision. I had no idea as to why they had taken my service-connected compensation away from me. Then John McMahon told me that they had me down as a *homosexual* in my records. The file stated I had been kicked out of two convents because of it and that I had been court-martialed twice because of *homosexual activities!* They had also labeled me a passive aggressive personality.

Personality disorders weren't considered to be service-connected illnesses. I was appalled. *I didn't even know what a homosexual was until I went in the service!* John told me he would take the case and not charge me anything unless he won. He was also going to write to the convent and prove this was a lie. I was to have a hearing on January 3, 1963. I can't express the outrage I felt.

Larry was discharged from the service in January, and he asked me to give our marriage a try. I told him I would as long as sex was excluded, and he agreed. Maybe our two beautiful children could help solidify our union. Meanwhile, Howard and I had a long talk. He loved my children, and we were in love, but what could we do? He was not a man to interfere because Larry was the father of the children. Howard kissed me good-bye and headed south.

John had set up our VA hearing for the first week in February. He had been diligently searching my records and wrote to the convent. The day of the hearing I was out of it mentally, and the VA took a hostile role against me—which was a total violation of their regulations. The hearing was a tragedy of errors, for I was not equipped to answer any questions properly. In March, I read John's rough draft of his memorandum in support of my appeal. The convent completely cleared me of their homosexual allegations. After reading John's brief, I was in a stupor. The depth of the VA's duplicity was very difficult for my mind to absorb.

The most significant part of his brief was the fact that while the VA doctors stated that they held a "staff conference" regarding my case on October 12, 1954, they jointly issued a written diagnosis dated September 27, 1954 (15 days before the "staff conference" took place). This finding showed that the diagnosis made at Downy the previous year was erroneous. (It said I was not suffering from *long term progressive disorder*, but that the correct diagnosis was "passive aggressive reaction." Then it recommended a severance of service-connected compensation.) Even in the nebulous realm of psychiatry, such prescience should raise eyebrows—but not with the VA.

Whenever I attempted to have my mental disability compensation restored, the rating authority relied upon the *1954 Downy report*. In fact, the diagnosis of various Veterans Administration hospitals had completed the cycle from schizophrenia to long term progressive disorder, and back to schizophrenia again. I supplied John with an affidavit denying that any of the four "psychiatrists" who signed the report ever treated me or discussed the case with me at the time of their so-called "10-hour conference." We hoped that this would cast some doubt upon the report.

I wanted out of this intolerable scenario. I did not consciously plan suicide, but I downed so much liquid chloral hydrate that I lost all track of time. (Larry provided me with an abundant supply.) I landed at the VA Hospital in Albany on March 28, 1963, and they didn't know what was wrong with me—except I had slurred speech and an unsteady gait. They gave me a Darvon and one barbiturate a day, but that wasn't enough for the withdrawal I was going through. Every nerve in my body was screaming. I literally begged nurses to give me something for my howling nerves, but I was ignored. I started to hallucinate that the light vents were wired. I thought I could hear doctors talking about sending me to Utica. With the last bit of sanity I had left, I went to the ward doctor and pleaded with him to put me out of my misery. He said he was sending me home the next day, and that I wasn't going to get any more sedatives. Then I lost it all in the chaos of a *grand mal* seizure.

I regained consciousness surrounded by doctors and nurses. They gave me a brain wave test, and even induced a seizure (which is traumatic at best). I convulsed while standing at the doctor's desk and then hit the floor. I suffered bruises, abrasions, and two black eyes. Then they decided to send me to Marshall Sanitarium, a private mental institution.

After the induced seizures, I felt relief from the terrible pressure in my brain. I no longer craved drugs, but I was acutely depressed when I arrived at Marshall's Sanitarium. I was furious at the VA for withdrawing me so brutally. They decided I should have Electro Convulsive Shock therapies. I had 20 of them, and each time I was scared beyond comprehension. On June 30, I was discharged as an outpatient, and told to return every week for therapy.

When I arrived home, another VA claim denial letter was waiting for me. What did I do to bar me from compensation and/or pension? They would not let me know, so I figured they were still saying I was a homosexual. They refused my attorney further access to my records, which was a violation of everything sacred and holy.

I was happy to see my two children. They had been placed in a home for one month while Larry went for surgery. I got them the very day I was discharged, and they hated the home. At this time I noticed that Larry had absolutely no patience with my son, and he was verbally abusive to both children. One morning he lost his temper with five-year-old Ricky and kicked him with his combat boots! I grabbed a butcher knife and went after him until he backed off. I told him I would kill him if he ever touched Ricky again.

In November I was becoming more and more depressed. On November 22, the day President Kennedy was assassinated, I was back as an inpatient at Marshall's sanitarium and was given seven more Electro Convulsive Shock treatments. I was discharged on December 26, but my children did have a nice Christmas. They opened their gifts the day I came home, and a letter from Howard was waiting for me.

Early in January, my sister Marie came over to accuse me of going to bed with her husband. We got into a wrestling match, and Larry took knives, scissors, and a Coke bottle away from her during the confrontation. She pressed charges against Larry, and all he had done was keep dangerous weapons out of her hand! We all landed in the police station telling our stories.

I received my retroactive Social Security in March, paid all my bills, and lent money to my mother. I would not get any more, even though I appealed. Now I would have no income source except Larry, but Howard would never let me down. Debi and Ricky really liked school. It was around this time that Larry was hired by the Albany VA Hospital. Larry's abusiveness toward Ricky was just too much, so I told him to get out. He started rooming at the VA hospital. I took him into Family Court for support and was granted it.

Howard came back from Florida, and we were all happy to see him. I was determined that nothing or no one was going to separate us again. His very presence spelled peace to my troubled heart and mind. I sensed that he wasn't feeling too well at the end of May, so I made him stay at my home. When he asked me for a sleeping pill, I knew something was really wrong. He didn't even take aspirins. His sister was concerned too.

I landed in the hospital at Saratoga for five days in June of 1964, and was back home only a day or two when Howard landed in the hospital with what appeared to be pneumonia. He was losing weight and strength. His doctor, whom I couldn't stand, thought Howard was getting worse and cancer was suspected. Almost overnight my love became as weak as a kitten, and it broke my heart. Howard's sister ignored the doctor's suggestion that she take him to the hospital by taxi and called an ambulance. Howard almost died on the way! (If she'd taken a taxi, Howard wouldn't have made it to the hospital!)

Tests showed Howard had cancer of the lungs, and there wasn't much hope. He had all kinds of tubes in him and really didn't know me. I cried out to God to let him live because I couldn't live without him. The children, Nanny, and I went to Tupper Lake for a while but my constant concern and worry was for Howard. I called his sister Mamie continually, but there was no change. Then one beautiful August day, Mamie called to tell me Howard had passed away. I went into shock. I had lost my best friend, and my children lost the only father symbol they knew. I got lost in barbiturates. When I went to the funeral parlor to see the shell of my beloved lying so still, it was all so unreal. He had wasted away to a mere 85 pounds. I wanted to take him to me and nurse him back to life. Every fiber of my being was dark with inconsolable grief.

Nanny got worse by the day with her wine and pills. I was still grieving, but sleeping pills kept me going. In December of 1964, we had a terrible ice storm. Many homes including ours were without power. We had a gas stove in the kitchen, so we did have some heat downstairs; and upstairs, Joe and Susie heated with a space heater. Nanny was really hitting the bottle. When her brother Joe went to her room, he came down and told me she had spilled wine on herself. However, it was blood, not wine, and I had her taken to the Saratoga Hospital.

Later, my mother came to see me and told me Nanny was not going to allow me to go back to Church Street. She told everyone I had tried to kill her by throwing her down a flight of stairs when I had actually saved her life! All we had were the clothes on our backs, and we were not allowed to go into her home to get anything. My sister Aurora was moving in with her, and they kept all our food and possessions.

Larry helped us move to a motel for two nights. Still we managed to give the kids a Christmas—we even had a turkey. We found an apartment and settled in for the new year of 1965. One night, the children were in bed and Larry was drinking (he wasn't to drink while living with us). I did not want to confront him so I went to sleep. I woke up to go to the bathroom and "Pow!" When I got back in bed, he hit me in the mouth and kept pounding me. Then suddenly he stopped and headed for the children's room, mumbling that he was going to "do them in." I quietly got a hammer and was going to hit him over the head, but he was too quick for me.

Larry knocked me down and beat on me. Debi jumped on his back, pulled his hair, and screamed at him to leave me alone. She tried to call the police but he would not let her use the phone. I hollered to her to call from the neighbors' place, and she did, saving our lives. My son hid under his bed in terror. He always felt bad that he couldn't rescue me that night (he was just a little boy!).

When Larry wouldn't stop hitting me, the police handcuffed him and threw him in jail. I had 27 marks to show for his night's work. He was sent to the Ballston County jail and received one year's probation so he could continue to support us. He moved back to the hospital.

Abe and Betty Kaye, my landlords, came and told me that they wanted me out of their place, even though I begged them not to do this to me and the kids. I asked Aunt Rose to help with a loan and she refused! Then a government check for $600 came in the mail for Larry. I forged his signature, cashed it, and told the Family Court what I did. I gave them a money order made out to Larry. I had divided the check into four and wrote him a note telling him his actions had caused our dilemma. Family Court mailed this to him, and I was never prosecuted.

I found another apartment and at the end of June, the landlord came to visit me. He made himself at home, and when I offered him coffee, he said he wanted to go to bed with me! I told him it was a sin. He responded: "How would you like to be evicted again?" I asked if he was kidding, and he assured me he meant every word. He knew I had no money to move again. I was forced to comply with his request in the most disgusting, downright sickening act one could conceive. When he finished, I burst out crying and turned my head. I had been honest and told him about my circumstances and he used them to blackmail me!

On July 11, 1965, something else really rocked my boat. One of Debi's cousins told me Debi had fallen on the sidewalk and she was in bad shape. When we got to the emergency room, I told them what little I knew about the accident and they sent Debi back home. Some kids showed me where Debi fell, and it wasn't just a "hole in the sidewalk," it was a *six-foot-deep concrete hole* loosely "covered" by a large grate! The grate had fallen in when the girls were running across it.

I knew Debi had a concussion, so Dr. Mintzer admitted her into the hospital. When John McMahon met me at the school with his camera to initiate a lawsuit, I was so upset that I offended him, and he politely walked out on the case. I felt badly because John had been so good to me.

Again, the landlord showed up, and he said he knew I was alone. He said he would like to impregnate me, and he would pay for the rearing of the baby. This was too much! I told him he wasn't going to touch me with his filthy hands—no matter what he did! Again he threatened eviction, but I told him to get out. As he left, he said in an ominous tone—"You will be sorry!" He told his wife lies about me, and the persecution began. First he barricaded the driveway, then his wife verbally assaulted me until I took a broom after her.

I found another apartment and Debi and Ricky at last were secure in their environment. Ricky was attending classes in order to make his First Communion, and Debi went to church school once a week. In 1956, we had a nice Thanksgiving turkey dinner at Jeanne's and we also had a super Christmas with friends. The kids didn't get a whole lot, but they were happy. On New Year's Eve, I thanked God for allowing me to have this place, and as my two precious children slept in the bedroom, I whispered to the Virgin Mary: "Maybe God doesn't hate me after all. Would you please go to Jesus and tell Him I love Him?"

The electrical wiring in my apartment was overloaded to the danger point. We were in a neighbor's apartment when the lights started to flicker. My friend asked to use the phone in my apartment and returned shouting that my place was on fire! I tried to open the door, but a wall of flames made me retreat. The blaze was finally extinguished, but the children's bedroom was trashed and so was the kitchen. All of my children's clothing was destroyed, and we had no money to replace it.

The next day, the paper said the fire was caused by a cigarette in the bedroom, which was not true. I was upset, and I told the landlord I was going to publicly refute this lie. He told me he said this so his insurance would cover the loss; otherwise he wouldn't get a dime. He said if I kept quiet, he would give us a furnished apartment on the second floor and would redo mine in fine style. I agreed to keep quiet because I didn't need another eviction.

I told Larry what happened and asked him to buy the kids some clothes, but he refused. My children again had decent clothes and a nice place to live thanks to Jim the landlord, the tenants, and the Red Cross. True to his word, Jim had the apartment finished in March. We now had a lovely new home. He even supplied new bunk beds for the kids.

In April, Roger asked me to live with Nanny at 69 Church Street again, for Nanny was terrified of living downstairs alone. I knew I'd have to be crazy to do that again, but after he left, my feelings began to soften toward Nanny. An invisible force prodded me to forgive and help her. It was like I was 15 years old again. I moved in with her in May, but with regrets. My sister had walked out on her after stripping the curtains off the windows and cleaning out what little food was in the house!

I was unhappy living with Nanny, so I compensated for my unhappiness with sleeping pills. Roger had reduced Nanny to the point of insolvency, but we managed to survive. The summer ended, and the kids were back in school. I was able to dress them—thanks to my Montgomery Ward account. At this time Debi's boyfriend's mother and her children became friends with me.

The beginning of 1967 found me in deep depression. Where would it all end? I did my best to keep the wine away from Nanny, but it was impossible to deny her fully. I weakened it with cranberry juice, and gave her vitamin pills (I told her they were sedatives). I had to hide my medicine from her. My children were affected by her behavior, but she loved them as much as she could love anyone. She said her rosary and novenas and prayed to all the saints nightly.

One day in January, Roger walked in and told her she had to go into a nursing home. He said he needed money so the house would have to be sold! He told me to pack my belongings and get an apartment. Nanny cried, and said she did not want to go to a nursing home. I knew Roger was rotten, but he had scraped the bottom of the barrel. I told him to get out, and then I called an attorney named James Murphy, Jr., and asked him to arrange legal papers so Roger could not force her hand.

Roger listened to my call, but he caustically told me he would be back to finish what he started. I screamed at him to leave. He then told me he was going to have me locked up because I was crazy. I explained everything to Jim Murphy, and he put the house in both Nanny's name and mine so it couldn't be sold without my signature.

This infuriated my mother, and she tried to talk Nanny into living with her. One day Nanny got mad and said, "I will go up and live with your mother." Less than a month had passed since the deed transaction. My mother and Roger spent endless months trying to get the deed changed so they could sell Nanny's house. They accused me of stealing it, but my conscience was clear. They knew that if Nanny left, it would leave me financially unable to pay the bills, so they hoped to force my hand; then they would sell. Every time my mother started something with me I reminded her that Nanny could come back anytime for it was her home.

This was breaking me down mentally. I needed help, so I got a woman to come and stay with my children for a few days and went to the Albany VA in March. They took me off Dilantin and phenobarbital, but my nerves were already shot. I went to the Psychiatric ward at Albany Medical Center under the care of Dr. William Hart, the head of the unit. To me, he was a god in his own right. When he suggested that I undergo a series of Electro-Convulsive shocks, I knew what these treatments would do to my mind and memory. I needed to find someone to care for my children without putting them in a home. I finally called Larry. He consented to care for them, but I told him he couldn't drink because of his violent history (he wasn't happy about it). I told Debi and Ricky that I had to be hospitalized, and that their father would care for them. I prayed nothing would happen.

I endured the shock treatments and wondered if I would ever wake up. Dr. Hart always "comforted" me and gave me liberal doses of tranquilizers and barbiturates. I clashed with the staff and trusted no one. I snapped out of the acute depression but got hooked on barbiturates. I was given four Amaytals a day and four Carbitals at night. I also had a private supply hidden in the bottom of the Kleenex box.

When I returned home, Larry told me to raise Joe and Susie's rent to keep the place out of Roger's hands. Larry was willing to help me with some bills, but not if Joe and Susie only paid $10 a month for a whole apartment. I asked for at least $40 a month and they were insulted. They would have no place to live if Roger got the house, but they wouldn't listen. They moved across the street from my mother's, paying $100 a month!

In July, Debi was hit by a car while riding her bicycle and suffered a broken leg. It was a miracle she wasn't killed because her bike went under the car. It was the driver's fault, and a law suit was initiated. Right after this, I received nine more shock treatments and came back home a complete mess. I was taking 19 sleeping pills every day! My new tenants helped me out a lot and Larry kept his word and helped to pay some of the bills, but by the end of August I was really robotized by the pills. I only lived to see Dr. Hart (and his pills).

Dr. Hart faithfully supplied the crutch I needed—drugs. I bounced between four druggists at a time, and I wasn't a bit afraid to alter a prescription. If the doctor gave me a script for 10, I just added another 0. I made sure I had enough Carbitals and Amaytals to satisfy my insatiable craving. Every fiber of my being screamed for more.

Dr. Hart was my main supplier, but I knew I had to get this drug monkey off my back. I was like a vegetable, existing to swallow more and more downers. Dr. Hart readmitted me for four more shock treatments and even more pills. I knew I had to do something drastic, or else take my life. Somehow, I knew that Dr. Hart wasn't going to get me off drugs. When I remembered that Marie went to Utica State Hospital to dry out, I asked Larry to drive me there. I also told my children what I was going to do. We started out late at night, for I dared not wait another day, or there wouldn't be many more tomorrows for me.

We arrived after midnight, and I had brought my pharmacy with me. I hadn't taken any pills for hours, but just before I went in the building I downed a couple to bolster my courage. I presented the doctor with my medicine stockpile, but then he told me they didn't treat drug addiction: they only treated mentally ill people. Then I asked him, "How disturbed does one have to be? If I'm taking up to 19 barbiturates coupled with tranquilizers every 24 hours, wouldn't I be a mental and emotional wreck?"

He called in another doctor while I asked myself, *Am I really trying to fight my way into an insane asylum?* I knew if they did not admit me, I had no where else to turn. I pleaded with them, and they agreed to keep me. They warned me that I would be placed on Utica's worst ward; it was the only ward where there was enough help for me should I convulse. I bid my husband good-bye and begged him to be good to the children. Then I was taken to the sixth floor and made to strip and shower. By this time my body was screaming for barbiturates and nicotine. I spent a weird night amidst strange noises in a twilight-like sleep, with no idea of what awaited me.

That morning I was told to get up and was given clothing. Then we were herded into a dayroom. Everyone looked horrible and scary. It was truly the classical "snake pit." My mind and body were in the throes of agony. I told a doctor I had to get out of there because I was going crazy, but this was Wednesday and Larry wasn't coming until Sunday. I was placed on a decreased withdrawal schedule and was allowed so many barbiturates a day. I came on Tuesday, and by Saturday I knew no real sleep. Night after night, when I would doze off, it was as though someone was choking me and I would wake up screaming. Every nerve in my body would jerk and convulse. I did what I was told, but it was far from easy.

I got along well with the charge nurse. She told me there were other patients of Dr. Hart's there, and all of them were addicted to drugs. She asked me never to go back to him. Visiting days were on Wednesdays and Sundays, and I was anxious to see my children. Sunday came, but I had no visitors. I was in despair. Why did Larry do this to me? I got a letter from Debi that said they hadn't visited because Larry couldn't get anybody to take his place at work, so I counted the hours until Wednesday. They all came and brought me a lot of goodies that I shared with other patients. When they left, I knew I would soon be home with a clear mind.

I was discharged with prescriptions for Librium, but I really missed Dr. Hart (I was "in love" with my "god"). I called his office, and the secretary asked me why I hadn't kept my last appointment. I told her I had gone to the Utica State Hospital for barbiturate withdrawal. I was given an appointment, and I counted the hours until I would see him again. Dr. Hart wasn't pleased that I had gone to Utica for drug withdrawal. He didn't approve of such drastic steps. I apologized for doing it without talking it over with him, and he appeared to be pleased with my submissive attitude. I left his office with a fresh prescription for 100 Carbitals! I told myself I'd go easy on them....

It was the holiday season, and I told Larry I would sign his income tax if he would co-sign a loan so the children could have a nice holiday. He agreed (this wasn't the first time I'd used this ploy). The children had a good Christmas, and we went to see Nanny, Aunt Rose, and my mother. I was shocked when I saw Nanny. She was emaciated, feeble, and much too thin. Marie told me privately that Nanny had been neglected for months. Because of the house situation, I knew that I would get nowhere by intervening. I left in tears.

In 1967, I had been hospitalized eight separate times, spending time in hospitals nine out of twelve months. I rationalized that there had to be a purpose for my life and as I popped a couple of Carbitals on New Years Eve, I was sure that a few would never hurt me and my moods would steady. "Oh what a tangled web we weave, when first we practice to deceive" (Sir Walter Scott).

I still managed to see Dr. Hart on a permanent basis. I had to have my supply of sedatives, and he was a constant outlet for these needs. I still worshiped him and wondered if I would ever get over the feeling of wanting to be around him. Larry was becoming more short-fused, and that wasn't a good sign. He complained about the attorney handling my daughter's two accident cases. Sure that something should be settled by now, he phoned Jim Murphy and blew his stack. I got Jim to agree to continue handling the case—if Larry had nothing to do with it. I finally told Larry to go back to Albany. (I feared another brainstorm.)

Shortly after Larry left, my mother told me she could no longer care for Nanny, and I would have to take her. She said Nanny was too sick to come to the phone, and that she was going to call Pat Simone and have him bring Nanny over via ambulance.

Pat Simone called to tell me that Nanny was dying—that is why they were sending her to me. He said she had lain in her own feces and urine and was truly vegetating. He was furious, and so was I! He said he had taken her to the hospital several times but they always denied her admission. I told him I had to take her in because this was really her home, and that nothing would surprise me concerning the care she got on White Street. After he hung up, Eugene (my mother's husband) showed up with a hospital bed. He put the bed up, hung up her clothes, and left saying, "Have fun."

When Pat came with Nanny…words cannot describe how bad she was. She was stark raving mad due to brain anemia and malnutrition. How could my mother, a nurse, do this? I cleaned her up as much as I could, but she had to be rehydrated, and she needed to be in a hospital. Her doctor was determined to put her in Utica State Hospital as a mental patient, but I told him her body had to be taken care of before I would ever consider Utica. I would fight the whole damn city before I would allow her to go to an insane asylum.

I asked a friend to make a bomb from a metal vacuum cleaner hose using hundreds of match tops. He planted it by the doctor's house and detonated it. I think he got the message, for he admitted Nanny to the Saratoga Hospital shortly thereafter. Her mind started to come back, and then she was placed in a nursing home in Greenfield Center until she was stronger. I vowed she would come home again.

I was an avid follower of Dr. Martin Luther King, Jr., and felt real sad when he was killed in April of 1968. I knew about Resurrection

City, and the Poor People's March in Washington, D.C. planned for June. I told the head of the NAACP in Saratoga that I would like to go to the march with my children. In June, we were watching TV and saw the reports of Robert Kennedy's murder. That was also the month Bernice Jefferson of the NAACP told me there was room for us to go to Washington. She said she would pick us up and drive us to Albany to catch their bus.

We boarded the bus at Albany and sat in the back. We went with a semi-militant organization called the "Brothers." I told them what happened to me in the Army, and they asked me to send them some of my evidence. There was a lot of drinking, although I was told there would be none. There was no bathroom on the bus so we had to make a 20-minute stop. When we got back on the bus, I popped a couple of pills to help me sleep. Suddenly I heard a siren wailing behind us. State troopers were pulling the bus over, and someone said, "What do the pigs want?"

As the trooper stood on the steps of the bus, I heard the men in the back say they would "take care of the pigs" if they dared to come onto the bus. I was afraid. The troopers said rings and jewelry had been stolen at our last stop, and one guy said he would "throw the stuff out the window" before he would let the pigs have it. (They had robbed the place.)

I was really disenchanted. I was coming to the march to add my voice to those of the poor and downtrodden from every race and color. Stealing and lawbreaking wasn't the answer. I kept my mouth shut, but I wished we had not come. I prayed the troopers would not board the bus, because it was a very tense situation. My prayer was answered.

We finally arrived in Washington and were given the number of our bus and the time to return. Then we were left on our own. We went to Arlington National Cemetery and saw 50,000 people there. I saw Resurrection City, with its booths and clothes hanging outside. In my ignorance I was looking for a worldly utopia. That was the first time I had ever seen hippies. The day was sizzling hot, so we sat by a pool soaking our feet.

Bill Cosby, Eartha Kitt, and Coretta Scott King spoke, and a telegram was read to us from Ethel Kennedy. It was a long, weary day, and I was exhausted. It was time to go to our bus, and Debi said she knew where it was. She went to make sure, while Ricky and I waited. Ricky was carrying my pocketbook, for I was completely drained. Debi didn't come, and I started to cry. So Ricky went to look for Debi. He told me to wait—now both of my children were lost! The next thing I knew, I was lying on the ground surrounded by people. I couldn't talk, and someone said my pulse was only 30. I tried to ask, "Where are my children?" and someone assured me my children were with the Southern Christian Leaders Association and being well cared for. They were with me when I passed out, but I had no memory of it.

An ambulance took me to George Washington Hospital where I was kept for several hours, and the bus left without us. The doctor wanted me to stay the night in the hospital, but I wanted to be with my kids. The SCLA man came with my kids to drive us to the bus station where he purchased our tickets and we boarded the bus. We would have to change buses in New York City to reach Albany. There we needed to catch still another bus to Saratoga.

We arrived in New York to learn we had a five-hour layover for the bus to Albany. It was midnight, and I wasn't about to keep my kids in a terminal all night, so we took a cab to the Times Square Hotel. In the morning, we ate and then took a cab to the bus terminal. I had left the bus tickets at the hotel gift shop, so I had to spend my dwindling supply of money to get us home. Wonder of wonders, we made it back safely. Herb Starr from TV Channel 10 arranged to interview me concerning the trip. I told them why I went and how I felt about it all. My children and I were the only whites from Saratoga who went to the march.

I went into the hospital two more times shortly after that for some painful tests on my spine. While I was undergoing therapy for my ulnar nerve, Dr. Hart let me have all the sleeping pills I wanted (while I was in or out of the hospital). I was allowed to call his home in Delmar, and I did many times. He always seemed to take my part in any confrontation I had with the staff. But one night, the charge nurse would not give me my allotted medications at bedtime. I told her I was going to call Dr. Hart at home, and she told me it was fine with her.

When I called Dr. Hart, he suddenly turned against me. I was abruptly transferred to a violent ward and locked in a seclusion room with only a mattress and a sheet. I was in shock. In the morning, I saw my "god," but he was as cold as an iceberg and would not answer my questions. I was absolutely dumbfounded. When I got home, I found out that Larry had attempted to choke Ricky for wetting his bed one night. He told my children he would get even with them if they told me. I wanted to kill Larry. I lit into that beast, knowing he was afraid of me because of my many mental problems. He knew I was as capable of murdering him as he was of me! I threatened to prosecute him for child brutality, and he left mumbling that I would be sorry.

On December 6, 1968, he came back with an electric utility man and cut off the electricity in the cold of winter! My bills outstripped my income, so I told the children we would have a meager Christmas. My tenants were unable to pay their rent, so on Christmas Eve the presents under the tree were as sparse as the food in our cupboard. The phone rang and a voice told me to go to the front porch. The children and I found two large boxes there: one was filled with wrapped Christmas presents and the other was filled with food. We had an exquisite Christmas, and on New Year's Eve we thanked God as we ushered in 1969. I kissed the kids goodnight and mused over how we would make it.

Ricky began to give me heartaches that year. He was stealing, vandalizing, and running around with a bad crowd. I especially couldn't stand one kid he hung around with; he lied, cheated, stole, and terrorized everyone. One day I told him to stay away from Ricky or I would wipe the streets with him. Ricky told me I was the only one this kid feared. I often thought that if Howard had lived, Ricky would have been different.

I called Dr. Hart for an appointment and learned *the VA would not pay for my care any longer*. Then I told him I had a Medicaid card that would pay for my therapy and that I was desperate. He reluctantly agreed to see me. I was thrilled to "return" to his good graces, but he had decided I was too much to handle *when the price wasn't right*. He finally released me as his patient, and I lost my little "god." I was left to pacify my pain with the cursed barbiturates.

Once again I became Nanny's self-appointed savior. I was still trying to reinstate myself with Dr. Hart, but I also found another doctor in Albany who would supply me with barbiturates—if I paid him $10 for each script. I couldn't see how we could possibly keep the house. We were behind on the mortgage and home insurance. The foundation was sinking, and the house desperately needed maintenance. Larry waited patiently for us to go under. He wanted me to sell the house to the man next door for $4000.

My legs were so bad that I couldn't even walk a block because of the pain. An orthopedic specialist urged my doctor to put me in the hospital so drastic measures could be taken to lower my weight. I told Debi I would run the house from the phone in the hospital because I did not want Larry coming up. She promised to care for Nanny until I got back.

One morning I was talking to a nurse about some sleeping medication when Dr. Feynaman (he had been Howard's doctor) said, "If you can't sleep, why don't you go home?" I told him off, reminding him in the process of how he had killed Howard through negligence. I told Dr. Carasavas what happened between me and Dr. Feynaman. He told me he had problems with him too. He was treating a woman whose drug addition was nursed by Dr. Feynaman. When I saw him again, I called him a mercenary killer as loud as I could and started naming some of his victims. He threatened to report me to Welfare and I laughed (I wasn't on Welfare). I was riled, and I had an audience. He fled down the stairs, and some nurses told me they were glad someone had told him off.

Ricky was running wild. One night he wasn't home and I was so upset I planned to leave the hospital. The charge nurse had the police locate Ricky, and he was back home at midnight. I was furious. Aunt Rose visited Nanny and gave her some cash, and Nanny ordered wine! Thank God my children intercepted it and prevented a tragedy. Nanny could not be trusted with money, and Aunt Rose felt awful.

I came home 27 pounds lighter but I was still in pain. Dr. Carasavas told me my knees would regenerate, but I was depressed, dreading the long winter months. I was in no condition to work. Then Social Security reversed its decision and told me I would receive retroactive money from 1964. At last the tide was turning!

Chapter 7

Early Seventies

The year of 1970 began with the news that my cousin had committed suicide after taking the lives of his wife and two children. He had never got over the death of his older brother who had made himself a human torch in New York protesting the Viet Nam War in 1968.

Debi and I testified in court about Debi's fall into the deep hole on school property, and she was awarded $2,500. I placed the money from the court settlement into a trust fund for Debi. Aunt Rose surprised me that month when she offered to loan me $300, and I took her up on her offer.

Dr. O'Connell kept his word and treated Nanny. He sent Jeanne Conway, a public health nurse, to the house to give her monthly injections of Vitamin B-12 for her pernicious anemia. When Jeanne started talking about God, I laughed in her face. When I recited one of my childhood poems for her, she shocked me by saying, "You had the Holy Spirit when you were fifteen."

Jeanne then said, "In the world ye shall have tribulation: but be of good cheer; I have overcome the world" (Jn. 16:33). I asked her where that came from, and she said Jesus said it and that it was recorded in the Bible. I wasn't allowed to read the Bible as a Catholic and I was amazed! *Surely it didn't apply to me?*

In February, the Social Security Administration began to send me monthly installments, back payments as well!

In March, a truant officer told me Ricky had been skipping school. Ricky told me he and his friend were jumping on some mattresses they had found an abandoned house, so I had a heart-to-heart talk with him. I told him to "turn over a new leaf"—or else! Then I was told that Ricky and his friends had stolen and destroyed merchandise at a "five and dime" store. When I threatened to place him in a juvenile detention home, he promised me he would straighten out. His report card showed me he was making an effort, so I had a glimmer of hope.

In late April, I received some money and decided to pay a number of bills. The last one on my list was Aunt Rose, and I gave her $300 to repay her for the loan she had given me. I returned only to learn that Officer Lyons had been there asking about Ricky and the bad company he was keeping. I called his home, and then I called the station and asked Sgt. Paul Cassier if Officer Lyons was around. He got flippant and told me he wouldn't tell Officer Lyons anything about my call. He also called me a liar. I slammed down the phone and called the Chief of Police at his home. I told him what had happened and said, "Paul Cassier is wrong, and he has no right to call me a liar." I shouted and blamed the Chief for all the actions of his department.

I was still raving when Ronnie Lyons knocked on my door! He had stopped by, and I was so glad to see him that I picked up the phone and called Cassier, and said: "Cassier, you're a schizoid paranoid, and you're like a kid who shines his brass every night in boot camp. If it's the last thing I do, I will get you!"

Lyons told me Ricky had been playing in a large tank filled with hay, and he could have either become stuck or it could catch fire. Later on, *I found out the truth* from another beat officer. He said the cops thought there were stolen goods in that barrel, and Lyons had said: "Let me go and get Ricky Higgins and have him crawl in there and see what's there. You know his mother is a wacko, so I'll go by myself." *This was the real reason Lyons came to my home and asked Nanny about Ricky.*

As Lyons was leaving, he explained that he had forgotten to write down on his report that he had stopped at my house. That was why Paul Cassier thought I was lying.

The next day, when a heavy knock came on the door, I answered, and there stood Paul Cassier, Ronnie Lyons, and Robert Gratton. I laughed—for here was the whole police department. Then Cassier said I was under arrest for "aggravated harassment over the phone"! I said, "You've got to be kidding!" He took my right wrist and started to twist it, and when I told him he was hurting me, he just twisted it harder. He said he had finally nailed me, and that they were going to throw the book at me. I wanted to kick him but I knew the law well enough to know that if I even touched his uniform, it would be a felony.

I also told him I would have my day in court. My daughter and her girlfriend came in and heard Cassier say, "Come on, we are taking you to the police station." When Debi said, "Not until she gets dressed," Lyons ordered Debi to be still, but Cassier said, "I'll let you get dressed, but on one condition: give me your gun." I told him it was perfectly legal and that no one was getting it. (I had a reputation for being a marksman, but I couldn't hit the broadside of a barn. I wanted them to believe I would blow their heads off if I got mad enough.)

He finally allowed me to go to my room, and as I was dressing I envisioned myself making a stand with my little Brownie rifle against three burly policemen with their .38 Magnums, tear gas, and billy clubs. (I might have been crazy, but I wasn't that crazy!)

Cassier yanked me while we were going up the police station steps and tore my coat. When they booked me, they told me I had to pay $25 for bail or go to jail. I refused to pay. I told them I always wanted to see what it looked like back in the jail, so they took my pocketbook and counted my money. I had over $500 in cash, and the booking officer said, "Come on, Theresa, why not pay the $25?" I told him I wasn't guilty and it was a matter of principle.

The jail cell sure wasn't the Ritz. It featured a hard bunk bed, a toilet, a sink, and no privacy. Lyons took my kids and fed them, and I started to read a book when Cassier came to my cell nice as pie and actually said he was sorry. (I thought, *My diagnosis was right; he is a schizoid.*) I had already left a message with my lawyer's wife.

Cassier brought me two cheeseburgers and I told him I only wanted one. He insisted, but I wouldn't give in. He even went out to get me catsup. I couldn't believe his about-face. This guy wasn't so bad after all; we were both cut out of the same stubborn cloth. My kids came to see me, and after they left, I told the police they had better get a nurse to stay with me all night and weekend because I was 100 percent disabled.

Jim Murphy was trying to reach Judge La Belle, who was at church, so Cassier invited me up front to wait. I told him I was under arrest and that I had to stay behind those cruel bars, but finally I did agree to wait in front. One would have thought nothing had happened and we were the best of friends, but the pain in my wrist kept reminding me of Cassier's deeds.

Judge La Belle released me to my lawyer's custody, but he warned me that if there was "any nonsense of any kind" on my part I'd be right back in jail without bail. I was infuriated when I appeared in court and read the charges. Cassier's complaint said that I had called him an "S.O.B.," and that was a lie. I told the judge I had two dogs, and I wouldn't want *either of them* to have Paul Cassier for a son! Later, I told the judge he had a lot of nerve signing this complaint against me since I wasn't even allowed to counter charge with the truth.

James Murphy, my lawyer, talked to the Commissioner of Public Safety and the cops who had come to my house. When Lyons confirmed to the Commissioner that I had not been abusive to Cassier, he told my lawyer to tell me to drop everything. But I was too pigheaded to do so, even though he believed I was telling the truth, and his own men testified to it.

The next day, my hand was black and blue and my wrist hurt. I went to the Saratoga Hospital Emergency room for x-rays, and Dr. Carasavas and a resident orthopedist told me I had a fracture. They put a cast on my wrist up to the elbow. I now knew I had a law suit for police brutality, and I decided I wanted an out-of-town lawyer. Three days later, my arm was hurting really bad at the elbow. The cast was so tight that it was causing my arm to bleed. I called Dr. Carasavas and asked him to do something about the cast. At that time he told me that my wrist was not fractured, but that he could not take it off "because he had no right to put it on." I offered to go to his office to have the cast removed, but he refused, so I told him he would live to regret his decision.

Armand Riccio, my attorney in Schenectady, was sure he would win "megabucks" for me. When I told him about my wrist and how the doctors wouldn't remove the cast, he took me to St. Clair's Hospital for x-rays and had them remove the cast. He took the remains of the cast for exhibit A for a new malpractice suit. My wrist had only been sprained, but it was still bruised and discolored. I had a good case against the police and an excellent one against the two doctors and the hospital.

My attorney was really excited about the law suits, and he again made me promise that I wouldn't drop them. I demanded that he proceed with the police brutality suit, for I wanted it in the paper as soon as possible. He asked me to wait until after my trial, for it could militate against me. I wanted it my way, so in May there was an article in the paper that stated I was suing the city of Saratoga Springs and its agent, Paul Cassier, alleging false arrest and mistreatment causing injury during the arrest.

In mid-June, Aunt Rose took a turn for the worse. I saw her at my mother's house, and Aunt Rose was gasping for breath. I told my mother to call an ambulance and she wouldn't, so I called one and went to the hospital with her.

Another time, Aunt Rose asked me to purchase two pair of pajamas for her and gave me a check for them. She was talking very softly, and she whispered that Roger was bleeding my mother for money. My mother did not like her talking to me alone, and they always asked her what we discussed.

One night Aunt Rose asked me to stay the night with her. When I got there, Aunt Rose was nearly dead thanks to the Percodan and sleeping pills my mother had given her! When Aunt Rose came to, I started to fix her bed and found even more pills in her bed. That night, my mother also took a lot of sleeping pills, but instead of going to sleep, she was especially talkative. She said she and Roger had broken Aunt Rose's metal box and read her will. The bulk of her money was going to my first cousin Ronnie, so my mother planned to ship Aunt Rose to Ronnie as soon as possible. She ranted and raved all night, while Aunt Rose listened. That morning, my aunt asked me to call her attorney so she could change her will in my favor. She was going to the hospital, so I told her to wait until she got out of the hospital.

Roger drove me to the hospital to see Aunt Rose, and when we got there she was in bad shape and shaking all over. When Roger left, she asked me to go to the bank in Mechanicville and withdraw her money. She said she would have the nurse call the bank on Monday. She told me to keep the money until she got better. I did not know until later that there was nearly seven thousand dollars in that bank. Then Roger came in suddenly, and I swear he knew what she asked me to do. Something was fishy. I didn't withdraw the money, and Aunt Rose passed away the next day.

Aunt Rose wanted to be cremated, and she allowed only one family viewing of her body. My mother told me this viewing was on Tuesday night, but when I went to the funeral parlor, I was shocked to learn that my mother had deliberately given me the wrong time! Aunt Rose's body had already been cremated! Mother never went to view Aunt Rose, and she made sure I wouldn't see her either.

Aunt Rose left most of her money to Ronnie, and I was amazed that she had left me $2,000 because I had told her to shove her money. She left my mother the same amount, and young Stewart received $1,000. My mother couldn't wait to throw Aunt Roses' remaining possessions into the dump.

I was addicted to barbiturates, and my knees were still in bad shape; I was taking a lot of Darvon compound for the pain. I had an unexpected visit from Dr. Carasavas after he'd received a court summons. He begged me to settle out of court. I told him to talk to my lawyer. I also told him I would not have initiated this law suit if he had been man enough to remove the cast. His own actions condemned him.

I had evaded Jeanne ever since she had told me about the "born again experience" with Jesus, but Jeanne was a persistent person. She told the notorious Theresa Higgins all about this Jesus who was in the business of transforming and changing lives.

I went to court July 24, 1970, before a jury of six. We each told our stories, and Officer Lyons even confirmed that I had not used abusive names over the phone. The jury deliberated for 15 minutes and found me guilty—despite the fact that Cassier was caught in an outright lie. Judge La Belle talked to my attorney and told him he made his mistake *when he put me on the stand.* I believe I blew it because I was hostile, sarcastic, and arrogant. I was to be sentenced on August 13 by Judge La Belle. This defeat was staggering for me and my Schenectady attorney. My sentence was "Don't call the cops unless you have to."

At the same time, the hospital called me to come in for knee surgery. Debi went to Greenfield and Ricky went to a law officer's home when I went in, but I was so addicted to sleeping pills that the hospital had to give me at least eight every 24 hours. I was a mess and they knew it. Dr. Edwards, the chief of orthopedics, said I couldn't survive an operation, and he refused to take my life on the table. I weighed nearly 250 pounds and had a severe drug addiction. I admired his integrity, and I know he was right.

Jeanne Conway and Nancy came to see me in the hospital, and I was a mess. Worries over my children and my health had taken their toll. They asked if they could pray for me, and I reluctantly bowed my head. Suddenly Nancy put her arms around me. I was embarrassed. Because with the homosexual allegations against me, I couldn't conceive of ever hugging a woman. Somehow I understood that Nancy's action was motivated by the Holy Spirit. She got a glimpse of the poor, hopeless person I was and the compassion of Christ poured out of her. In August, Jeanne Conway invited me to a "brown bag lunch" for September 1 at a state park with Nancy, Dorrene, and Pat.

They kept praising the Lord, and I thought they were a bunch of nuts, but when I got home I felt a ton lighter.

Dorrene asked me to go to a Full Gospel Breakfast, and for some reason I agreed to go. Kenneth Hagin was scheduled to speak, but first a former nun with a guitar told her story and sang a song that touched the very fiber of my heart. One line said, "It's no disgrace if you fall, for I want to tell you a secret, My blood has covered it all." That day God started to heal my damaged emotions. Kenneth Hagin gave a powerful testimony, and to say I was shook up is putting it mildly. I even received the baptism of the Holy Spirit! For the first time in my life, I was given a Bible to read.

That month, my congressman told me the VA said the decisions of its Board of Veterans Appeals were final. I had to have new and material evidence to reopen my case. John McMahon's brief proved I was not a homosexual or an alcoholic, but I was denied again.

The VA gave me a "non-service connected pension" in 1970, and I was puzzled. They said no veteran with a personality disorder and/or a "Willful Misconduct" citation (homosexuality, alcoholism, and drug addiction) can receive compensation. They accused me of the first two, but never the last one. It was all too mysterious. I knew my condition was service-connected, and I wasn't going to give up.

Ricky got interested in football, and I was pleased. This was a constructive move on his part. One day he passed out, and the doctor said he had epilepsy, ending his football career. They later admitted Ricky did not have epilepsy, but he never wanted to play football again. He went further down the path of self-destruction.

In October, I started to go to a Pentecostal church with Dorrene. I began to know another God and a Jesus who was no longer in a box that only priests could open. I heard sermons that were all substantiated by the Bible. I immersed myself in the Bible, and was anointed with joy. One day the Holy Spirit seemed to say, "Theresa, you must give up your hate for your mother." I wrote Mother a letter, and I mailed it to her.

At the end of the year, my daughter's second accident case was settled, and she was awarded $1,750 for injuries she suffered when she was run over by a car. I decided to ask Larry up for the holidays and try to forgive him, and on Christmas day, there was peace in our home. I was thankful for God's gifts. Debi, Diane (Debi's friend), and I had all accepted the Lord as personal Savior at the end of this year.

Larry went back to his apartment after the holidays, and the flu I battled over Christmas got worse by the day. In mid-January, I began to hallucinate because of malnutrition and dehydration. The last meal I'd eaten was on Christmas day, but my children didn't know how ill I was.

I was to see my orthopedic doctor on January 26, and when Larry arrived to take me, he was surprised to see the condition I was in. He and the kids dressed me and drove me to Albany Medical Center. They were told I would have to be admitted. My hemoglobin was so low that if I had waited much longer I would have just fallen asleep and never awakened.

My husband stayed with the kids, and I got better, but Dr. Balanti wanted to do a biopsy of the small bowel. He returned with a mile-wide smile on his face; the biopsy was non-malignant.

The law suits were now on the front burner, but I was really into the Bible. One night the words jumped from the page—"*sue no man.*" Without hesitation, I wrote a letter to the mayor and told him: "In the name of our Lord and Savior Jesus Christ, I am dropping the suit against the city." I then contacted my attorney and told him to drop the malpractice suits. He was furious and told me I was crazy. I told him Jesus told me to do this through the Bible, and I was going to obey Him. I sent the lawyer $200 for his time.

Debi, Diane, and I went to a monthly all-night "Consecration" prayer meeting. At 2:30 a.m., we went to a restaurant where there were a lot of inebriated people. A fight broke out and I popped up and said: "Don't fight. Why don't you come to church with us?" We took them back to the church and the three of them accepted the Lord. Some of the members didn't like the idea that they had been drinking, but we were tickled pink that we had helped bring three men to Christ.

Debi turned 15 on May 24, and I had enough money to invite four couples to an exclusive restaurant. Her boyfriend pretended he was taking her out to dinner, and Diane's mother and I hid until she came in. Everyone yelled "Happy Birthday, Debi!" Afterward, we went to her girlfriend's house; but one of the boys had booze and that ended the party.

Ricky often came home late. I knew he was on drugs, but I didn't know where he got them. One night we heard a blood-curdling scream, and found Ricky flaked out—sitting up in bed with a wash-cloth and a can of Pam. We found a six empty cans of Pam in his room (he had even stolen some from stores). Years later I was to find out that Ricky and a friend were also visiting an older man who gave them beer. Ricky has never admitted it, but I believe this man sexually abused him.

God was speaking to my spirit about my sleeping pill addiction. In 1971, I began to buy pills from the black market to supplement the drugs obtained at two different drug stores. I knew the pills distorted my reasoning, and I knew that I would die if I didn't do something.

One Saturday, I gave all my pills to Dorrene (after hiding a bottle under a couch cushion). I asked her and her companions to pray with me that I would have no seizures when I tried to withdraw "cold turkey" from my addiction. I feared I would take a massive overdose in my depression, so they began to pray. Mom Russell was kneeling near me, and the Holy Spirit nudged my conscience about the bottle I had hidden. I told Mom Russell about them and relinquished them as well. When they left with my complete "pharmacy," I felt absolutely alone and riddled with fear.

Barbiturate withdrawal is highly dangerous and can be fatal. By Tuesday I was in terrible shape. I asked Dorrene and Marian Crandall to call the Oral Roberts Prayer Tower for prayer. I was nauseated and couldn't retain any food or liquids. Dorrene called Nat Tate, and he told her to give me toast and tea. By Wednesday I was long-gone mentally.

I had hallucinations and even started a fire in my kitchen! On Saturday (one week later), I was taken to a woman named Pat Brooks for deliverance. They feared I would have to be sent to Utica if something didn't break. I told Dorrene I would come out of it in ten days, but she was worried. I should not have been taken for deliverance because I couldn't be held accountable for any of my actions—I was sick.

On the tenth day, Debi stayed home from school to watch me. I heard Debi and Dorrene's voices, and my mind suddenly came back. I never truly got addicted to barbiturates again even though I was to go back to them at a later time.

That summer, I was baptized by immersion along with Debi and Diane in Lake George by the pastor and his son. It was a glorious day and God was in His Heaven. At the end of the year, Ricky and another boy ran away. The police in Oneonta called us to pick them up. On the way back, we stopped to eat but I was so angry that I wouldn't let Ricky eat. I felt very badly about this later on, but I had to give it to Jesus.

Stewart and Gwen accepted the Lord and attended church with me. On New Year's Eve, Stewart came downstairs to party. Ricky wanted to drink, so Stewart said why not. I didn't know Ricky was already an alcoholic, but he drank until he passed out and threw up everywhere.

Nanny was ever so sweet. I really loved her at this time. When I told her about the baptism, she said she was willing to be baptized in the tub. This touched the very core of my being. Debi was doing well. When she turned sixteen she went to work at the supermarket. One of the sorriest moments of 1971 was when Diane, a precious child of God whom I loved deeply, ran away for no known reason.

Late that year, with Nanny's consent, I put Stewart's name on the deed. He shared all expenses with us, and did the maintenance around the house. His wife, Gwen, stayed with Nanny and made her feel important.

New Year's Eve of 1971 found me sitting alone at watchnight services at the Soul Saving Station. My children didn't come, and I was sad that my family would not enjoy bringing in a New Year with Jesus.

Early in 1972, I was hobbling around the streets with my crutches telling people about Jesus and attending a Bible study at Malta and another at the church. The more I knew about Jesus, the more I loved Him. Larry and I were trying again, and he came to church with me at times, as did Debi and Ricky.

I gave my spiritual mother a hard time when she would quote Isaiah, "...with His stripes we are healed" (Is. 53:5b). I got furious because I lived in pain and I wasn't healed. I told her that if she told me this one more time I would take a gun and shoot her. At a Bible study in church, I freaked out when the Pastor read, "...Jacob have I loved, but Esau have I hated" (Rom. 9:13). All my life, I'd felt God was unjust, and now I was flying high with the Lord. Now the Bible says God loved one person and not the other! I said I didn't want to serve a God who was partial. The pastor's wife tried to calm me, but it was to take time for me to see what God meant by this.

It seemed that things were becoming a whole lot better at home as I got to know Jesus. Even Ricky appeared to be serious, but I was to find out later how well he could truly con me. I still did not want to believe all the things the cops said he did. He seemed sincere in church, but he did his own thing.

Larry and I seemed to get along better because I tried to keep my mouth shut, but I would not allow him to physically or verbally abuse Ricky. Debi was nearly 16, and he basically left her alone. In May, Larry cosigned with me for a new Dodge Coronet. We had agreed that he would pay the bills and I would buy the groceries. This satisfied me and gave me spending money for things of the Lord.

Late that month, Nanny didn't get up for breakfast. I found her lying lopsided on her bed with blood coming out of her mouth. She had had a stroke but was still alive. My 84-year-old aunt was feverish and unresponsive. Her doctor said she could die. I begged her not to die, and she pulled through, but was still on the critical list. Mother and Aunt Vina just told me to "let her go."

I went home and slept, but when I woke up, I discovered that all of my medicine and money had been stolen by Aurora and Marie! At first they vehemently denied their theft, but later they admitted that Aurora took the pills and Marie took the money. Nanny lived, but she was placed in the hospital nursing home where she reverted back to being a child. I visited often, but she didn't even know me.

Ricky's school told me his work was unsatisfactory, and I admitted that I was at my wit's end with him. The school officials didn't know how to deal with his behavior problems either. I noticed that he spent a lot of time caring for his hair, so since his hair meant so much to him, I told him I would see that he got a crew cut if he did not improve fast. The stress with my sisters, my aunt's illness, and Ricky wiped me out.

Jeanne Conway asked me to go to C.F.O. (Camps Farthest Out) with her in late August. The Lord opened every door, and the trip was awesome. After an unfortunate series of events, I met Bernice Girard, one of the main speakers. She told me that people like me would get in the Kingdom of Heaven quicker than others, and that either God or satan would win out with me here in Nova Scotia. I felt an overwhelming sense of peace come over me. I found out later that nearly 80 people were praying for me at the time. This broke satan's stranglehold on me, and I was set free. The veil of oppression and depression lifted.

I asked God the impossible: to use me someday like he was using Bernice. I joined a prayer group of seven to nine people, led by Dr. Bob Metcalfe, an internist from Nashville, Tennessee. That afternoon, they formed a circle and prayed for me, and I realized that I had separated the Father from His Son, Jesus. I actually thought the Father was a bogeyman! I cried uncontrollably, and my "bogeyman" Father God wiped my tears away and covered me with His love and forgiveness. I told Dr. Metcalfe, "I came a thousand miles to find out that I was consciously afraid of God the Father!" Dr. Metcalfe said: "It would be worth traveling 5,000 miles for that." I was alive and effervescent, and different people gravitated toward me at every meal.

One day I was sitting alone in the prayer room, basking in God's presence. I asked Him to forgive me, and I enjoyed a relationship with the Heavenly Father that, for the first time, was void of fear. Then a sense of awe came over me, and a breeze blew through the windows. I knew it was the Holy Spirit. These words (and many others) dropped into my spirit directly from Heaven:

"You are a child of the King. You are somebody. But without the King, you are nobody. You are somebody because you are a child of the King.

"...Your prayers and requests are made known to Me. I will not fail you. I will sustain you, but you must discipline yourself...You must take time everyday My child to read the Bible. I will answer many of your problems through it. You must be stable in your Christian Fellowship.

"Stop looking at people, Theresa. Love them, but don't worry about their faults. I will not leave you, and I will let you know what I have in mind for you to do for My Kingdom. If it is My will, nothing will defeat you. You must give up as many pills as possible. I will always be near you. I love you, My child. Remember what I told you...Everlasting Eternal Love, your Dad."

The following day I told Dorrene I was now ready to do anything and everything for Jesus. However, when I went back to the Soul Saving Station (I had been away from there for around six weeks), they were convinced I was mentally ill, and their judgments laid heavy on me.

Larry finally accepted the Lord as his Savior, but he wanted to remain a Catholic, which was all right with me. He did come to some services with me. I continued to see Nanny on a regular basis and saw to her needs. I wanted this to be the best Christmas ever. I purchased a mini-bike for Ricky because I wanted to please him, hoping he would be different. He was suspended for three days, and I had to go to school with him in order for him to be readmitted. He acted repentant and I was praying.

On December 1, 1972, Larry and I renewed our marriage vows at the Soul Saving Station. Chuck and Dorrene stood up for us, and both of our children attended. The church gave us a lovely reception, but I knew something was missing—and I believe it was God's blessing. That night I gave myself to Larry cold sober, but it was a bust. I pretended to be satisfied, but I hated myself because I knew I was a phony.

One night, I heard Larry hollering at the kids as usual. He said it wasn't funny for someone to call and say he had won a thousand dollars. My ears perked up, and I got out of bed. I had secretly entered his name in a contest, and he had really won. (Larry never so much as thanked me, but when he cashed the check, I made sure I was there to get my share).

The day after Christmas, Ricky ran away with a boy up the street. In two days, a New York Port Authority policeman called. He had picked up the boys. He said they would have to go into a detention home if the we did not pay their way back. I told him to put my son in the home to teach him a lesson, but he sent Ricky home instead.

In 1973, my daughter was still going with the boy who had taken her to the prom. They had an Episcopalian youth group that was un-chaperoned. One day I walked into the room where they met and caught my daughter and others necking. I spoke to the leaders of the church and to some of the parents.

Once again I threw Larry out because of his cruelty to my children, especially to Ricky. At this time, Ricky stole some sleeping pills and money from me and gave the pills to some kids at a game, so I reported him. The kids signed papers against him, and Ricky had to go to court. I got him a lawyer, and he got one year of probation. Still he continued to do his own thing.

Jeanne told me at one time that she had felt the Lord wanted me to start a Christian Book Store in Saratoga, but it didn't pan out. I couldn't seem to find my niche in life. I wanted to do more than be just a housewife and mother, but I was bogged down with multiple physical and mental problems.

One day I stopped at Betty Alford's home and told her about Jesus. She told me her nine-year-old daughter was impossible. Since I had a way with children, I told Betty that I would care for Amy for a week so that she could go away and have a nice time.

In February, Betty Alford offered to pay me well if I would care for Amy for a longer time, so I took Amy into my home. She tried to pull a few things, but when I told her to do something, she obeyed me. She ate and slept well. When her parents called, they were happy that I had no problems with their daughter. My children were dumb-founded when they saw the way she was with me and the way I was with her. When her parents came for her, I refused their money.

By April, I weighed over 260 pounds. My legs were shot, and so was I. The Saratoga Hospital emergency room sent me to the Veteran's Hospital in Albany, and Larry accompanied me. I craved water, and couldn't get enough. The doctors suspected that I might have Diabetes Insipidus, but tests ruled this out. I would have to stay in the hospital, and I was put on a strict 500-calorie diet. I was killing myself. I had an enlarged heart and bad tremors, and the doctors didn't know why.

I had to go to physical therapy once a day and have my knees hot packed. I needed to do the exercises while I was lying down. Every four hours I was given pain medication, along with Valium. I got along fairly well with the help for the first time in my life. The staff couldn't believe that the tiger they had known had turned docile, so I told them it was the transforming power of Jesus Christ.

I had a marvelous opportunity to witness to a number of men at the VA. I told them I was a born-again Christian, and that I was also very human; God was not finished with me yet. We played cards over coffee, and they knew I would leave if they started swearing. It thrilled my soul that they actually tried to control their language.

My husband was the nicest he had ever been to me during this hospitalization. When I went home on pass he bought me special food. In early June, my children fled to my mother's house because Larry had gone berserk again. I got a 72-hour pass to straighten out the mess.

While I was there a nurse named Carol told me something that sickened me. She said her husband, a plumber at the VA, was called to the seventh floor to fix a leaky faucet on the ward where Larry worked. He walked into the room and saw Larry beating up and shoving an old man around. Lou got angry and stopped Larry, who promptly shouted for the head nurse (from whom he had accrued many brownie points). He told her Lou was "interfering with his work" and caused him a lot of trouble. I wanted to kill Larry, but the Holy Spirit whispered to me, "Vengeance is Mine" (Rom. 12:19).

I returned from the hospital to find that Larry had bought me a freezer, two cabinets, and a new bike for Debi. We all went to the bowling alley (although I could not bowl, even though I tried). We played a game of miniature golf as well. It was rare for us to do things as a family unit. I was 27 pounds lighter, and I felt good about myself.

I borrowed a book on Dr. Atkins diet and bought some kito sticks, eager to try this amazing diet. Franny had warned me not to do it, but I wouldn't listen. As usual, I did it with an overabundance of enthusiasm, went into ketosis, and became drenched with perspiration. I went to the emergency room and was warned to get off the diet. Truly, I had almost done myself in.

In the fall, I attended a Full Gospel Convention in Harrisburg, Pennsylvania, with Dorrene, Natalie, Jeanne, and Debi. Jeanne disapproved of my smoking, so I reserved a private room on the ground floor near the front of the building. Debi went with the others in one room instead of sharing my room with me, and that night, I sat at dinner by myself, feeling the others didn't need me. I went back to my room, smoked some cigarettes, and wished I was dead.

I stuck it out and talked with Malcom Smith, one of the speakers. At that convention I learned from Judson Cornwall the power that was in the avenue of praise. And at the end of that day, I was ready to fly. I heard John Poole speak for the second time. He broke down in front of everyone under the unction of the Holy Spirit—I was touched and moved. Then satan came after me full force, and I gave into my feelings of rejection. I made arrangements to catch a flight home to Albany. (One of my psychiatrists had told me I was supersensitive. He was right.)

I didn't follow through. Instead, I attended the meetings and was blessed. Willy Murphy lead the music, and he was superlative. Music had always affected me, so God's music was something else. The conference was wonderful. It renewed my faith and my walk with God. My battery had been recharged.

When I returned home, I again told Larry we should try again. Also at this time, I had a real vivid dream. I was in a nursery where babies were lying in their cribs. A baby boy lay in one of them marked, "For Chuck and Dorrene." I told them of my vision, but Chuck was very negative. He thought I was trying to get them to adopt my niece's yet unborn baby. (I didn't even know my niece Patty, was pregnant.) Dorrene helped arrange for Patty to go to Booth's Memorial Hospital in Buffalo, New York.

The next day I visited Patty and took her to a Full Gospel breakfast where she accepted Christ. Then I offered to drive her to Buffalo and buy her the clothes she needed. It was a long tiresome drive to Buffalo, and we were to see a social worker at noon. I admired the social worker and the Salvation Army for having a place like this. Patty wanted to give up the baby for adoption and start all over. She had lost her two boys from a previous marriage. Less than a week after I drove Patty to Buffalo, I found out she was leaving the home and returning on the bus. I was ready to personally "do her in," but some friends ushered me out of the city. Patty kept the little black baby—with tragic results.

I drove another niece (one of the daughters of my deceased brother, Stanley) to Albany in November to see a doctor. She was pregnant and had tried to take her life. This doctor had managed to salvage her hand (which was dangling by a thread), and her life as well.

As I looked back on 1973, I thanked God. Debi now liked a boy at church. She was stable in the Lord, in school, and in her work. She delighted my heart, but I cried out to God for my only son. Nanny was holding her own, but was not with it mentally; and Stewart and Gwen had separated. My mother's husband was having sexual relations with members of the family, and although they thought they were fooling her, she knew what was going on. It was sickening, maddening, and immoral.

I again spent New Year's Eve in church, and testified to the glory of God with my children by my side.

Chapter 8

The Mid-Seventies

I was determined to follow Jesus no matter what in 1974. With a friend like Dorrene, a daughter like Debi, and a church family, I was sure I would make it. My mother was confined to a wheelchair, and my sister Marie was attending "AA" meetings, which was perhaps the first constructive step of her life. Early that year, Dorrene asked me to minister to a woman who wanted to commit suicide. Phyllis was an alcoholic with three sons and a married daughter. I ministered to her, and then we all prayed for her.

In February, Larry retired from the VA after 30 years of service with a Civil Service pension, plus his Army pension. We all went to a Full Gospel dinner as a family, and it thrilled me. Ricky was hanging around with a kid up the street, and I found out the older man who had been giving beer to them had skipped town real fast. I suspected this man was a pedophile, but had no proof. I begged Ricky not to hang around this boy, but he would not listen or take advice from anyone.

Marie stayed sober, attended her meetings, and received psychotherapy. She moved out of my mother's house and shared an apartment with her daughter Denise. Larry and I helped her get settled, hoping this would help break her psychological dependence on Mother.

In March, I got my mother to attend a revival at the Soul Saving Station. She wasn't healed, but the lively service shook her up enough to give her nightmares. Mother, a die-hard Catholic, thought it was all satanic.

Marie's neurologist, Dr. K, was interested in my facial affliction, but I couldn't figure her out. Her son was always sleeping on a couch at her home office. I suspected drugs, but she said he had "tired blood." Ricky was released from probation in March. I tried unsuccessfully to prove to authorities that he needed help. Of course, his relationship with his father was non-existent, and I sensed he was headed for serious trouble. I faithfully attended Soul Saving Station and it sustained me. Dorrene never condemned me, even though her husband was upset over my frequent phone calls.

I hoped that Larry and I would establish a rapport, but the only way he could show affection was by waiting on me hand and foot. At times it was nice, but I considered him to be effeminate. My friends thought I had it made because he did the house cleaning, but I would rather have had a dirty floor and true affection for me and the children.

Marie hit the bottle again, and one night, Dorrene and a friend were ministering to her. They told me she was in bad shape. (Several days prior to this, she had taken an overdose of medicine.) I told Dorrene to take the Drano and any lighter fluid or cleaning fluid with them when they left (Marie had once taken Drano). I hung up, but the Holy Spirit quickened me to call back and tell them to bring Marie in their car, pick me up, and we would rush her to the hospital. Doctors pumped her stomach, and although she was failing fast, she managed to survive.

Ricky was taking drugs and drinking. One night he and a group of boys were caught sniffing Carbone (a cleaning fluid). The cops escorted Ricky home, and we learned the next day that one of the boys had died because of the Carbone. When Debi turned 18 in May, it seemed that she had been waiting for the day she would not have to mind me. One night I pulled her hair and called her names, and I knew I had lost her. This supersensitive young lady had had it with me.

Debi's rebellion, Ricky's tricks, and Larry's ugliness made me wonder where God was. Everything had looked so bright at the beginning of the year, but now everything was messed up. We were pulling farther and farther apart. Aurora moved in with my mother to care for her, but Aurora was addicted to drugs and alcohol, and my mother was hooked on sleeping pills. She had lost all desire to live. She prayed a lot, and her priest gave her communion, but Mother didn't have much to look forward to. Her grandson, Stewart, whom she had raised, was a human parasite. My mother realized too late that she had helped to make him what he was.

All hell broke loose with Larry and me, and I told him I hated him and didn't care if I ever saw him again. Debi and I also got into it—hot and heavy. I threw orange juice in her face and told her I hated her. She had planned to leave until she talked to Dorrene. Dorrene told her to stick it out, for she was going to graduate soon.

Larry was making all kinds of money at different jobs, but he didn't give me a penny while I spent what I had on good causes, or just gambled it away. Roger drove me to the bank so I could borrow $3000, and Larry agreed to cosign on the loan (but he would not give me a penny from his pensions and earnings). Roger got some of the $3000 for setting up the loan with his friend, a top gun at the bank. I gave money away and gambled until we were deep in debt.

Debi graduated from high school, and it was hard to believe that my little girl had grown up. Jack, my roomer upstairs, did a lot of little things for me around the house. He was intelligent and a gifted painter and poet. Diane, my other upstairs tenant, had her eye on Jack. Jack felt sorry for her because her husband had left her, but I warned them that there better not be any "goings on." I ran the house on Christian principles and sex outside of marriage was wrong.

On July 5, 1974, my world went spinning into a mad pit of chaos and sorrow. Debi and I got into a fight over something we can't even remember. I told her that if she did not shut up I would kill her. She became afraid and ran out of the house. I started to worry that something might have happened to her, and I sensed that she was at Sister Tate's, but no one answered. I called up Dorrene and told her what happened. Debi called me a few days later; she wanted to get her clothes. On Sunday, I heard a knock at the door. I was shocked to see that Dorrene and Sister Tate (my pastor's wife) had come with Debi to get her clothes. Dorrene's husband waited for them outside. I wondered, *How could Dorrene be a part of this foul deed?*

Sister Tate admitted that she had taken Debi in the night she ran away. She hadn't answered the phone because they were afraid of what I might do. The ultimate betrayal was that Dorrene and Chuck were going to take Debi into their home! Debi thought Dorrene's home was a utopia, but I never dreamt that Dorrene would turn on me like a viper! I told them all to get out of my living room. Tommy and Ricky helped with Debi's things while I delivered a tirade of curses. I wanted to mentally bury Debi, Dorrene, and Sister Tate, and never let their ugly heads resurrect in my life again.

I got some sleeping pills from Dr. K. and lost all desire for life. On Tuesday, Marie walked in and told me Dr. K. was afraid that I had overdosed. She wanted me to go to the Mental Health Unit, so I did. There I met Rodney, who would sell his soul for Valium; Chris, who had tried to hang himself in jail; and Phil, who was very effeminate and was trying to break his bondage to his mother. They became my family. My second night there, Dorrene showed up! She asked to see me alone because she had come to ask my forgiveness. I told her that if I had to go to hell I would never forgive her.

One night I had a confrontation with a nurse. I was trying to clean up a mess with a mop when the nurse told me to hurry up. I threw the mop down called the nurse every name in the book. I said I was going to leave. I ranted and raved, but I finally calmed down. I expected to be locked up, but no one touched me. They just let me calm down.

Franny, who was now my roommate, got into an argument with me over our "dueling radios," and Franny was about to hit me with her tape deck when the attendant caught her hand. They put her in a secluded room, but she sat outside the door all night.

In mid-July, I saw a woman walk by the door. I asked Rodney who she was. He said, "She's Claire Stratford, and she's tough." Later I went to group therapy and Claire was in charge. She was one of the very few people who could psych me out. Franny began alluding to an incident the night before, and I told her I did not need it. I started for the door, but to my amazement, Claire gently asked me to come back into the group. I don't change my mind easily, but I went back.

The next day, Dr. Robert Flynn urged me to kick Ricky out. I knew I would rant and rave, cajole and threaten, but I would never throw Ricky to the proverbial wolves. I decided to leave the hospital, so Roger came for me. As he was putting my things in his car, I was planning to end it all. As I headed for the door, Claire asked me to stay another day or two. My weak arguments and plans of self-destruction faded away. I didn't know why she even cared about me. I went back to my room, and Roger gave me six Doridans. I took three of them. I was high when Claire came in, and I handed her the rest of the pills.

Someone had told me that she handpicked her clients, but the night before my discharge she told me I was to see her the following week. I tried to tell her that I just wanted to say good-bye and leave it at that, but she said she'd see me in the morning.

I wrote a letter that night telling Claire I couldn't take the appointment because I did not want to go through transference again, (my experiences with Dr. Hart were still fixed firmly in my mind). I rambled on and on. She called me into her office, and I showed her the letter. She called it a bunch of baloney and said she was saving the time for me. She explained that it was up to me if I wanted to stand her up. She saw beyond my ugliness and glimpsed a little girl who was crying, "Please help me!"

Claire sustained me through my heartbreak with Ricky, Debi, and Larry. In late July, Ricky was caught robbing an elderly lady. I retained Jim Murphy as his attorney, and he got 90 days. He got out in October and returned to school. Would he stay straight? Jack and Diane were having an affair, so I kicked them both out. Debi came up to therapy with me. We talked it out, and she returned home. I knew I had to forgive Dorrene. I rather reluctantly went back to church, but I was not comfortable. I made peace with God. Dorrene and I were now talking, but our relationship was to take a long time to heal.

Claire continued to sustain me. Debi, Ricky, Larry, and I lived under one roof, but we were all waiting for a bomb to explode. My mother died in her sleep on November 15, 1974 at the age of 77. She was laid out on my birthday and buried on November 18. Ricky was one of the pall bearers. Finally she was at peace. As I stood by the grave, I knew for sure we would meet again. Mother left her house to my brother Freddy; Eugene, her husband; and Stewart, her grandson. Freddy was to bury her, and divide the proceeds of the sale of the place. Shortly afterward, Stewart took off, and Marie moved to another state. She came back and set up house with my stepfather. So what else is new? Debi, Ricky, Larry, and I were miles apart—mentally and spiritually. Ricky was still hell-bent on the road to destruction. Debi was working, but far from happy; and I felt diminished by my mother's passing.

Around Christmas, Ricky made a sarcastic remark to me, and Larry jumped in and told him he was not to talk to me like that. Ricky challenged Larry, and he took him up on it. Ricky decked him, breaking his glasses and making the blood flow. While Larry was grasping blindly for his glasses, Ricky stood still. He did not come in to further his advantage. I admired him for that, but years later, he told me, "All the drugs in the world could not have given me the high I had when I saw him on the floor. I hoped he would try again. I was waiting to kill him, Ma. That is why I stood back." I had known that Ricky would physically give Larry a good beating some day, but I didn't expect murder!

Christmas was a sham. We exchanged presents, but there was no joy in our home. We had all withdrawn into our own private worlds. The fight had crushed my world, and I ended the year with sadness. As January of 1975 opened, the tension in our home was so thick you could have cut it with a knife. I was undergoing in-depth psychotherapy with Claire, and I was going through the "poor me" syndrome. Still, she persistently worked with me. She wasn't a Christian, but she had more Christianity in her little finger than most of us have in our whole bodies.

Jim Murphy was threatening to sue me if I did not pay a $400 legal bill from Ricky's last episode. Larry and I wanted to go to Texas to get away from it all, so we borrowed money and paid Murphy. Before we left for Texas, I said good-bye to Debi and Claire, and we took off.

Larry literally courted me all over again, so I felt there might be hope for our marriage. We never had a cross word. In Missouri, we ran into a snow squall and stopped for the night. It was here that I started to bleed profusely through the rectum. We arrived at my brother's house on Saturday, and I was admitted to a hospital in Lubbock, Texas, for five days with a peptic ulcer and diverticulosis.

Billy wanted me and Larry to settle down in Texas, but it was too hot for me. Billy was an amputee, and we now got acquainted for the first time in our lives. He was a proud man whose infirmities had humbled him. One night he took me to a professional card game at a motel. We left with modest winnings. Then we went to a restaurant and talked for hours. In the morning, his wife Jackie accused Billy of loving me more than her!

The next night, Billy and Larry got drunk, and they came home drunk. The next morning I hauled off and hit Larry because he'd broken his promise to me. Billy's wife was so furious that she went to live with her sister. It was time for us to head East. We started back, but I could not enjoy the trip because I wasn't at peace with myself. The bright spot was my platonic relationship with Larry. Except for the time I had whacked him, we were getting along much better. I made out a will before I left, leaving him one third of the proceeds of the house.

In May, Larry suddenly told me that I was to handle the money! He was going to give me his government checks and only keep the money he made on the side. Ricky also called to beg for money to come back from Florida. Although he had run away at the beginning of the year, he now promised to abide by the rules of the house. I made him swear to it and sent him the money. This rankled Larry and he picked a fight with me then and got his old room back on Phila Street. The next thing I knew, Larry was dead drunk and riding on the rims of his car when he was picked up for D.W.I. Tragically, Larry had been right about Ricky; he returned the same as when he left. What would happen next?

In late June, Larry actually agreed to attend a Kaythryn Kuhlman miracle service with me. As I waited for the service to begin, I noticed that Larry was reading a book about Kathryn Kuhlman. To say the least, he appeared to be impressed!

That month, my new congressman forwarded my VA file to the VA Congressional Liaison in Washington, who turned the matter over to the Chief Benefits Director. Unfortunately, I again was told that the decisions of the past could not be appealed without new evidence.

Ricky was arrested for assaulting and robbing an elderly man, a felony offense. I put up the house for bail money, and I hired John McMahon as his lawyer. Larry said he would pay the fees. In just a few days, Ricky was arrested for possession of marijuana and the sale of illegal fireworks. He begged me to bail him out again, but I would not allow him to disappoint me again.

Bernice was going to be at a Camps Furthest Out (C.F.O.) in Long Island, and Larry agreed to go with me. Larry and I needed a spiritual shower and a healing of memories through the power of Jesus, and the C.F.O. could be a marvelous beginning. I saw Bernice, Corolla, and Bob again, and every night Larry and I went to our motel room and studied the Bible. In the day, he waded in the ocean while I sat on the beach. On Friday night, we were asked to be members of the council for the next camp. Larry asked Alex, the council leader, who told him to ask us, and Alex answered, "The Holy Spirit." This was the greatest honor in my life.

I marveled at the power of God. I actually felt close to Larry for the first time in my life! I could do nothing without God, and the same was true of Larry. If God could forgive me, how dare I not forgive him? Things went well back in Saratoga; I took a lot of medicine but no sleeping pills. My disposition improved immensely, but I still had a short fuse. Larry and I read the Bible for a whole week together when we got home. Freddy was getting my mother's home ready to sell and Larry helped him. I continued therapy with Claire, and Ricky accepted the Lord in jail and asked to go to Teen Challenge (a Christian drug and alcohol rehabilitation organization). Judge Brown consented, but reminded Ricky he was on probation and that he would have to serve his time there. He came home for two days and I gave him my only suitcase filled with new clothes. David Tate drove him to Teen Challenge.

Then Larry began to act strange. We got into an argument and he said he was going back to Phila street. Then he took off for Minnesota! What happened to the beautiful time we had together? It didn't make sense. I begged him not to do this, but he warned me to put the house in someone else's name, he was going to file bankruptcy. "Oh God," I cried, "Why?"

After I was admitted to the Mental Health Unit late in September, and I received a note that really broke my spirit:

Dear Theresa and Larry: Just a quickie to say we are looking forward to when you come—and send love and blessings meanwhile...Love and Joy in His Presence—Corolla.

We were supposed to go to our first council ring meeting. How could I possibly tell her what happened? Claire was my only hope, but I wondered how Claire (who was not a Christian) could possibly believe in Jesus if He did this to me? I was too depressed to do anything at the unit. Marlene, the charge nurse, insisted that I get dressed and I refused. How could she know the utter despair I felt? Later, I learned that Marlene had once been where I was at. She knew pity wasn't the answer. When I heard that a woman in the unit had hung herself, I wondered how she did it. Could this be my way out? Several days later, one of Debi's friends told me that Debi said she wouldn't know what to do if I killed myself. That gave me a ray of hope. Maybe someone did care if I lived or died. Nevertheless, a dark heaviness consumed me. I could hardly breathe because of the oppression and mental agony I was experiencing. I began to devise ways to commit suicide, but today, I know God intervened to steer me away from a path bent on total destruction (doom).

I began to take an interest in other people's problems. I also asked God to make Himself real to me. I was fuming over an altercation with another patient when the Holy Spirit told me to forgive the man. I asked him for forgiveness, and he also apologized for what he did.

I got a positive note from Ricky's probation officer just as I was ready to go home. Debi was going to be staying with me, and maybe Ricky would be able to come home for the holidays! There was hope, praise God! I had been home only a few days when my world caved in again. Ricky had run away from Teen Challenge, and the judge issued a warrant for his arrest. Words can't express the pain I felt, for my son had been lost, then found, and now he was lost again. Only Debi kept me from slashing my wrists. I told Corolla about Larry and Ricky. I was crushed beyond consolation, but I knew many prayers would go up for us from this council ring.

For the first time, Debi did not give me a birthday card. After staying with me for two months, she moved to a friend's house. Through it all, my Bible study group was very supportive, and none of them forgot the day I was born. Corolla sent me money for my birthday, and for the rest of 1975 she frequently sent words of encouragement. I also received a letter from Bernice. She was impressed by my book, and she gave me some tips, and I decided to take a creative writing course.

Jeanne invited me to go to her home for Thanksgiving, and I went even though I didn't like the idea of not being able to smoke while I was there. I weathered the storm, for as usual she was a gracious hostess. I had an attack of Melkerrsdon's Syndrome Friday night. Although Jeanne was a nurse, she wasn't very sympathetic. On Saturday, Jeanne took my car to work (hers was being fixed), and I felt a strong compulsion to go home that day.

That invisible Presence was wooing me back to Church Street—but for what? I went home and was there less than an hour when the hospital called: Nanny was in critical condition. I rushed there to discover that the nurse couldn't get any blood pressure or pulse, and she was cold. I could not see her breathe. I knew it was the end, so I said to God: "So this is the way You want me to end it all?" Then I whispered into Nanny's ear: "Please don't die. If you do, I will not be able to take it, Nanny. Everyone has left me, and I just cannot survive if you die right now." My sister Marie came up, and we stayed all night. I believe Nanny returned from the dead. God knew I just couldn't bear any more sorrow.

I invited Debi, and her friends, Jan and Arnold, over for Christmas dinner, for they had nothing, not even a tree. I told her I would put up a tree, make a turkey dinner, and buy some presents. I was scraping the bottom of the financial barrel, but I had more than they did.

A few days before Christmas, Larry told me the bankruptcy was going through, and that I had better get the house out of my name. I told him I was not going to be a part of this fraud. I told him God would punish him. And miracle of miracles, I received a card and a wristwatch from Ricky, who was in the Bahamas. He didn't explain anything; he just sent the card and gift. At least I knew he was alive and cared.

I put up a tree, bought presents, and planed a nice turkey dinner. Debi, Jan, and Arnold arrived on Christmas Eve, but Arnold was sick; so he went right to bed. Debi told me that she and Jan were going to a party for an hour or so. They promised to be back around eight. I stayed, nursed Arnold with sips of ginger ale, and waited. The evening was going fast, and still Jan and Debi did not return. I couldn't believe that they would leave Arnold alone and go off partying. At 10:00 p.m., Jan called me (Debi never liked to talk to me when she knew I might holler). She told me they would be right home, I told her what I thought about her leaving her husband. They didn't come in until 3:00 a.m.! I was so hurt that I dared not talk.

I finished fixing the dinner and then left to go to Marie's for dinner. Again my daughter broke my heart. I had always felt that Debi was selfish and ungrateful, but now I could not stand this human parasite whom I had loved so much. I was beginning to again become hard inside. I doubted my relationships in my family, my church, and everywhere else. My life had been a chain of disappointments, and I knew I just could not handle another major one. I alternately believed and doubted God. I had little to look forward too. The shocks of 1975 had done me in. Would I ever recuperate?

Chapter 9

The Rest of the Seventies

Early in 1976, I was deep in depression. How I could I get by without Larry's financial help? I petitioned the authorities in St. Cloud, Minnesota, for support from Larry, but I didn't know what 1976 held for me. The anguish I endured in January was indescribable. I received a little over $200 a month, and my bills were mounting. My congressman contacted Larry's bankruptcy judge in Minnesota on my behalf, and I hoped that justice would triumph. I didn't want to file personal bankruptcy, except as a last resort. I got my aunt's written permission to sell the house, I put it up for sale.

By March, my bowels and ulcer were really acting up. I had to take Gelusil at all times, and it seemed like my string of hospitalizations and daily drug doses was unbroken. I had severe choking spells at night, and I had to have regular injections in my knees. Every day, I took as many as 15 Darvons for pain, eight Lomotil for diarrhea, and four Valiums and two chloral hydrates at night time for sleep!

I enrolled in the creative writing course at Skidmore after someone helped me pay for it, and I battled with the utility company and the Public Service Commission. Larry was having no problem, but I was getting all kinds of threats from our creditors. I prayed to God to do something about it, but I still thought I had a second-class standing with Him.

The house wasn't selling, and I was terrified of becoming financially destitute. I trusted no one. I talked regularly with Dorrene, Nancy, Jeanne, and Natalie, but I no longer attended the Soul Saving Station. I forgave Sister Tate, and I told God that I would go back to church, but He would have to make it real to me. He did. I began a 12-week creative writing course at Skidmore College and really enjoyed the class. Now I had two things to look forward to weekly—therapy and school, and the rest of the time I dipped in and out of depression.

One day Jeanne came to visit me and asked, *"How is your idol?"* (referring to Claire). I was shocked to hear her say this. She and my other so-called Christian friends thought I should go to Bible school, but what did they expect me to do—Steal the money to go? Disgusted, I told her I didn't need her or anybody else, and she left.

My writing instructor, Dora, was impressed with my writings. She even came to my home to talk about my abilities. She took off her shoes and rapped with me for a couple of hours, and it really built my ego. At the end of February I was shocked to find out that Kathryn Kuhlman died. I can still hear her say the first question she was going to ask Jesus was, "Why didn't everyone get healed?"

I was tipping the scales at 300 and my knees were in bad shape. I was also in a constant state of depression. I had a razor blade ready at all times, and I came close to ending it all many times. I almost quit the writing course, but I didn't. The electric company was going to turn off my power on March 26. About this time I decided I couldn't trust Claire (a temporary mood swing). I called Albany and Washington and told lies about Claire, which caused quite a stink. Despite my actions, she still stood ready to help me.

Larry's bankruptcy went through, and there was nothing I could do about it. Debi had moved to Albany to live with a man, and I wasn't too happy. I got into a disagreement with Lou, Diane's mother, over Debi's situation. I had a real problem when it came to forgiveness. I just could not forgive when someone hurt me. I was a miserable mess. Jeanne wrote me a letter filled with love, but I refused to even talk to her.

In October, I put the house in Debi's name at my attorney's recommendation because of Larry's bankruptcy. I was receiving Supplemental Social Security, and an educational grant to attend Empire State College. Because of my disabilities, the teachers would come to my house. Debi introduced me to her boyfriend, and we did not hit it off. But what could I expect?

Late that summer, Ricky called. He was a "caretaker" for a rich man in Florida who was willing to send him to college. He said he no longer took drugs, and he even sent me some money. In the fall, he called to say he was coming home to give himself up to clear his name. He was going to Texas first to see a friend, then he would fly to Albany. I was thrilled to see that God was indeed working miracles.

A week later, "Billy B." called from Houston and said he was a friend of Ricky's. He said a wealthy older man had befriended Ricky for homosexual reasons. Ricky had been "turning tricks" (as a male prostitute) when this man, "Peter C.," picked him up and fell in love with him. This man had followed Ricky to Texas to plead with him to return to Florida. Instead of coming home, Ricky went back to Florida to live this homosexual life. Billy warned me not to let the man in Florida know I knew he was a homosexual because he would take Ricky to Europe. He had property there and he had already taken him there once. Billy said if he took Ricky back to Europe, there was a chance I would never see my son again. I was devastated, but I had to play it cool. A few nights later Ricky called to say the reason he did not come home was because the judge would put him in jail. I was nauseated when I thought of the trap Ricky was in.

The millionaire himself called to say my son had overdosed, and tried to slash his wrists, but he would live. The hounds of heaven were indeed chasing him, and God did not allow him to die. Shortly after Christmas, Ricky wrote, "Mom, I am sorry for getting you involved with my ordeals. ...I would like to thank you for all the good times you showed me...[and] Especially for keeping us together through thick and thin...You always provided for us...So in my book you did alright, as a mother...I'm not sure if you understand me. So when you get the time to write back, please tell me how you feel about me. It's really important to me. With all my love—Ricky."

In November, I feared that I had cancer of the bowels, and I had to sleep on rubber all the time. In December, doctors ordered me to bed to recover from a bad case of the flu. (I got a call telling me that Nanny was real bad, but I couldn't go to her. Claire was going to go, but Nanny died before she could get to her. I wasn't even able to view her body or attend her funeral.) But I had prearranged her funeral and granted her wish to be buried next to her husband.

Debi and Alan came up around Christmas time and gave me some lovely gifts. Lou and I were friends again, and she invited all three of us to her home for dinner. I still wasn't talking to Jeanne (that forgiveness problem again), but she sent me a Christmas card and told me she was really sorry that she had let me down when I needed her. My brother Billy's daughter, Renee, died that month. After a simple D & C, she had contracted a staph infection and died 10 days later at the age of 28. I spent 90 percent of 1976 steeped in depression and suicidal thoughts, but God was there all the time.

Peter Claydon, the millionaire, called to tell me Ricky had stabbed someone while high on drugs. Only the power of prayer saved the boy whom Ricky had stabbed. I wanted desperately to tell off Peter Claydon, but I remembered Billy B.'s warning (although I am sure my hate radiated through the phone line). A week later, Claydon told me Ricky was in the Dade County jail for the possession and sale of drugs. He said he was going to get Ricky psychiatric help and asked me to write an encouraging letter to Ricky.

I poured out my heart to Ricky in a letter, and a week after I mailed it, Claydon called to say he had opened my letter and thought it was too depressing. He wasn't going to give it to Ricky, and he said "there is no such thing" as a Jesus and God. He said Ricky didn't believe in such "nonsense" and I said Ricky knew Jesus personally. Then Claydon made fun of my grammar, jeered at me, and again declared his atheism. If I had been well, I believe I would have hitch-hiked to Florida just to blow this arrogant man's brains out!

Another week passed, and Claydon called to say he had used his money to bail Ricky out again, but Ricky had flipped out, tore a telephone off the wall, and had gone completely berserk. Claydon had to have him reincarcerated. New York State told Florida that they did not want Ricky back; if he returned they would put him in jail, so they gave Florida full license over him.

I decided to file for bankruptcy, and Judge La Belle was my angel of mercy. He knew of my plight and had empathy for me. He handled it for me. It was great having a friend like him. His secretary, Barb, was always doing something to encourage me.

My suicidal thoughts became worse early in February, and I knew Claire was soon to go away to South America for a whole year. I was admitted to the Mental Health Unit on February 2. Claire entered my room and told me that Dr. Flynn wanted to see all of us in the dining room. When I got in there, Dr. Flynn told us that a patient who had been discharged a few days earlier had gone home and shot himself. I suddenly felt Claire's hands reaching for mine...she knew this news shook me up. After I heard this, I was released from the spirit of suicide. I found it difficult to go on at times, but never again did I contemplate suicide. This was the last in-patient hospitalization I was to have in a Mental Health Unit.

I phoned Ricky at the Dade county jail, and he confirmed everything Billy B. had told me about Peter Claydon. After that Claydon called to ask why I had phoned my son. He asked me with saccharin-sweetness to send my letters to his Post Office box because Ricky was locked up in a Rehabilitation Center and could not write to anyone for a year.

In April, after 24 phone calls, I reached the office of Judge Herbert M. Klein in Florida only to learn that Ricky had been *released to the custody of his uncle–Peter Claydon!* Who did this rich creep think he was, saying he was Ricky's uncle? I got the name and phone number of the drug center where Ricky had been, and they referred me to someone else who urged me to compile all my information and forward it to the judge. I did just that. I also wrote to the producers of the "60 Minutes" TV program, to the President of the United States, and many others as well. Ricky confirmed later that Mr. Claydon feared me. Judge Klein's office notified me that Ricky was now back in custody. My letter had pulled Ricky out of Claydon's claws!

In April I became a full-time student at Empire State College. Even though I had been accepted in July of 1976, it wasn't until April 25 that my mentor came to my home. Something was amiss. Then I received a contract in the mail that I didn't know anything about. Mr. Bragle, my mentor, told me to just study psychology and history and not to worry about the dates. (He had sent me a contract that had already expired.) Something wasn't kosher, but I took his advice and began my studies.

Claire made arrangements for me to meet the man who was replacing her, but my heart was breaking. I didn't know how I could get by without her for a whole year. She was the only one who had never really given up on me. With tears, I walked away from the most important person in my life.

Debi was now talking to me, but her soon-to-be-husband wanted no part of me. Debi reluctantly invited me to her July wedding, and I wasn't going to go. Then Alan's mother told me she wasn't going to the wedding either. She was very bitter toward her son's actions regarding her. (I thought I was bitter, but she beat me by a mile!) I set aside a lot of time to diligently seek God's will for my life. I felt the Lord tell me to go to the wedding, and I told Him I would—if He would provide me with a dress and shoes.

God supplied everything exactly as I asked, so I told Debi I was coming to her wedding. Debi then asked me to come to their house in the morning to have pictures taken. Unfortunately, there was a schism a mile long between us, and I just couldn't stand the man she was marrying. Debi and Alan had needed to work hard for their big day because Larry was stingy, as usual, and would not finance the event. They were married at a nuptial mass, and it was a beautiful ceremony. I was glad I went, for I had humbled myself. I went back home and prayed for Alan's mother, who had not attended the wedding. I understood how she felt for we had similar lives and our children had truly been a disappointment to us, but hadn't we been one to them also? A few days later. Debi called from Niagara Falls to ask for $150. I managed to dig it up and send it to them.

I was hoping to move to where I could live within my monthly income. Family Court initiated action against Larry for support, but he was fighting this and initiating divorce proceedings in Minnesota (they had a "no fault" divorce law). My renters were behind in their rent, and my assets were depleting fast. I had not been able to pay any taxes on the house in two years, and I could not even sell the house, for it was in Debi's name and she was not willing to turn it back over to me!

On August 29, Debi took me to Glenridge Hospital because of pain in my knees and back and difficulty in breathing. Dr. Ming Lee told me I had arthritis of the spine and that there was little that could be done for me. Debi took me to a restaurant, and this was the first occasion in a long time that she was actually nice to me. She even sent me a thank you card for the wedding gifts.

Eugene, my "stepfather and brother-in-law" visited me and said he was lonely. He said he had a brother in the state insane asylum in Ogdensburg whom he had not seen in over 20 years. I had money from my school grant, so I rented a car and drove him there in September. My heart went out to these men. They lay in bed, day and night, without hope. There was no water in their pitchers either, so I filled them up and gave each man some water and told them about Jesus.

On the way back we stopped at a motel in Tupper Lake, and I found that Eugene had ulterior motives for having me take this trip with him. I quickly put him in his place. Later I found out that he had seen his brother just a year ago. I took him into small claims court and made him pay for half of the trip!

In September I officially initiated my bankruptcy proceedings, and I had finished my psychology and history courses. However, I could not get Mr. Bragle to come and test me, so I reported him. He finally came, and I taped what he said. He knew I was trying to trap him, so we had it out and he never did come again. I was assigned the Associate Dean, Evangela, as my mentor. I gave her a hard time because by this point I did not trust anyone at this college. I told Evangela how I felt, and after a while I began to like her. I confounded her when in five days I had written three papers in Sociology and had taken a 714-question test—and passed it. I wanted to prove to her that I could do my work.

Ricky called regularly, and he was getting out of jail on the last day of August. I was still going to the Soul Saving Station, and the Lord was prodding me to tell the church to concentrate on Him and not on who was coming in or going out. He also told me to tell them that 10 people were to fast and pray for a certain man who had backslid and that He would bring him back. Finally, He said He was going to remove one of us. Dorrene told me, "The messenger has to deliver the message," so I did it—with fear and trepidation. Ten people volunteered to fast and pray for Al (the backslider), and two weeks later, a member of the church had a couple of heart seizures and died. At her funeral, the pastor said she had come to him and said, "If it's me, I am ready."

After giving this message, I came home and reached for my pack of cigarettes, and a jolt like electricity went through my arm and the Spirit said, "You'll never need another cigarette, for obedience is greater than sacrifice." I was totally delivered from nicotine. (Before this time I had tried to quit 19 times.)

Claire was writing me letters now, and Debi sent me a beautiful birthday card. In December, the Holy Spirit told me to continue on with my book, and Corolla and Bob Williams sent me an IBM typewriter. My bankruptcy went through, and Judge La Belle signed a note for me for $300. I told him I would pay it as soon as I was able to sell the house. Debi and Alan came up for Christmas and we exchanged gifts. They gave me just what I wanted and needed—a backrest. They knew I did a lot of studying in bed to save heat.

I fought the divorce, but everything seemed to be falling in place for Larry, while everything was falling apart for me. Ricky was up to his old tricks again; he was now living in Texas with another man. I was owed well over $300.00 in back rent, and my health was failing. Judge La Belle helped me get a lawyer in Minnesota. He said I would have to come there to contest the divorce, but my health was too bad.

In January, my nephew, Roger, Jr., asked to stay with me. His parents had kicked him out because of his drinking. He was 35 years old and had a very promising future, but alcohol was destroying him. I let him stay, but reminded him I would not take any of his nonsense. If he came in drunk and caused a scene, he would be out on his head. He accepted my rules and abided by them.

I got a letter from Alan's mother, and I knew we were birds of a feather. Her son had hurt her as much as my daughter had hurt me. Alan lost his job and Debi was pregnant and needed help, so at the end of April, Debi and Alan moved everything up to my place. On May 3, I had what I thought was a weird attack of Melkerrsdon's, with growths on the outside and inside of my mouth. A dermatologist told me he had never seen such a thing. I actually had a serious staph infection. One doctor told me he found it hard to believe I was still alive. In June, Alan won his case against the restaurant where he had worked and was awarded backpayments for unemployment. This helped them to get back their dignity, but until they received their money, I helped them.

My first grandchild was born on June 26, 1978, and she was Debi all over again. I had to withdraw from Empire State College because of my health, and Larry's divorce from me was granted. Larry La Belle told Debi to turn the house back over to me, for I had been listed in a public registry for outstanding property taxes. Debi threw the letter at me and said, "I hate you, and I could slap you in the face!" The anger in her eyes was something to behold.

I was now closer to God than I had ever been since I had lain prostrate on the floor of St Peter's Church as a child years ago. He told me to go to Debi and to humble myself, but I thought, "How can I ask her forgiveness when I had done nothing but good for her?" I finally told Debi I was sorry for my lousy attitude, and asked her to forgive me. She said she didn't know if she could forgive me, and I was choking at this humiliation. Still I had obeyed God and that was all that counted. Then He told me to go to Alan too. I was really dying a horrible death to self. I put my arms around Alan and asked his forgiveness.

In the fall of 1978, I saw Claire again, and I knew when I saw her that I would never need her again for therapy. God was now my Divine Therapist. She told me she felt my prayers had kept a bus she was on from going over the edge of a mountain road, and this really encouraged me. She went back to work at the Mental Health Unit.

Nancy asked me to go to a week-end C.F.O. retreat, but my physical and financial problems made it impossible. Jeanne had applied for a scholarship for me and it came through. I knew God had something waiting for me at the retreat. Al Allen had a healing ministry, and he was praying for people at one of the meetings. When he asked me, "What do you need from God?" I told him I needed a "general overhaul." He touched my head and all Heaven broke loose!

The Lord told me He would deliver me from all that was not like Him. In a few seconds' time, He told me He had planned on taking me home in July, but He had asked His Father to stay His hand so that my life might glorify Him! Al told the people to look at my face because it was aglow with God's glory. I was standing before a sea of faces and yet looking only at *one* face. For the first time in my life, I perceived truths that had evaded me for years! To this day, revelations from that moment in time are still being given to me because I couldn't grasp it all at once. I still felt pain, but now I had faith to believe things would get better. My healing had begun, and Theresa would never again be the same! The next morning, I set aside my crutches actually danced with my friends before the Lord!

Late in November, that still small voice told me to get rid of the chloral hydrate and Valium. I told Dr. McKinley, and he said I was religious, and suggested I come off the medication gradually, but I flushed all my sedatives down the drain. I began to actively participate in Bible studies, and every day was a new adventure. Debi asked me to pray that Alan would get a job, and I sensed by the Spirit that he was going to get a job, but it would be close by, and I told her so. In November, he got a job a stone's throw from where we lived.

The Lord told me to write Larry, so I wrote him and asked his forgiveness. What a release this was! He wrote back and even sent me

$25 for Christmas. Then the Lord told me to call Peter Claydon and wish him a blessed Christmas, even though Ricky was no longer with him. At the end of December, Debi was afraid she'd be fired, because her boss wanted to see her the next day. I told her that her attitude was getting her in trouble and that if she was willing to change, she would get another chance. I was able to minister to her like I never had before! The next day, she told me that someone had complained about her, and her boss had intended to fire her. He didn't know why he changed his mind, but he let her stay on.

Claire came to see me and I told her my story, embraced her, and said, "Wherever you go, whatever you do, my life will be better because of you." I had finally set her free, and she knew it.

I began 1979 on fire for the Lord, who had finally become real to me. I still faced many of the problems that had plagued me before, but I knew that God would see me through. I even started *walking* to the store (a miracle of major proportions!). Alan and Debi watched from their window in amazement.

The bills were mounting, and I needed to sell the house. The highest offer I had for it was $4000, and my taxes were more than that. Debi had still not signed the house back to me. I let her know we could both be on the street if the house was again advertised for taxes and someone picked up the place for the amount owed. This sure gave her food for thought.

I made a tape of my testimony and invited friends in to hear it. I wanted to read it in church but was not allowed to. Even Claire came to listen to it. In February I went to see Dr. Litts, and I shared my testimony with him. I told him I would not be coming to see him any more for I felt that God would take care of me—he was very nice and he told me if I ever needed him to call, and he asked me for a tape of my testimony. I was also led to send Peter Claydon one of my testimony tapes with a letter telling him how much Jesus loved him. He called to thank me, but he said it was difficult to believe. I told him I would pray him into the Kingdom.

Things had deteriorated at the Soul Saving Station to the point where Pastor Tate's son, Nat Tate, who was leading the services, would not acknowledge me when I wanted to get up to testify. I asked his forgiveness if I had offended him, and he would not even answer me. The church was planning to build a new facility, but the deed to the land would not belong to them, which Chuck absolutely opposed. One Sunday, Dorrene, Chuck, and I walked out of the church for good. Later, Chuck called me up and told me he now knew I had my act together, and he would go the extra mile with me. He was instrumental in letting me borrow money until I was able to sell the house.

I wrote to Corolla and Bob Williams and told them about the miracle in my life. Corolla wrote back to say they were thrilled to hear from me, and she believed God was going to publish my testimony.

I also felt that the Holy Spirit was telling me to call Larry and ask him to come back, for now I believed I could be a good wife. I called Larry and told him I loved him in Christ. He cussed me out and told me never to bother him again. I felt badly because I felt that God was going to provide for me through Larry and his return to my life. However, we cannot "out-guess" God.

A friend of mine who was going to Sister Tate's Bible study at the Soul Saving Station brought me a tape of her lesson. It was the first and last time I ever was given a tape of Sister Tate's. I was flabbergasted to hear these words spoken by Sister Tate: "Look at the woman at the well. Jesus evangelized her overnight, and she saved the whole town. But if she were in our church, we wouldn't use her, for condemnation would be on her." Pastor Tate had prophesied to me that I would be "the woman at the well" in Saratoga—how strange that Sister Tate would say this.

After Judge La Belle intervened, Debi finally turned the house back over to me, and now it was up to God to send a buyer. The motorcycle shop next door had changed hands and the new owner was interested in it. He wanted to tear it down and use the land to expand his business, but nothing was written in stone.

Dorrene worked faithfully with me to find a source to publish my testimony, but without success. She had friends who were good friends of Jamie Buckingham (now deceased), and she asked them if they would bring a condensed form of my testimony to him. They did, but he wrote us to say that he wasn't able to do the book. We also sent it to Logos, but they too rejected it. It was all in God's hands, I had finished what He told me to do, so now the ball was in His court. I felt I was ready for anything, but if Moses had to be on the back side of the desert for 40 years, why should I have my desires instantly?

I was on no drugs and saw no doctors, but I got pneumonia and this was truly to be a testing of my faith. I believed God was going to heal me. A nurse named Grace was told by God to come and put a mustard plaster on my chest, but at first she disobeyed. She finally obeyed and applied the plaster and I got better. I knew from previous episodes that it was pneumonia, but the mustard plaster loosened up the congestion.

This was the year I was to see Sister Anna Roberta, the high school teacher who had meant so much to me. I found out that she was teaching in Amsterdam, New York, so Dorrene took me to visit this nun. She was very happy to see me again, and she told me that I made her day. She had not changed much, and it was nice to sit with her and relive some of the past.

At this time, I was really spending time on my book, and I knew I had to get some medical records. I started in Illinois and moved to the other states and the Army, and I managed to obtain a lot of my medical records. The Albany VA told me I would have to come down for a psychiatric consultation before my records could be released to me. I asked John McMahon for a copy of what he sent to the VA in 1963, and he sent it to me. I called Dorrene and asked her if she would take me to the Albany VA in September. She said she would meet me, and then she pulled up with a truck! I asked her, "Why the truck?" And she said, "I thought we would need it because of the multitude of records you must have." It was hilarious! We still laugh about it to this day.

Alan and Debi wanted to go to Florida for a week, and they asked me to stay with Jennifer in October of 1979. At first, a spirit of fear came over me, and I was afraid of staying in the house alone with my granddaughter. Could I do it? It would be a giant step, but the Holy

Spirit let me know I would be okay. It was one precious week for me. I slept upstairs in the room next to Jennifer. She would wake up in the morning and jump up and down and chatter at me until I got up. Then I would change her and give her breakfast. One day Claire came for lunch, and I put Jennifer in her crib. She could see where we were sitting and was determined not to miss a trick. Claire said, "She's another Theresa." She even took her first steps that week.

When Debi and Alan came back, I went to the unemployment office to take a battery of tests to determine what field I was best suited for. They called me back and said my scores were higher than most college graduates. They told me that there were only two things I could not be, a doctor and or a pharmacist. I decided to take a two-hour civil service exam for the 1980 Census and passed it.

Natalie was teaching me all about golf in her back yard, so I actually went on a golf course with her in the fall of 1979. I was shocked at my ability to do this, for truly I had come back from a living death. I even started to bowl again (with fear and trepidation). I was determined to bowl. In truth, I was a new creature in Christ.

At the end of the year, I accepted a job working in the hospital. I was one of the sitters who was providing round-the-clock care for a woman whose daughter was a Christian school teacher. Jan wanted Christians to care for her mom, and I really needed the income. On Christmas Eve, the woman's daughter asked me to stay all night with her mother, and I slept on a rug on the floor while Muriel (the woman's name) was sleeping. I again celebrated the holidays with Alan's mother and uncle, and we exchanged gifts. I was invited to spend the night with Dorrene and Chuck on New Year's Eve, and New Year's Day was so nice that Dorrene and I played golf in the backyard!

This was a great year. I had finished the book, but we were unable to find an avenue for publication. I now also owed Chuck over $1,000. I heard rumors that the motorcycle shop was interested in buying the house, and I prayed to God that this was true because I had to sell or lose the place for taxes. I was learning to rest in Him. One other thing bears telling. Dorrene and I had a prison ministry with the woman in Warren County jail. We went there faithfully every Saturday to sing songs, share our testimonies, and read the Bible. Only in eternity will we know what good came out of all this.

Chapter 10

Early Eighties

In January of 1980, I received many of the missing records I needed for my autobiography. I also moved to Schuylerville to care for Muriel, Jan's mother. By mid-January, Muriel began to get confused, so I slept in a room next to her. I told her sister, Harriet, what God had done for me, and she thought I was a kook. One night Muriel's lips turned blue and her breathing was labored, so I called an ambulance. I slipped on the snowy walk and fell flat on my back on the way out, nearly breaking my back. God's power was protected me. Muriel was admitted to the hospital and seemed to be recovering.

Later on, I went to the hospital to visit and I saw a woman sitting with Muriel. She told me Jan had hired her, and I was shocked. Jan explained, "You have done a good job with my mother, but Aunt Harriet doesn't want you around her; she thinks you are crazy." I had been fired because of my testimony!

I visited Aunt Vina for a few days, and she told me a lot about my mother and father. When I returned to Saratoga in February, I discovered the man next door definitely wanted the house. I left it in God's hands, and the man offered me $25,000 for a house that wasn't worth $5,000! The sale proceeded rapidly, and at my request for bankruptcy, my attorney had settled my debts for 25 cents on the dollar! My creditors considered my debt paid in full! I planned to pay my attorney $1,000 for defending my son in 1975 and for his work on closing the house sale. I was also planning to pay a $1,000 pledge made in 1979 to Marilyn Hickey and $2,000 to Roger for his 1975 Buick. I decided to give $2,500 to Debi for a downpayment on a house, for she was pregnant again and desperate. I also planned repay Chuck and Dorrene $1,000 and Judge La Belle $300.

At the closing in March, I endorsed the $25,000 check over to my attorney to take care of all my obligations. Then I took the remainder of the funds to the Adirondack Bank. The vice-president told me to show the check to the loan officer who had once been so nasty to me! After I satisfied my financial obligations, paid my tithes, and gave to Debi and Alan, I bought furniture for the apartment I was moving to on April 1.

I was returning from a national Christian rally in Washington, D.C., when God told me to go to Pete Pemberton, the Chief of Police, and confess my crimes. The next day I told Pete about breaking into the county building, setting a fire on Regent Street, breaking windows, and everything else. He said the way I had lived for the past few years had more than made up for my past infractions! I felt like a ton of bricks had been lifted from me. I praised and thanked God for the exoneration.

I knew the $2,000 I had left wouldn't last long, but I was believing God. I had done everything I was supposed to do with this money, so I knew God would honor me. I was also convinced He was going to have my testimony published. By June, I was really desperate. Jesus said, "Ask, and ye shall receive" (Jn. 16:24b), so I asked, and on June 11, I received a call from the U.S. Census Bureau. I answered the phone with a "Praise the Lord!" And I was asked if I was interested in working for the census. After an interview, I was told I would be a substitute, which meant I'd get limited hours. I told God I needed more than three days' work to sustain my needs, and I sensed that I would be put on full time.

I was told to go to the two-day training and then it would depend on someone's leaving if I would receive work. At the training a man was let go because of an attitude problem, and I was put on full time.

Later I asked my crew chief why I wasn't put on full time from the beginning, and she said it had been because I had answered the phone with "Praise the Lord," and she thought I might be a religious fanatic. Through this I learned that there was a time and place for everything, so I ceased to answer the phone this way.

I called Social Security, Medicare, and the VA and told them that I did not want my benefits any longer, for God had healed me. They couldn't believe that I was of a sound mind and able to work. They ignored me and continued my benefits, but I'd tried. On August 7, 1980, my grandson, Ryan Alan, was born at the Saratoga Hospital. At the end of August, I was asked to care for a 72-year-old widow with terminal cancer in Schenectady. I worked two full days and nights at minimum wage caring for Theresa, an ex-schoolteacher and the former chairwoman for the Republican Party in Schenectady. She only weighed around 80 pounds. She had no children, and her brother and sister-in-law in Indiana kept track of her finances. Theresa had memory losses, but she was an elegant lady.

I joined a bowling league, and took a CETA clerk/typist course while I was I working with Theresa. After I started, the lady who oversaw her care had back problems, and I began to oversee Theresa's care full time. I scheduled other caretakers to watch Theresa when I was at class or bowling in the evening. During the first week of clerical school, Theresa loved to correct my homework and test me in spelling. But the second week, she really took a turn for the worse. She had a flu-like illness that doctors said would soon cause her death, not the cancer. I called her relatives in the Midwest, and they returned to comfort her.

I knew Theresa would never be coming back. Her nephew and his family came to the hospital, but Theresa kept on calling my name. Although her vital signs weren't good, her nephew wanted to leave anyway, even though a nurse said she was failing fast. I stayed by her side, and the last thing she said was "Theresa." She fell into a semicoma, and reached upward for something that she saw with a beautiful smile. I knew she had seen something celestial and beautiful. I held her hands and prayed. She died at 4:00 a.m. After the funeral, her family gave me an extra week's pay and thanked me for staying with her.

Bob and Corolla Williams sent a Christmas card that year, and Claire sent me a special candle. She also came to my apartment with groceries to make lunch. Christmas found me with Alan's uncle and mother at Debi and Alan's place. Alan's mother was filled with unforgiveness—like a mirror image of my former self. I told her there was a better way, but she couldn't see it. So I prayed up a storm for her.

I spent New Years at church with my friends. I remembered a concert where a man told how a pearl was made. He said friction and pain were necessary for a pearl to became genuine. Then the Holy Spirit whispered, "You are no longer a 'Child of Fear.' You are a 'Pearl of Great Price.' " (My real given name is *Pearl* Theresa—praise God!)

January of 1981 was very cold, and Joan called me around midnight one night and told me her kids had not eaten for days. She asked me to bring them something to eat. I pillaged my cupboards and refrigerator and brought them food. Joan's husband drove a new Cadillac, wore starched shirts, and was "one of the elect" at the Soul Saving Station—yet his family went hungry! I applied for jobs, I also had lunch with Claire, which was always a special time. I invited my nephew, Stewart, and his girlfriend to a Full Gospel Businessmen's Fellowship breakfast at the Quaker House Restaurant in South Glens Falls. They both openly professed Jesus Christ as Lord!

On January 31, a Christian archaeologist who published a booklet called "Bible and Spades," hired me part time. In February, Ricky called from Arizona to ask for money, and I sent him part of my rent money. (It was probably used for drugs. I always bought what he said "hook, line, and sinker.") I started my new job with Bryant, the archaeologist, and I wrote Larry and told him what had happened in my life. I asked him to send some money to help me, and within a week he sent me $300!

Claire was moving to Cleveland, so we had lunch. I said good-bye with tears in my eyes. In mid-May, Bryant went to the Holy Land for an archaeological dig and left me in charge of the mailings and the office. He took my book with him, hoping to ask a friend of his to edit it if he came to the States. He tried unsuccessfully to get the book published through several avenues. The ministry was funded mostly by offerings in the mail. I prayed fervently that God would supply. I handled the mailings and sent out books that people ordered. While I was there we kept our heads above water, so God answered my prayers.

Late in June, my friend Mark asked me to go to the White Mountains with him, and he would pay all expenses. Nothing of a sexual nature ever happened between us, but I told him someone else would have to go with us. He lent some money to Joan, so we enjoyed a wonderful trip. Bryant returned and said I had done a fabulous job while he was gone. He had even brought me a gift from Egypt. I walked a mile every day, golfed, and nearly lived in the bowling alley. On August 1, I went with my sisters to the farmhouse where I was born, visited Aunt Rose's grave, and drove to Plattsburgh to see Aunt Vina. On the way back, I had it out hot and heavy with Marie.

Ricky was in jail in Texas, so I called Stewart and asked him to visit him. He and Roger, Jr., couldn't see him because it wasn't a visiting day, so I left it with the Lord. I made the TV bowling eliminations. I travelled to Schenectady to tape the tournament Friday night for broadcast on Sunday. I finished fourth, and then went out to eat with friends and family. Joan had absolutely no home life. Her boys were doing their own thing, and her husband locked her out of the bedroom so she had to sleep in the living room. Bryant was leaving for the Middle East again on October 20, leaving the ministry in my hands.

Meanwhile, things were really crowding in on me financially. Larry wasn't going to help me, and I couldn't afford to stay where I was. Joan and I applied for a job caring for Tessie Mae, a 92-year-old woman in Ballston Spa, where my office was. There was an empty apartment in the same building. When I got the job, we took the apartment that day. Joan and I settled in by the end of the week. I also worked as a waitress at noon for Annie, a local restaurant owner, and took care of the office (as a volunteer at times). Late in November, excruciating pain in my back kept me awake all night. I became violently ill and was burning up with fever. For five days I lay there in bed believe the Lord to heal me, and the Lord was telling me to return to the doctor. When Dorrene took me to Dr. Litts' office, he took one look at me and sent me to the hospital.

I spent 13 days at the Saratoga Hospital. They were sure a kidney stone had caused the problem, but they thought it had passed—or was small enough to pass on its own. On December 22, Debi showed up at our apartment with Larry! When I embraced him, *all bitterness had gone!* I returned to work with Jessie Mae and discovered that the night woman had told her I had an infectious disease because she was jealous of my relationship with Jessie Mae. Bryant came back, and I spent the holidays at Debi's with Larry, and Alan's mother and uncle. Larry gave me a card with a $100 bill in it. We all had a super time, especially our two beautiful grandchildren. In all, 1981 was an amazing year for a person who had been "a vegetable" just a short time ago!

I decided not to return to Empire State because Evangela told me not bring God so much into my writings. In 1982, I continued to work at the office, the restaurant, and at Jessie Mae's. Bryant told me that Dr. Wilson, who he had hoped would edit my book, was not coming to the U.S. I wanted to go home and unburden my disappointment to Joan, but she wasn't there! She'd returned to her husband. A deep loneliness overtook me, and Joan's departure forced me to work more hours at Jessie Mae's. Bea, the night woman, continued to cause problems, but Jessie Mae gave me several bonuses that winter and a ten-dollar gold piece. I told her about Jesus, but she believed more in Norman Vincent Peale. She had lived a good life, so she felt she didn't have to do anthing else.

On February 10, the transmission went in my car. Jo and her son, Tom, bailed me out. I kissed Larry good-bye, for he was returning to Minnesota the next day. He put new tires on my car and helped me a lot, and I hated to see him go. I wasn't feeling too well because of urinary tract problems. Jessie Mae was enjoying me more, and she began to trust me implicitly, even though she tended to be wary of everyone. Whittaker House was not interested in publishing my book, but Logos (now Bridge Publishing) said they would consider looking at it for a nominal fee. The pastor's wife and Kathy edited it, and Jo Lucas retyped the text.

Ricky sent me a heart-rending letter telling me everything he had done since he ran away from Teen Challenge. He was in jail again, but what could I do? Jessie Mae gave me $900 to go to Texas, but God told me to return it and I did, with much thanks. I still bowled in three summer leagues and worked three jobs. On May 21, I mailed a portion of *Pearl at a Great Price* to Bridge Publishing. Jessie Mae and I were real close, but Bea still tried to turn her against me. I got fed up with the strife, and I told Bea she could have the job and packed to leave. Jessie Mae begged me not to leave her, so I stayed, but I told Bea to cool it. I told her that if I wasn't a Christian, she would not have a job. In June, we had it out again because Bea wanted to "work" six nights a week while being paid for it (she slept all night while Jessie Mae slept), and leave at 6:00 a.m. I told her she should give the others two nights each and take her fair share of the day shifts, but she refused. I was burnt out. I asked God to direct me, and I resigned June 12.

Depressed, I told Annie I couldn't work at the restaurant, and I wrote a letter of resignation for Bryant. In three days, I got on my face before God and repented. I went back to Annie's to work, and I never gave Bryant the resignation letter. A specialist in Albany discovered that I had a kidney stone with jagged edges that I was unable to pass, so I had surgery. Natalie took me to her home to recuperate on July 8. She and her husband, Marty, were very nice to me. I returned to my apartment on the seventeenth and thanked Marty and Natalie. The reply from Bridge Publishing was in my mailbox. It said my manuscript had merit, but it needed to be redone and resubmitted. I never did it. My support group for the book met for communion. We had a lovely time in the Lord, and again I knew I had to trust in Him to meet all of my needs.

On July 28, my brother Billy took me out to lunch and I drove his new Cadillac. We had a super time together, and he met a lot of my friends. We talked a lot. He also got in trouble with Jackie for being with me so long, and was unable to see me again because of her jealousy. In August, I was working for Bryant again, but I was in despair. My friends faithfully supported me, Larry sent me money, and Jo was helping me at the office, but I could see no light. I had to sell the gold coins Jessie Mae had given me to pay some bills, and I had stopped bowling because of the surgery. On August 22, I bowled for the first time since surgery, but I discovered one of my friends had committed suicide. That really rocked me.

On August 25, 1982, Ricky arrived by bus, and I saw him for the first time in seven years. He told me he was sick with a flare up of hepatitis, so I got him medical attention. I went to hear Kenneth Copeland and Rev. Schambaugh, and met with family members in September. When I got back, Danny Doyle was with Ricky, and I knew they were up to no good. (Doyle was a mental patient I'd taken in for a month in 1979.) I confronted Ricky and told him I knew he was taking mind-controlling substances and he got angry and went to live with Marie for two days. He came back and I took him to the hospital to get straightened out. Then Ricky left me a note: "Mom: Bye thanks for everything. Will send some money when I get some. Love, Ricky." I cried for days.

I had a lovely Thanksgiving dinner at Debi's, but I found out that Larry had a heart attack and that Ricky was back in jail. Ricky got out of jail on December 2, and Larry got out of the hospital at the same time. I spent a fabulous Christmas afternoon at Debi's, and on New Year's day, I worked for five hours in the office, then I came home, had dinner, and worked on office work at home. I thanked God for holding me up during a very difficult year. In January of 1983, I prayed about the situation with my gall bladder. On January 13, I called the doctor to schedule surgery at the end of the month. Bryant was taking a tour to Israel in April. If we got ten people for the tour, he said he could take me along as his assistant. I really believed we would get ten people, if not more, so on January 20, Dorrene took me for my passport pictures.

On January 25, Kathy and Ron came to my place, and we had communion before they drove me to the Saratoga Hospital for the surgery. The surgeon confirmed that I had several large stones and an enlarged gall bladder. I was discharged nine days later, and within two days, Ricky returned and asked if he could stay with me. I told him I wouldn't tolerate any drug use. Bryant supplied me with work at home (I needed the income), and Dorrene and the others visited me. February 13 was Ricky's twenty-fifth birthday, the first birthday he had spent with me in eight years. Debi, Alan, and their kids came over. We all had ice cream and cake. It didn't take long for Ricky to mess up. Eight days later he came in stoned, and I ordered him out. Six days after that, Ricky was in jail for shoplifting, possession, and violating his probation.

I began to work at the office again, and Bryant gave me his doctoral dissertation to type on top of everything else. I finally got it done a month later, but after much prayer, I felt the Lord had released me from this job. I gave my letter of resignation to Bryant, effective April 1. Ricky asked me to tell the jail's doctor that he couldn't digest fatty foods due to hepatitis. Dr. Peacock feared that Ricky would infect the jail population, so he told the sheriff to let Ricky go. He also told me that Ricky would never live to see 40. Ricky left the jail, but I did not want him to stay with me. Marie took him to her apartment out in the country. I visited him there and made meals for him.

I was instrumental in helping Jo to realize she had to attend her daughter's wedding on April 16, 1983. It was a sit-down dinner, and everything went great. I was supposed to go to Israel on April 21; however, we fell one short of the minimum, so I stayed home. Larry returned and stayed with Debi, but he visited me often. He helped me financially in May after I left my job with Bryant. Alan's mother suffered a stroke but seemed to be recovering. Larry and I visited her together a couple of times throughout May. One evening I even made a super dinner for Larry, our family, and our friends. Larry stayed the night with Jennifer that night. Ever since his heart attack, he hadn't felt very well, so bypass surgery was indicated. One day he said sadly, "I would never be able just to not do anything. I really couldn't live very long like that." For the first time, I realized that Larry was a wounded little boy at heart, and my heart went out to him.

I hoped God was going to put Larry and I back together; because with the way Larry was acting toward me, I actually felt love for him (although it was not a physical or romantic love). Another evening Larry spent the night at my place with Ryan and Jennifer, and we took the kids to Bingo. We were together a lot. I even went to Mass every Sunday with him and the grandchildren. Ricky was still with my sister Marie. I talked to him on the phone, but I did not get overly involved with him or Marie. At the end of June, Ricky got a job. He began living with his cousin Karen in town. He bought a bike, and I prayed that he would keep his job and stay out of trouble.

On June 23, I took Ricky to work at the dentist's office. Then I went to do my volunteer work at the local battered women's shelter. But when I got home, I discovered Ricky was in jail. He was accused of stealing a credit card from the receptionist at the dentist office. (The police found the credit card on Ricky, and he said he had found it.) When he was taken for arraignment, he escaped! He called Larry at Debi's and asked him to pick him up at Dr. Litts' office and take him to Karen's. Larry put a note on the door to tell Debi that he was driving Ricky to Karen's. The cops saw the note, and so did Debi. She went over to Karen's, where Ricky threatened her with a bicycle chain. (She was pregnant at the time.) The cops surrounded the building.

I finally got there and reasoned with him. He agreed to surrender peacefully. I talked to Judge La Belle, and saw Ricky at the hospital. I also went to Karen's and found other cards that belonged to the receptionist. I learned that Ricky had gotten a lot of groceries for Karen. I had to tell the police, but before I did, I drove around the lake and cried out to God. My heart was breaking over my son who had no conscience. He was a liar and a cheat, and it broke my heart. Then I gave the evidence to the police.

On July 1, 1983, Mary Thornhill, a former bowling partner, asked me to consider caring for a man in Schuylerville. She came in his car, and we picked him up and came back to my apartment. Leon Rafael was a 72-year-old widower with one daughter, whom he was alienated from, and a sister-in-law in New York City. He had worked as an engineer at Espey's for years, but now he could not care for himself. He hated the home, and he wanted to live in Mary's house, but she had a husband and children. I told him I would run a tight ship because he was a diabetic. He was used to being his own boss, but I let him know that I would have to be the boss. I wasn't too crazy about Leon Raffael's personality and arrogance. Leon told Mary I was too bossy and feisty, and that I didn't have enough finesse. I told Mary he was right.

Larry and I picked strawberries for Debi. He also helped me plant tomatoes on my patio. Then he and the kids came to spend the night. It was a miracle we got along so well. We took Ryan and Jennifer to Plattsburgh and stayed overnight. Later that month, we took the grandkids to see "Snow White," and to Browns Beach. We really were learning to enjoy each other through the grandkids. Although I was applying for numerous jobs, I wasn't hired anywhere.

On July 20, 1983, Mary Thornhill said Leon was in the Glens Falls Hospital, and he wanted to see me. He had eaten a lot of cookies and nearly went into a diabetic coma. He was in critical condition. His former boss had gone to see him. He had Leon make a will when he was not capable of doing it. He got Power of Attorney from Leon, and was now in charge of his affairs. He didn't want Leon to give everything he had to Mary.

Sol Pinsely was very wealthy, but he did not want Leon's money going to Mary. They had no witnesses there to see Leon sign the will, so it was taken to the lawyer's office and signed later by an alleged witness (I found this out later). I now believed God really wanted me to care for Leon, so I put another bed in my living room. Sol Pinsely and I made arrangements for his care, and I asked Larry to help me with Leon. Without warning, Larry took off for Minnesota on July 21.

I took classes at the hospital to help Leon lose 30 pounds so he would not have to take insulin. Leon came to my home, and I started him on his special diet. Leon's real disposition soon showed. He had a dirty mind, and he annoyed me when I tried to read my Bible. Everytime I went by him, he tried to be fresh; so I lit into him. Sex was all in his mind (he was totally impotent), but he was determined to make others believe he was a man in his twenties. After prayer one night, I told Dorrene I felt God wanted me to marry Leon! Dorrene smiled at me. In essence she was telling me it was probably what God wanted me to do.

Two days later Leon asked me to marry him. He said his sister-in-law wanted him to buy a house in New York City for her family, and she wanted Leon to live with them. Leon wanted to marry me so she would leave him alone. He bought a ring and called Sol to ask him if it was all right with him. Sol gave us his blessings, and we set the date for September 4, 1983. Sol secretly asked me to sign a pre-nuptial agreement and I signed it, for I knew God was my source. I felt I was to enter this marriage of convenience, and it was confirmed to me by other good Christians.

Chuck and Dorrene stood up for us, Jennifer was my flower girl, and Ryan was the ring bearer. Leon insisted on rising from his wheelchair to take the vows. We had a beautiful double-ring ceremony, and then we headed for a real swanky restaurant in the mountains for a sit down dinner. We headed for home and bed. I kissed Leon and he kissed me, and that was the extent of our lovemaking. The next day, we spent the day with my grandchildren, and Leon was a miserable mess. Finally I took him home and took the kids to get something to eat, intending to bring something back for Leon.

I sent someone back to the apartment to see how he was, and Leon said he was going to bring desertion charges against me! When I got home, he threw a glass of water in my face, and I slapped his face. He pounded the table as hard as he could, but I let him know he did not scare me. The next day I called Sol and Mary, and Leon agreed to see a psychiatrist. We wanted to buy a mobile home, and we found the one we wanted. I took Leon to the White Mountains on September 9, and he actually rode in the cog railroad to the top of the mountain. We stayed for two nights and had a fabulous time. I was bowling three times a week, but I took Leon for a ride every day. We ate out a lot, and while he stayed on his diet and dropped pounds, I was picking them up in the restaurants.

On September 16, Leon had a weird drug reaction to "Halcyon" that paralyzed him. The hospital put him in the Mental Health Unit for two nights, and I threw all those pills away. He still did weird things, but the doctors kept telling me it was all in his head. On September 29, I found Leon on the floor. His breath was sickeningly sweet, indicating acidosis. I called an ambulance and decided that I wasn't going to buy anything they said. Something was really wrong with Leon, and I was determined to make the doctors listen.

The hospital wanted me to take him home again, but I demanded diagnostic tests. They even put Leon in a wheelchair and urged me to take him to Dr. Litts, but I wasn't that stupid! I knew the minute I removed Leon from the hospital premises, they were off the hook. I called Sol Pinsley, and he sent an attorney to the hospital. Dr. Litts didn't want to be involved with any attorneys, but I told him Leon needed help, so he admitted him. The attorney scared the hospital so much that they didn't dare send him back home.

Meanwhile, Sol Pinsley and an attorney took care of the mobile home deal. We put a substantial amount down, and we wanted to get in by October. We wanted a ramp for Leon's wheelchair, along with central air conditioning and a paved driveway. Leon's wedding gift to me was to go anywhere I wanted, and I told him I wanted to go to Israel. But first I wanted to get to know him better and take care of him before I traveled abroad. I had all I wanted, but I was not in charge of Leon's money (and that was fine with me). On October 18, I spent my the first night in our new mobile home. Leon and I talked by telephone constantly. I visited him regularly, but he was anxious to occupy his new home.

At the end of October, a neurologist confirmed that Leon had water on the brain and scheduled an operation to put in a shunt to release pressure on his brain. The surgery was successful, and on November 8, Leon saw his new home for the first time. After this Leon began giving me a real hard time through his disposition and his actions to get even with me for bowling, and for not being with him every minute. We argued, and he tried to hit me over the head with his cane. Once he punched me in the breast, but I gave back more than he gave. Sol told me to leave him, for he was just plain rotten. He had known Leon for over 40 years, and he said Leon used to throw his lighter on the floor and say to his first wife, "Pick it up, slave."

I told Leon I was willing to do almost anything for him, but I wouldn't let him be mean to me. I needed time and space too, but I always made sure that he had someone with him, and I never neglected him. He said he was better than me and that I was his slave. He said he would do anything he pleased to make me miserable, but I told him I'd live in a shack before I would let him continue this way. I told him what Sol said, and I warned him that I wouldn't stay with him unless he started treating me like a human being. I gave him time to think it over. Later he told me he was sorry. He promised he would try to be different if I didn't leave him. He said he really cared for me, but that he had never gotten along very well with anyone. He still thought he was superior to me, but he also knew I wouldn't take his physical and mental abuse. Sol was on my side, and this really worried him.

Sol Pinsley, the lawyer, and an engineer came over for champagne and hors d'oeuvres. Leon felt ten feet tall when they congratulated him on marrying me and having such a lovely place. Then they asked him to work about 10 hours a week on a project he'd worked on before his illness. (They were trying to pick his brains because he was considered to be an electronics genius.) Leon later told me he was afraid to go back to work; he had lost confidence in his mental ability. I told him there was nothing wrong with telling the truth, so I told Sol the next day.

Marie and Eugene came to visit, and I built a fire for Leon that morning because it was a cold day. I left Marie and Eugene there and went bowling, but I let the fire go out in the fireplace before I left. When I got home, we had a nice chat and everyone went to bed. At 3:00 a.m., a neighbor woke us up because our porch was on fire! The fire department put the fire out, but there was extensive damage on the front porch. Eugene had placed the ashes in a cardboard box on the porch next to some clothes; however, the ashes had been still very much alive. Sol remarked, "I heard you had a house warming!" Insurance took care of it, and no one was hurt.

Leon and I still had heated arguments . He wanted to possess me, but I wanted freedom—and I got it. I took him to Plattsburgh to see Aunt Vina in December, and he was nice because he had me all to himself. He wasn't in love with me. He simply wanted my undivided attention. When we returned, he messed all over the place. His doctors confirmed he was doing it on purpose because there was no physical reason for him to do it. They told me to put Leon in the hospital.

Sol told me to leave Leon because he would make my life miserable. I was reaching the end of my rope. On December 22, Leon called from the hospital to say he was sorry, and he was brought home for Christmas Eve. We opened our presents and had Christmas dinner at Debi's. On New Year's Eve, Ron and Kathy prayed for me and Leon. It was one hectic year, and it took Leon to show me how really human I was. At times, Leon discussed God in a favorable way. He also talked about his younger years in West Virginia. He was kicked out of college for making booze in a bathtub, and his father had been a religious fanatic. Also Leon had been a spy during World War II. I found a different name on his passport, and he said he'd gone to Italy to work in a factory to gather submarine information. He had gone to Japan several times after the war as well, as a consultant. When I told him about my life, he listened with awe. He was amazed when I told him how rotten I was, despite the fact that I loved God. I told him that everytime I had to physically or verbally defend myself against him, I would go in my room and cry out to God because I wasn't what He wanted me to be. This confession eventually led Leon to come to the Lord.

Chapter 11

The Mid-Eighties

On January 2, 1984, Shawn Michael Coombs, my third grand-child, was born. Alan and I took care of Jennifer and Ryan until Debi came home. Shawn reminded me of my side of the family. On January 7, I again qualified for the TV tournament on Channel 6. The man I was to compete with told someone, "If I bowl her, she will be a cinch." He found out that all he had to do to see me at my best was to stir up my French temper. I beat him on TV, won the championship, and received $375 for my heroic efforts.

On January 15, Leon had a mini-stroke, and the next day in the hospital he was totally out of his mind. On the twenty-sixth, I brought Leon home and stayed with him that night. The next morning, I found him lying in the bathtub stark naked! Dr. Litts thought he had what is called "Sundowners Syndrome," meaning after the sun went down he would lose it. On February 3, Leon was hostile and talked crazy most of the time. I tried to go to the hospital every day, but I couldn't take Leon's verbal abusiveness. I sometimes stayed away for a day or two.

I had a long talk with Sol Pinsley about Leon, and he told me he had plans for Leon. I asked him what he meant, and he told me to just wait. On March 2, Leon went off again mentally, and he had to be watched closely. I could not depend on Ricky for he was taking mind controlling drugs again. Leon got into it with me on March 6, so I talked to Sol. A few days later, Leon was served a court paper initiated by Sol Pinsley, his best friend. It essentially took away his assets and ordered that he be put in a nursing home as mentally unstable!

Leon could not believe that his dearest friend would do this to him. He tried to contact the lawyer, but the lawyer didn't want to touch the case with a ten-foot pole. Leon was afraid, and he begged me to do something. I told him that he had been so miserable to me and everyone else that everyone thought he was out of his mind. I asked Sol why he did this, and he said it was because no one should be subjected to what Leon was putting me through. He said I would be able to keep the home along with the $6,000 in the checking account, and perhaps his stocks. He told me I would be better off physically and mentally when this was over.

I knew I couldn't let anyone take away Leon's dignity. I had vowed to care for Leon, and I was going to fight Pinsley if need be. I got Judge La Belle and others to certify my ability to handle Leon's affairs, and Sol Pinsley backed down. By April, everything was put in my name, along with Leon's. Leon found out that Sol had me sign a pre-nuptial agreement and he was furious. He immediately made a new will, leaving everything to me. Despite all of our problems, he knew I had saved him from being put away as an alleged mental case. He often said it was because of me that he was still alive.

The hospital tried to charge Leon thousands of dollars for "staying too long" in the hospital. At a Utilization and Review Board hearing, I argued that Leon had fallen in the bathtub and could have seriously injured himself when they sent him home prematurely. They had also said nothing was wrong and sent him home when he actually had water on the brain. I told them we would not pay since all of his hospitalizations were legitimate. I never was billed again. I hired Joan Foster to stay with us for $100 a week, and I let her plant a garden on our land. I promised Leon I would only bowl one league in the summer, and that made him happy. At times it was rough, but he seemed to try harder after the legal episode with Sol.

Now Leon used a cane. He was severely hunchbacked, and he had to have operations on his legs to correct circulatory problems. I tried to make him walk around on the porch several times a day, and I ordered a wheelchair for him because I'd promised him we were going to take several trips. We headed for Cape Cod with Jennifer and Joan, and we had a great time. Then I told Joan she could go home while Leon and I took a senior citizen tour to Wildwood, New Jersey. We also headed for Atlantic City and went to the Tropicana Casino. After we got back home, I dressed up like a clown for Jennifer's sixth birthday and had a lot of fun with my big nose. On July 5, Leon and I left with Joan to Amish Country. We stayed for almost a week, then headed for home. It was a marvelous trip.

Leon let me bet $200 on baseball games, and I promised him I would double it. Within a month I had made over $600 on the games, but I quit as I promised. We also made trips to Ausable Chasm, and the 1000 Acres Dude Ranch at Stoney Creek. When we got to the ranch, Leon told me he did not want to stay. I respected his feelings, for I could see he was uncomfortable.

Larry had heart by-pass surgery and felt much better. He wrote me a nice letter when he found out I had married. On August 13, I purchased a new moped and rode it home while Tommy drove my car home. I went for a nice ride that night and loved it. On August 15, I told Joan and Leon that we would go out to have ice cream when I got back from an errand on the moped.

I thought of taking my helmet off because of the heat but decided not to. I saw another red moped just like mine on the side of the road way ahead of me. When I reached it, the moped pulled out in front of me. I hit it and went flying in the air. My head hit the pavement several times, and the helmet came off. When I looked up, I was on the other side of the road and an 18-wheeler was bearing down on me. He managed to stop, and I managed to crawl off to the side of the road. When the sheriff came, I told him what had happened. Then the ambulance transported both of us to the hospital. The girl on the other moped was only 15, and she said she had been making a left turn (she actually drove straight across the road without looking to her left).

I was lying on a stretcher when the deputy gave me a ticket for following too close! This was not true and later God vindicated me. I was admitted to the hospital with a broken rib, a partially collapsed lung, multiple contusions, bruises, and road burns. The girl fractured her ankle but went home that night. I told Judge La Belle what had happened. Back home, Marie was telling Joan that my behavior was unsuitable. The chaos and verbal assaults of my sister Marie, along with her distorted versions of my medical situation, caused Joan to leave. Marie even told Joan that I did not want to see her. Joan couldn't take care of Leon in that atmosphere.

Everything was a mess after Joan left. Someone had to care for Leon, so praise God, Larry stepped in. Leon gave him a hard time, but Larry stuck it out. Leon came to visit me in the hospital, and I was a sorry mess for days. I spent 13 days in the hospital, and I had terrible nightmares for some time. Larry stayed on and drove me to the doctors. Leon was as nasty as could be because Larry was what he called "the boss."

Ricky called to apologize to me for stealing money from me when he had left in May, and he sent $20 back. In August, I found out that Ricky had hit an airline hostess and a man with a crow bar. The woman was in critical condition in the hospital, but the man was in better shape. Ricky was tried for drug intoxication and got six years.

I had a long talk with Leon, and I told him there was nothing between Larry and me. I explained that if it hadn't been for Larry, he would be in a home for no one could care for him. I also told him that we were going to Skyline Drive as he'd requested, and our talk seemed to help. On September 22, Ron, Kathy, Leon, and I headed for majestic Skyline Drive and Luray Caverns. Then we headed for the Carolinas and visited Heritage Village. Next we moved on to Virginia Beach, Virginia. We were right on the ocean, and it was a fantastic sight. We visited the Christian Broadcasting Network (CBN), and we joined the audience for Pat Robertson's "The 700 Club." That night, Leon and I looked out at the ocean and held hands in beautiful communion with each other. The next morning we headed for Atlantic City, but we couldn't get a room. We ended up in a dumpy hotel that we were glad to leave. Our trip spanned nine states.

After we returned, I found blood in the toilet after Leon went to the bathroom. Leon knew about it prior to our trip, but he feared I'd cancel the trip if he told me. Leon's surgeon and the oncologist told Leon he had cancer of the bowel. Because of his general health, Leon underwent a "cauterization" procedure and came home October 24.

From the day Leon came home he was unable to control his bowels. On October 27, he was readmitted to the hospital. The surgeon was afraid Leon wouldn't survive colostomy surgery, but it was the only answer to his problem. I prayed with Leon and made sure that he wanted the surgery. He wanted it because he wanted to come back home with me. Ironically, Leon's roommate was the father of my childhood friend, Polly Claydon, and we reminisced over old times together.

On the eighteenth, I held Leon's hands and prayed, and I received assurance that Leon would make it. The same day, the surgeon said he did not believe Leon would survive. I told him Leon would live because we had prayed, and he shrugged his shoulders and walked away. Leon came through the surgery the next day without a hitch! On December 21, Leon had some trouble with his heart and was placed in intensive care, but in a few days he was able to go back to his regular room. I took lessons to learn about his colostomy, but no matter how much they tried to have Leon help himself, he would not cooperate.

Leon couldn't come home because he refused to help himself. He was no vegetable, and I told him so. On Christmas day, I picked him up at the hospital, and we went to Debi's for gifts and for dinner. Leon was very weak, so I returned him to the hospital. Dr. Litts said Leon should go to a nursing home until he got stronger and learned how to help himself. He felt Leon would be too much for me to handle. so I put him in a private room at a nursing home in Schulerville for $1,000 a month. He seemed to like the place.

On New Year's Day, I asked God to guide and direct me in 1985, and on January 2, I picked up Leon and took him for a ride and dinner. Then returned I him to the nursing home. Larry was staying with me and doing odd jobs around the house. I told Leon this was what I wanted, for I did not care to live alone in the winter. Besides, Larry was paying half the expenses, and it was a purely platonic relationship.

On January 10, Claire came to visit me. I had not seen her in three-and-a-half years, and we had a nice two-hour visit. I was volunteering every Monday afternoon for the Special Olympics as a bowling coach and scorekeeper. The Olympians gravitated to me, and I had a lot of patience with them. I got to know them all and respected them as individuals. Ricky was in a Louisiana state prison, and Larry and I agreed to each send him $20 a month. I made it a point to visit Leon several times a week, and when the weather permitted, I took him out. He did well in the home, but he refused to help himself. Several times they had found him on the floor. I urged him to straighten out so he could return to his home.

I had planned to bring Leon home in March, but when the home told me the things he was doing, I changed my mind. He stole a woman's cigarettes and was caught smoking all alone downstairs around midnight. (The building was old and made of wood.) He was also urinating in waste baskets. He was hostile and unwilling to deal with his colostomy. I told him that when he wanted to stop his nastiness, I would bring him home.

On March 27, Leon fell and was taken to the hospital. There were no broken bones, but he was sore. I took a stress test and was put on a beta blocker by a cardiologist. On Easter Sunday, I fell into acute depression. I lost direction in my life, and I was running faster and faster to escape what I feared—Leon's condition and my inability to handle it. Because of my years in mental institutions I was terrified to be around a person whose mind was confused. I wasn't seeking God; I was depending on my own strength. Dorrene knew what was going on without me saying a word.

Larry returned to Minnesota for medical consultation with the VA, and would not be returning until May. I really didn't cherish living alone. In May, I applied for a job as a sitter in the emergency room for alcoholics. On Mother's Day, Alan's mother suffered a severe stroke and went into a deep coma. Dorrene and I prayed for her, and she came out of the coma, but she was placed in a nursing home. Aurora's boyfriend died suddenly of pancreatic cancer, and she was lost without him. I brought her to my home, and while heavily sedated, she managed to set fire to one of my chairs. Something told me to get up. I found Aurora sitting unconscious in the chair while it was on fire!

When Larry came back, I asked him to help with Leon. I took Leon out of the nursing home on June 3, but he still had a mental block about the colostomy. Larry helped in every way possible, but Leon was abrasive in actions and words. I became impatient and inconsiderate at times. I started to take Leon out more and more to dinners to ease the pressure. Larry spent most of his time at Debi's, and I cared for Leon. However, I did not want Leon alone at night when I worked. Whenever Larry tried to assume any authority over Leon, I reminded him I was in charge. This worked out well for Leon, but it drained my energy bank.

Larry was a compulsive talker, but I had learned to tune him out. It was still annoying. On July 30, Larry started rambling while Leon and I were watching a movie. Leon hollered, "Shut up!" and Larry told me Leon had no right to talk that way. I reminded him that it was Leon's home and he was watching a movie. It would have been better if Leon had said, "Please be still," but it was still Leon's home. The next morning Larry left and had words with Leon on his way out. I was depressed because I really didn't want to stay alone with Leon. After a long talk we put the house up for sale. Leon assured me he would be fine when I worked nights. His mind was good, maybe this was God's way of giving Leon more dignity and me less fear. On August 25, Larry left for Minnesota.

At the end of September, Leon and I went for a day ride to Tupper Lake, and I began to spend more time with my grandchildren. Leon seemed to care for them too. I had Aurora with me as well because of the depression that she was experiencing that month. On November 1, I had a big blowout with Leon, and he got physical, but I defended myself. We made up and I took him to the movie *Jagged Edge*. On November 27, Leon and I talked until 7:00 a.m., and Leon told me he could listen to me all night every night. Two days later, my knees got so bad that I could not walk. The doctor sent me to the emergency room for treatment. Jo and Tom drove me home, and Jennifer and Ryan spent the night with me. Leon started in on the kids, but I scolded him, so he settled down.

On December 29, 1985, Aunt Vina died. Leon, Pauline, my brother Freddy, and I headed for Plattsburgh to Aunt Vina's wake. Later we all went to the Spa Brauhaus for New Year's Eve dinner. That night I moved Leon into the back room to give him more privacy. Leon kept saying to me, "Hit me"; he thought I moved him to the back room because I didn't want to be near him. But I explained to him that he deserved his own privacy.

I spent most of January, 1986, shoveling and chopping ice, while Leon spent a lot of time sleeping—his health was failing. One day Leon grabbed my wrist and started to twist it until I slapped him. He seemed to thrive on dissension and strife, and every day was a new adventure. By March, Leon was failing before my eyes. I took him to the Emergency Room on March 5, and on March 6, my fourth grandchild, little Jason, was born. I called Larry the next day to tell him the news. On March 23, the weather was good and I took Leon for a nice ride and dinner. He rewarded me by messing up the whole place again. On March 29, Debi and Alan sent me a beautiful arrangement of flowers in appreciation for all I had done for them.

Leon's disposition was so ingrained that it was hard for him to be nice, but I had glimpsed a little boy hiding behind his gruff facade. In March, we began to talk about God more than ever before. He claimed to be an atheist, but I told him for me there was nothing worth living for if there wasn't a God. I told him the whole plan of redemption through God's Son, Jesus Christ, and I told him I had to forgive him or God could not forgive me. That is why he had to forgive his daughter and Sol Pinsley. He digested everything I said, but the old man dies hard.

On April 22, Leon's urologist told him he would eventually have to go on dialysis, but Leon said he would never allow it. In May, Larry returned from Minnesota and stayed with us on the condition that he would have nothing to do with Leon's care unless an emergency came up. Leon loved opera, so I surprised him with two tickets to the opera *Carmen*. We went to the opera on June 22, and Leon really enjoyed it. I told him I appreciated all he had given to me. (Leon was going to send me to Hawaii in September as a gift.)

In mid-July, Larry said he'd had it with Debi and that He was going back to Minnesota. Leon and I were preparing to go out, but I told Larry not to leave this way, urged him to think it over, and left in tears. When Leon and I got back, the keys were on the stand, so we knew he had left. Leon went to his room to lie down. My spirit was wounded and I got on my knees before Leon's bed. It was July 15, 1986, when I held Leon's hand and asked his forgiveness for my meanness. I laid my head on his chest, and we both cried for our transgressions. The spirit of heaviness lifted from me, and I knew that God had worked some kind of miracle in both of us. The next day, I opened the door and found Larry sitting on the porch. I told him to go in and go to bed, and he stayed.

On August 1, Leon started to act strange and confused. I took him to the Emergency Room, and I felt he had a mini-stroke. Leon seemed to recover, and he came home August 9, but a nurse came to see him for a while. On the nineteenth, my brother Billy, his granddaughter Amy, Jennifer, Ryan, Shawn, Debi and I all went to Hoffman's's Playland and had a great time. On August 22, Leon turned 76 years old. I took him to the Spa Brauhaus for dinner. He had a cake and they sang "Happy Birthday."

I purchased my tickets for my Hawaii trip, and Larry returned to Minnesota for a VA appointment. Arrangements were made for Leon to stay with Ron and Kathy when I went on the trip. While Larry was gone Leon was miserable but I couldn't help him. One night he cried and asked me how he could reach God. He wanted the faith I had. I told him, "Leon, all you have to do is ask Him into your heart, and He will be with you"—and He did! I told him that God was as near as his next breath. He seemed to have more peace than he had ever had.

On September 11, Leon called me into his room, and I noticed he had a lot more edema (swelling) in his leg than usual. I checked his lungs and they were very congested. I became concerned about congestive heart failure. Leon was admitted to the hospital with fluid on his lungs. I got back home after midnight, but I woke up with chills and fever with an attack of Melkerrsdon's syndrome. On September 14, Leon wasn't doing too well. When I entered his room, I started to cry because of the drastic change in him. He had nasal oxygen. He also had a big patch on his arm because he had fallen during the night and had required stitches. Leon saw me and started to get out of the bed and put his hands on top of my head. The nurses couldn't believe how he was when he saw me; he perked right up. I made him lie back down and told the floor nurse I wanted to know his blood, urine, and oxygen level. She made the mistake of telling me she couldn't tell me. I told her I wanted to see the charge nurse—I had a right to know my husband's condition. Leon got a kick out of it, and he perked up even more.

Of course the nurse had to give me the information I sought. I asked for the doctor on duty, and Dr. Wharton talked to me. I told her I wanted Leon in Intensive Care. He was so sick that he had fallen during the night, and when I came to see him he looked like death warmed over. She said he wasn't bad enough for I.C.U., and I disagreed with her. When she asked me what I perceived, I said, "Death!" I told her that I was going to call an ambulance and have him transferred to Albany unless he was put in Intensive Care. He was put in Intensive Care. Even though I was sick, I wasn't about to leave him until he was moved.

I wasn't home a half hour when I received a call telling me Leon had suffered a heart attack. I went back to the hospital, and again Leon perked up. Dr. Del Giacco said Leon wasn't good, but they would keep a good check on him. I went home reassured that the doctor would be there all night. Dr. Litts called at 10:30 a.m. Leon had been put on a respirator because his heart had stopped. When I got there, Leon was in bad shape but conscious. I told him that he was in God's hands. Ron, Kathy, Alan, and Debi came to the hospital, so I went to Dr. Litts's office about my mouth infection. The hospital called there to tell Dr. Litts that Leon had pulled everything out, and

Dr. Litts wanted to know what I wanted to do. I told them to "put everything back in."

I hadn't eaten, so I decided to go to get some soup with Ron and Kathy while Debi and Alan stayed in the hospital. At the restaurant, we prayed that God's will would be done and returned to the hospital. When I buzzed the nurse, she came out and told me Leon had died. He pulled everything out after I left. I asked them why they hadn't come and talked to my daughter, and they said they had but that Debi and Alan hadn't heard them. Leon had a peaceful look on his face and a little boy smile. I gently kissed him and walked away. The last thing I said that night was: "Dear Leon, I'm so glad you have reached your final home." (Leon died exactly two months to the day I had knelt down by his bed and we had both asked forgiveness and wept.)

The pastor who had married us also officiated at Leon's funeral. On September 17, I woke up with chills and fever, but I got my hair done and went to the funeral home with Alan. Sol Pinsley came with a friend of his and gave his stamp of approval, but I did not need it. I called Leon's daughter, but she would not come to the phone. Leon's sister-in-law and her husband came for the funeral.

I kept busy and tried to go on with life. In October, Larry moved into the back room and shared expenses with me. He went his way and I went mine, but it was nice to have someone living with me, even though Larry wasn't home much. On October 17, Ron and Kathy took me to the airport, and I prepared to fly the friendly skies of United to Hawaii with Sally, Kathy's mother. Hours later as I looked out the window over the Pacific Ocean, I looked at the sky and silently said, "Thanks, Leon."

Sally and I arrived in Hawaii in the afternoon. We were met there by Kathy and Ron's sister, Diane, and her daughter, Kim. After a quick stop at McDonald's, we went to Pearl Harbor to wait for Diane's husband, Eric, to come in on the submarine that he served on. Pearl Harbor meant a lot to me. We reached Diane's place after 7:00 p.m., and it was beautiful. Sally had the guest room, and Kim gave me her bedroom. I felt right at home. We did all of the usual tourist things, but one day Diane took Sally and I to Pearl Harbor, and we actually boarded Eric's submarine! We submerged and they gave us nausea pills. I even steered the sub and fired a torpedo slug! I visited various areas of the ship (not the nuclear room). We saw a movie and played cards. We got back to Pearl Harbor at 6:00 p.m., ending an experience I'll never forget.

Sally, Diane, and I went to see the Don Ho Show (which was Sally's dream). We had dinner and a birthday cake for Sally, and Don Ho autographed pictures and kissed Sally for her birthday. It was a dream that came true for her, and we all had a super time. Finally, the time came for Diane and Kim to drive us to the airport, so we bid *Aloha* to beautiful Hawaii. Debi, Alan, Ryan, and Shawn met us at the airport, and when we got home, there was a big sign outside that said, "Welcome Home."

In December, I went to see Bill Shea, a veteran's counselor, about reopening my VA case, and we started the process again. I "rang in the new year" of 1987 with Kathy, Ron, Eric, Diane, Kim, Rachel, Sarah, and Eric's mom and dad. January fifteenth was Larry's sixty-eighth birthday, and we all went to dinner at the Weathervane. That night, Lou LeMyre, Diane's mother, told me that Diane had died of cancer. I was really upset because I loved this girl, and I had really believed she would beat the cancer. On January 25, Jennifer and Ryan came to stay the night. Larry began to verbally abuse them. I made it clear that I would not allow him to hurt my grandchildren like he had hurt my children. That month Larry was told he was a diabetic, so I took his blood sugar every morning and night. He monitored his eating and finally stabilized his blood sugar.

After I reopened my VA case with Bill Shea, the VA sent me for a gynecological exam, even though I was stating my nervous disorder had incurred in, and was aggravated by, the service. I spent two hours talking with Bill Shea, and he was upset to hear that the VA had possibly shredded Dr. Wasserman's notes (who gave me insulin shock therapy in 1953). The records I had obtained from Downey did not have his name on them, so Shea wrote to the Regional Office and told them we were filing for a service-connected nervous disability.

About that time I heard over the news that a man had beat up his baby. I bowled with the baby's mother and grandmother, so Kathy and I went to Albany Medical to pray for the baby. I held the baby in my arms and prayed for him. He lived, but it was tragic that he suffered the injuries he did. His mother and father were forbidden to come near the baby, and the grandmother eventually got custody of the child. One morning in June, someone banged on my door. It was Dave, a Special Olympian I'd befriended. He said his 26-year-old sister was dead. She was a taxi driver and had one daughter. I comforted Dave as much as possible, and Dorrene and I went to the wake.

On June 10, I went to see Bill Shea, because he had been giving me flack about my case. He didn't seem to know where to go with my case. I got tired of his excuses and walked out with my records. I prayed about the problem, and in the morning I sensed in my spirit that I should call the library. I asked if they had a book with doctor's names in it. When they said yes, I had them look up Dr. Wasserman in their book. They said he was listed as a resident physician at Downey in 1953, and they gave me his address. Dr. Wasserman remembered me, and he had given me insulin shock treatments at Downey in 1953. With his letter, I could now prove that he was my doctor, just like I'd said all along. But where were his notes?

Dorrene went with me to Johnstown to pick up a notarized statement from Dot, who was my best friend before I went in the service. She affirmed that I hadn't even known what homosexuality was before I went into the service. She said she knew this because she had been with me and another friend at a bar when a woman had begun to buy me drinks. I kept giving them to Ruth and Dot, and thanking the woman—totally unaware that the woman was a lesbian and that she was making a pass at me. She said that she and Ruth had gone into the bathroom and laughed because of my innocence.

I asked the Legal Aid Society to help me with my VA case, but they told me so much time had passed that my case couldn't be litigated. I also went to see an attorney referred by Larry La Belle, and he said the case was not winnable. Soon after that Jeanne and I went to Silver Bay for a C.F.O. meeting. Malcom Smith was the main speaker. I was shocked to learn that he had left his wife, remarried, and was going to live in England; he was the one who had said I had to stay with Larry!

My case was now in the hands of the Disabled American Veterans. One night I asked Nancy to agree with me in prayer that if the DAV didn't want to handle the case, I would have a "burning of my records" party at my home and invite all my friends. I had carried this burden for too many years, and I was now willing to give it to God. In September, I started walking two miles a day, and Julia and I were still golfing. On September 9, I received a letter from the DAV, and they also felt my case was not winnable because too much time had elapsed. I was ready for my paper burning party, but I got a check in my spirit. The Lord wanted me to wait on Him a litle longer. I went for my usual two-mile walks and told no one about the letter.

On September 11, I felt led to call the VA in Albany. I thought it was ridiculous, but I was compelled to call. I was told to contact a Mr. Wilson in Schenectady and was given the phone number. I said, "God, I am willing to give you this case. But why should I call Schenectady? I live in Saratoga County." Then a still small voice said, "I work in strange and mysterious ways," so I called the number and asked for Mr. Wilson.

A man answered and told me that Mr. Wilson wasn't there. Then he asked if he could help me. I told him about my VA case and he told me he was interested. A half-hour later, he asked me to bring my evidence to Schenectady, and I asked who was I talking to. He said his name was Earl Wallace—the same man whom I had spoken to one day in 1977, telling him he would one day handle my VA case. He had taught school, and had worked for the Health Department. He had started working as a Veteran's Counselor only two months before! Dorrene and I went to Earl's office several times in September, and we started on the long journey with my case.

In October I called Debi's home, and Jennifer answered. I could hear Larry swearing at her in the background, and I became livid. I told Jennifer that I wanted to talk to him. When he came to the phone I chewed him out for shouting and swearing at Jennifer. He told me I could get another person to live at my place, and I told him his stuff would be on the porch. He came for it the next day and cleaned his room. Two weeks later he called me up and asked me if the room was still available, so I let him come back.

I met a Christian man at the end of October at the VA and he wanted to go out with me. I gave him my number and said he could call, but after thinking about it, I thought I did not want to get involved with anyone so when he called, I told him so. I spent New Year's Eve at the Spa Brauhaus with Eric, Diane, Sally, Kathy, Roy, and Ron's mother.

Chapter 12

The Late Eighties

I spent most of New Year's Day in 1988 relaxing at home. After the New Year, Debi lost her job because the telephone company had a big layoff. It was totally unexpected. My friend Julia told me about a class in abnormal psychology at St. Peter's School in Saratoga under the auspices of Adirondack Community College, and my ears perked up. She wanted to attend this course, so I told her I would try it too and see what it was like. On Monday, January 18, it was icy, but I managed to get to my first class at school with Julia. Our teacher worked as a social worker in a mental health hospital.

Julie and I seemed to almost compete in the class, and I considered it healthy. Julia seemed to enjoy the course, but on the twenty-ninth, our first class papers were returned. I received an A, but when the teacher went and told Julia he wanted to see her at break time, she exploded! She used the "f" word, and walked out of the class. The next week, the instructor asked me to ask Julia to come and talk to him. I told him that Julia wasn't even talking to me. I could not reach her.

I didn't understand until later that the instructor felt she had copied her paper from a book. Julia swore to me that she didn't. I truly missed her friendship. I knew I had done nothing to her, but it would have to take time for her healing. On March 3, Ricky called.

He was out of prison, and he wanted to come home. Larry and I split the cost and sent him a bus ticket with food money. Ricky arrived two days later, and Larry picked him up. He looked cold and hardened. The next day was Jason's second birthday, and Debi came over to celebrate.

On March 9, I found Ricky stoned, so I told him I wanted him out of the house by the next day. Ricky took off on a wild binge of drug abuse and confrontation with the law that ended in a mental institution a week later. I called Mental Health in Saratoga, and I was told to have him leave my home and go to Social Services, but Ricky accused me of putting a head trip on him.

The State Police picked Ricky up Wednesday and took him to the Saratoga Hospital. He had drugs in his shorts, but he took them too fast for the police to stop him. No doctor went near him, and when I asked about blood toxemia, nothing was done. He was sent to Capital District Psychiatric Center in Albany and then was turned away! After a whole series of official goofs and pass-offs, Ricky was committed to Hutchins in Syracuse. I told the officials involved that I wanted a complete investigation, along with proof that something was being done to the people responsible for this mental hell my son and family went through because of their actions.

From Hutchins, Ricky was sent to a regular hospital in Syracuse where he was strapped down and guarded. His platelet count was real low, and they wanted to do a bone marrow test, but he would not cooperate. He said they would have to take off the restraints before he would let them test him. Eventually, they gave up on him. In April, he landed back in jail in Troy.

Also in April, Jo's husband Tom had to have quadruple by-pass surgery. Praise God he came out of it fairly well. On April 22, Ricky called for a ride because he was now out of jail. I picked him up at Loudonville, and I laid down the ground rules. He went to the VA hospital with me several times, for I was having grief therapy with a wonderful doctor whose name was Knoblauch. And he helped me whenever I asked him to. On May 9, I took my final exam in abnormal psychology and got an A in the course. Larry put in one beautiful garden, and I suspected that Ricky was up to his old tricks. He turned over a bottle of cough syrup to me (this was one way he was getting high).

In the beginning of June I went to Congressman Solomon's office. I asked Patti Raucci if she could get my confidential medical file from the VA. I told her I had been trying for years to get it. I had recently requested it again, but I was being completely ignored. She assured me that she would get it for me. My nephew, Stewart, had settled down and was getting married. I attended his wedding, and when I came home around 2:00 a.m., I caught Ricky stoned out of his mind. I told him I wanted him out in the morning, and he took off. He came back stoned again and pleaded with me to let him stay. When I told him I was going to call the state police, he took off again. He knew I meant it. He was such a sickening sight that I couldn't stand it anymore. I felt like taking a knife and stabbing myself in the heart. I never wanted to see or hear from him again.

Debi went back to work for the telephone company again. Ricky then called her to say he was in Albany county jail and that he was wanted in Louisiana. Earl and I were really working on my VA case. We needed new evidence to counter what we believed to be their continued claims that I was a homosexual with a passive aggressive personality. I had to find some people who could refute their allegations. Dr. Bob Flynn was one of them, so I went to him and discussed my case. I also located the nurse named Joyce who had been so nice to me at Downey (I still had her wedding invitation). I traced her to California, and she called us. She promised to write a statement and send the book of poems I gave her many years ago.

I decided to locate Marie and Ginny because I knew they would verify that I could never be a lesbian. Nothing could hurt them now by telling the truth. After much research, I contacted their nephews, and both of them had died of female cancer—and of course they had never married. Marie achieved her dream of owning a home, and Ginny had worked as a photographer with NASA.

Dr. Flynn wrote a super statement for me, and my newest thera-pist, Dr. Knoblauch, did likewise, as did Claire. All three of them ex-onerated me from having a personality disorder and from being a lesbian. I also had a three-hour evaluation at the Alcoholic Services in Saratoga to prove I was not an alcoholic. We were building up new evidence.

On July 5, 1988, my "C-file" arrived at my home. I was amazed at the things I discovered. The biggest surprise was that they no longer considered me a homosexual or a person with passive aggressive per-sonality disorder. They had conveniently changed their diagnosis to "sociopath addicted to alcohol." I had to get to the bottom of this. They had gotten the diagnosis from a five-day hospitalization at the psychiatric center in Albany, New York, in April 1961. The diagnosis had been made by a Dr. Eisele, and further investigation showed that he was now working in California as an anesthesiologist. He had not even been licensed until 1962. Also his primary speciality was anes-thesiology, his secondary speciality was pulmonary diseases, his terti-ary speciality was clinical pharmacology. Therefore his diagnosis of me in 1961 was invalid and fraudulent. He had never been in the psy-chiatric field.

The Albany Medical Center finally conceded this fact after they knew we were not interested in initiating a law suit but rather seeking justice for a long-term wrong.

That summer the Saratoga Hospital was found to be negligent in letting Ricky escape, and they initiated a whole new set of rules for se-curity. On July 9, a state trooper came to my home with his hand close to his gun, and asked about Ricky. I told him all I knew, and I'm sure that at first he was sure I was hiding him. On August 27, I worked for hours on my VA papers—organization was the key. On August 31, I worked for hours with Earl to prepare the VA case. It was my job to coordinate the information and type it out it onto the forms. I took everything home.

From September 2 through 7, I spent nearly every waking hour working on my case and organizing my evidence. My new statements provided new and material evidence. They also proved that the VA had indeed done a number on me. Dr. Flynn's mother became critically ill, and he earnestly sought my prayers and the prayers of my friends. His mother had a strong will, and he was concerned about her struggling in vain with the inevitable. He wrote me a lovely thank you card and told me how his mother had called him and told him she was now going to sleep. She slipped right on into eternity.

Since I did so well in abnormal psychology, I signed up for a criminal justice course in September at Adirondack Community College. I also started coaching for Special Olympics in September and began bowling again in my Wednesday night league. On September 26, I went to Earl's office to deliver the mass of evidence I had prepared for the VA Regional Office.

Larry was not well at all, and the VA was giving him a runaround. He had a high bilirubin count and probably needed surgery. His doctors didn't want to operate on him because of his heart problems. But something had to be done for him because his gall bladder was severely diseased. He was suffering a lot, and he begged them to do something. He was unable to eat and was failing right before my eyes. What could I do? I told Larry to call the VA and ask for emergency admission, but he was denied.

On Saturday, October 15, Larry could hardly make it to the bed. I knew he was one sick man, but legally I was no longer a family member. I quietly went into my room, closed the door, and called Debi. Since Debi was his daughter, she had some legal leverage. I told her not to allow the hospital to send him back because he needed help. Since the VA refused him admission, he would have to go to the Saratoga Hospital. He was so sick that, for once, there was no argument on his part. The hospital didn't want to keep him, and the doctor basically told Debi he was a dying man. We called his family in the Dakotas and Minnesota.

The cardiologist felt he would not survive surgery, but there was no alternative because his gall bladder was so bad. He hadn't eaten anything for days. When Larry knew the situation, he said he wanted to change his will. He wanted to be buried with me. He also appointed me, upon Debi's request, as executrix of his will. He wanted to divide everything he had from his insurances between his grand-children, Debi, and me. He didn't want Ricky to have anything because of his history of drug abuse. A lawyer came to the hospital and made the changes.

On October 17, Larry seemed very upbeat about his surgery, and he felt he would make it. I felt it was all in God's hands. The next day we saw him before he went to surgery and stayed there until he was out. There was no malignancy, but Larry was put on a respirator in Intensive Care. He acknowledged us with his head and his hands. Considering all he had been through, he looked great. On my way out I threw him a kiss, and he acknowledged it. I felt he was going to make it. Prior to surgery, I told him I would put him in the front room near the bathroom so I could care for him. He told me he wanted his old room back when he got better. At 11:00 a.m. on the twentieth of October, I received a call from his doctor. Larry had taken a turn for the worse after they'd removed the respirator. He had stopped breathing, and they were having a difficult time resusitating him. I called Debi and we all went to the hospital. He was not conscious, but they managed to get his heart going again. I had a perfect peace about it all. At 3:00 a.m. on October 21, Larry had a fever of 104. Two hours later, Debi called me to say that Larry had died.

Larry's mass was held at St. Peter's. It was pouring rain, but he still had his three-gun salute. He was buried in St. Peter's cemetery, and everyone went to Debi's after the graveside services. I went to the VA and told them I did not appreciate the way they had treated Larry. I also told them they should pay for his hospitalizations at the Saratoga Hospital, but they didn't pay a dime. I missed Larry. Although there was no real love, it had been a miracle that we were able to live under the same roof for two years with only one minor separation. On October 28, Alan's mother died and we attended the wake.

Earl sent some of our new evidence to the VA's New York Regional office in October. That office sent us a letter that said in part, "We have determined that the evidence you submitted to reopen your previously disallowed claim is not new and material...we can make no change in our previous decision." This of course was all baloney, and it wasn't until a few years later that Earl and I realized that the New York Regional Office could not make a decision on my case. Nevertheless, they played tiddley winks with me for over four-and-a-half years. (Friends, you have no idea of the corruption in high places.)

I found out in November that my academic record qualified me to become a member of the Phi Theta Kappa National Honor Fraternity, but I would have to travel to Glens Falls for this, so I chose not to be a member. Earl was helping me to get Larry's stone, and on November 14, I found out to my great surprise that Larry had left me an annuity providing me with well over $500 a month for the rest of my life! At this time, I also received the shocking news that an insurance company had offered to settle in my 1984 moped accident case for $25,000!

By the end of 1988, I was facing 1989 knowing I had not come to grips with Larry's death. His presence was in the garden and in the shed he put up. After he died. I went out and took pictures in the twilight. I went in the shed. I sat on the lawn mower, and I cried and cried for what might have been, although I knew we could have never made it as a happily married couple. That wasn't what was bothering me; despite his rambling and faults, I missed his presence. His greatest virtue was stability. I could always depend on him when I needed him. Who would warm up my car, shovel the snow, and drive me to school in bad weather? I did make some nice meals for him as a way of saying thank you, and I took him out to dinner. But there was something deeper that made me cry. I searched it out. I realized it was the universal sadness for all of us—the Larrys and Theresas of this world who, because of personality differences and cultural backgrounds, could not stabilize a relationship as deep as a marriage should be. I had hated him with a passion, and I still got angry with him. I knew only the presence of God could have kept us together for this period of time. God had given me a compassion for this man who seemingly had no real emotions, or did he? Had he buried them so deeply that he was unable to express them? Or had he found it safer not to manifest any caring and love? Instead, he had substituted anger, shouting, and criticism.

I took a long look at myself: Even with all my emotions and caring, had I not withdrawn from the pain of existence for many years? By my hate for Larry, had I not brought out the worst in him? I cried not because I wanted him back, but because I genuinely missed him. I had to admit it to myself. I could only think of his virtues, not his faults. I will be eternally grateful that Larry and I met on common ground before he died. I no longer hated him. We didn't live together as man and wife, but as two different, struggling human beings. This was God's miracle to me. As I dried my tears and locked the shed, I glanced at his garden that was now dying. I admitted to myself that I had to allow myself time to grieve because I was a human being. There was nothing wrong with me missing him at times, just like he, as a farmer, had to see his gardens die year after year. They would again be planted and come up again. Unless a seed falls in the ground and dies, it cannot have eternal life (see Jn. 12:24). As the days passed, I managed to get by, and the loss abated. Thank God for that time sitting on the lawn mower. I had come to grips with Larry's death.

The day after New Year's Day in 1989, my expensive fire alarm system went off, and kept going off for well over an hour—even when I pulled it off the wall! Finally Freddy and Alan had to dismantle the alarm system. After all this, we found out that the noise had been a *radio*! What a way to start a new year!

The next day, I was bowling when I suddenly felt weak and turned as white as a ghost. I went to the Emergency Room and found out that my blood oxygen level was low. I had to stay on oxygen until midnight, and undergo follow-up tests, but everything appeared to be all right.

My schedule was getting packed. I was still coaching for the Special Olympics on Monday afternoons, and I took a college writing course on Monday evenings. On Tuesday, I worked all the phases of Bingo at the Ambulance Corps, and I had my bowling league on Wednesdays. I was studying "the History of England from 1485 to

1815" on Thursdays at the college, and on Friday night I bowled in a late-night mixed league.

In mid-January, I again went to the Veterans Administration office with Jo and then to lunch. She agreed to help me type my papers, and I was thrilled—she is an excellent typist.

The VA Regional Office contacted me on January 26 with the latest in more than 30 years of bad news. They rejected my latest appeal, and their decision clearly ignored every bit of the new evidence I sent them! They requoted the old 1952 decision, saying, "Diagnosis on above rating stated that the examination of service medical records together with factual history contained in the current hospital report impels the conclusion that an early psychosis was in evidence at the time of discharge but *not existing to a compensable degree."*

It also quoted from the outrageous rating given in 1962, that actually said, "The following discussion was noted on this rating: the accumulated medical evidence has clearly established the fact that the veteran suffers from a long time progressive disorder characterized by extreme passive dependency, homosexuality, addiction to barbiturates and alcohol. *These disabilities were the result of the veteran's own willful misconduct."*

Three more times in the letter, including the most recent decision, they quoted the statement that irritated and hurt me the most:

"REASON FOR DECISION:
"The veteran has had an alleged nervous condition prior to her entry into service and therefore her current claim for service connection for a nervous condition is again denied. We have also considered whether veteran's condition was aggravated during service and same is not established.
"The veteran's condition was also due to her willful misconduct."

Those infamous words, *"willful misconduct"* devastated me. We had sent them clear proof that I was not a homosexual, despite the fact I had been initiated to this life in the service. I was not an alcoholic, although it is true I was addicted to legal drugs for years. However, my addiction had started with the administration giving me massive doses of addictive drugs.

What we did not realize then was that they were strictly concentrating on the actions from 1953 to 1964 and that *they had no jurisdiction over this case whatsoever!* We learned that it had to be decided solely on the basis of new and material evidence by the Board of Veterans Appeals *in Washington D.C.*, not New York.

Because of our lack of knowledge, Earl again sent the regional office more evidence, and in March, I again received bad news using the same phrases, logic, and tone. They were determined to ignore the truth, but I was equally determined to press my point until the truth came out!

Early in February, I received a lovely card from Dr. Knoblauch with this note in it (it was a "thank you" note for a gift certificate I sent to her after her baby was born).

"Dear Theresa:

"As you can probably tell from the date on the check and the Christmas card, I've had some trouble figuring out just what I wanted to say to you. It's been so long since you gave me your gift after my baby was born. I was very touched by your thoughtfulness and generosity, yet I have always felt that it was really too generous. I very much want you to accept this money from me because it will make it much easier to remember the part of your gift that was loving and thoughtful. I think of you often and wonder how you are. You are a very special person, and I will always remember your strength and your honesty. Most of all, though, I remember your beautiful, loving heart. I have the rug you gave me where I see it often, and I see the hard work and love that went into creating it, and I think of the hard work and love that have made you into who you are. I have a lot of respect for you. Please do something nice for yourself with this money—that will be a true gift to me. I love you and wish you much happiness."

Arlene Knoblauch

I wrote her back and thanked her for who she was and what she had been to me. I accepted the money graciously as she desired. To this day I do not know where she is, but that is not important—what counts was the beautiful and productive time we shared together. Like Claire, she will always be a bright and shining star for me.

On February 4, I was making candy, and a toothpick accidentally went into the side of my foot right through my sock. I called Ron, but he couldn't get it out. It was deeply embedded—about one-and-a-half inches into the side of my foot, so he took me to the emergency room. The doctor numbed my foot, and I watched him take it out. It bled profusely, and the wound required four stitches. I was incapacitated for approximately five days.

That same day I bought two tickets for the play *Nunsense*. Julia and I went to Proctor's in Schenectady and truly enjoyed this hilarious play. As former Catholics we could appreciate this comedy about nuns.

Also in February, Barb, Judge La Belle's secretary, filed probate papers necessary to properly claim Larry's $10,000 insurance policy. Debi and Ricky would each get around $1,400 from his survivor's benefit plan (despite the fact that Larry stated in his will that he did not want Ricky to receive any money). None of us knew where Ricky was, but eventually he got the money and used it mainly for drugs and booze.

Kathy K. and I decided to go in the candy business for Easter. I landed most of the orders and helped make some of the candy. We prepared a display for potential customers and I had no problems getting orders.

Besides making candy, doing my homework, bowling, and working bingo, I was very busy with other things. When the bumper on my 1976 Oldsmobile rusted out I went to Izzo's and purchased a 1987 Buick Le Sabre. I knew the first minute I sat in it that it was my car. There were only 22,000 miles on it. I bought it on March 1 from a Christian. He gave me a Kenneth Copeland tape that I played in my car. I thanked Jesus for the beautiful car and dedicated it to Him.

In the middle of March I bowled in a weekend city tournament. At the same time, Kathy and I were delivering a lot of our candy orders. On March 20, I wanted to deliver candy orders to the Public Health nurses, but I needed Kathy to meet me there because she had things in the back of her car. When she arrived, she blew her top at me in front of everybody, even though I hadn't done anything to her. I was angry with her, and the next day I delivered a lot of orders myself.

Diane, Kathy's sister, made some negative remarks to Debi about the whole thing, and Debi told me what she said. When I went bowling the next night, I saw Diane. She remarked that she wanted to stay out of it. I told her, "For someone who wants to stay out of it you are doing a lot of talking." She got mad and walked out of the bowling alley and quit the league. I didn't bowl that night either; I was upset over the whole mess.

I was selling raffle tickets for the ARC Ball, and I hoped to sell anywhere from $500 to $700 worth of them. I knew that it would require a lot of running around, but at the end of March I had another attack of Melkerrsdon's.

I still managed to collect all the money for the candy business, and I figured out how much each of us should get, but I had a problem with giving Kathy half when she pulled what she did. I had to do everything to fulfill all the orders, including making and delivering the rest of the candy. I was really angry, but God directed me to do the right thing.

On March 27, I asked Kathy's husband to come to my home, and I gave him $521.55, which was half of the money we made on the candy. I told Ron I felt that God wanted me to give Kathy her part, but that I was still trying to forgive and allow God to heal my wounds over the whole thing. On March 29, I called Diane and apologized to her. I really had no right to verbally attack her in the bowling alley.

On April 6, I went to Adirondack Community College to meet my new counselor, Jane Owens. She seemed nice, and she said if I wanted to achieve my goal, I would eventually have to take two courses I dreaded: algebra and biology. In my college writing class, I began to realize that my teacher had a bias toward certain styles of writing (and mine wasn't her favorite). The dean of student affairs at the college said he definitely felt that there was a bias regarding styles of writing, but he also felt it wasn't maliciously intended. In the end he left the ball in my court. I thought about our discussion and decided to drop the issue. I was rewarded in many ways by other teachers, and eventually I took much more difficult literature courses and "aced" them all.

On April 21, I missed a step and fell, landing with most of my weight on my right hand. My X-rays showed that my pinky was fractured so it was put in a splint.

Kathy and I were now talking again and forgetting the past like the Bible says we should. Julia's daughter, Kay, began to come by frequently. I got along with her, but I had a hard time liking her. There was something about her that did not ring true, and she was very bold about helping herself to things in my home.

In May, I accomplished nothing short of a miracle by finishing my two college courses, including all of the papers and reports I had to do. I got a "B+" in the writing class. I really enjoyed my history class with Mr. Heighton. I wrote such a long paper on Mary Tudor that he told the class he had to buy a new set of glasses! He invited the class to his house, and we all watched *A Fish Called Wanda* and had refreshments. We also met his gracious wife, who was also a teacher, and their 7-year-old daughter, Joceylyn, who was an absolute doll. I promptly signed up for another history course and ended up meeting Ellie, the ex-wife of Sol Pinsley's lawyer. I hit it off with her right away and met several other people in the class.

In May, I went to Glens Falls with Diane to bowl in the state tournament and did very well. I also ordered Larry's headstone that month (it was put in place in July). I went to the cemetery to see if his military stone was in yet. It hadn't been put in. I knew it had arrived during the winter, but I could not make them put it in until they were ready.

Some of Larry's life insurance money came in, and I had the authority to dispense it, but the major check had not arrived as yet. It was a pain in the neck, and I wouldn't agree to take care of all that again for all the tea in China.

Debi and Alan were looking at a camper, and I told them they could get it with the kids' money from their grandfather, but someday they would have to give the money back. All the kids agreed, so I made arrangements for them to have it. That camper has been a blessing to them all. They still have it, and I know Larry would have agreed with this transaction.

Julia finally came to my home on June 3. I was happy indeed for I really like her. She is a real person. Although we had been talking for a while I had not seen much of her, so this was a pleasant surprise. On June 4 I went to Lake George to bowl in another tournament. Afterward I went to Tupper Lake and back with a friend. At this time I started betting baseball games with a bookie. I was fairly lucky, and I really looked forward to this. I guess I have the family gambling blood in me. I was also spending quality time with Julia. We watched movies together, and she got meals for me while I worked on my big class paper.

On July 10, I found out I was exempt from finals because I had earned A or an A-. Shortly after that, I picked up Jo and Jennifer and we went to the ballet at the Saratoga Performing Arts Center. And on July 14, I went to a picnic at Believer's Fellowship with Kathy, Kay, and Julia. I met a lot of old friends there.

Still nagged by the problem with Larry's military grave marker, I called St Peter's on July 17 and asked why Larry Higggins' military stone was not in place yet. I was shocked when they told me that the lot had not yet been paid for! I called Simone and asked him why he had not paid the money for the plot. He apologized and promised to go right up there and pay the money he owed. Needless to say, I was infuriated over the whole thing.

On Sunday, July 23, Julia, Kay, and I went to the Performing Arts Center to hear Amy Grant in Concert. It was so loud that we walked out and went back to my home. I also had it out with Kay for always helping herself in my home.

Through my daughter, I met a man who had a two-year-old son, and he was down on his luck. I said he could have my back room until he got on his feet.

In August we found out that Ricky was in jail in Louisiana. He was contesting his father's will, and I had to retain a lawyer (of course, Ricky did not win). At this time I also found out that a friend of mine died suddenly.

On August 7, I decided to put my home up for sale for $30,000 because I wanted to move into town. I was planning on a full schedule in school in the fall, and I wasn't too crazy about driving in bad weather. I was interested in purchasing a mobile home in the park my brother lived in.

In the middle of August Kathy and I went to some Christian tent meetings. I was doing a lot of work on VA papers in conjunction with Earl and Patti. I also had a bad attack of Melkerrsdon's.

On August 24, I found out that someone was interested in my place, but when they came to look, Mike's room was so messy that they got disgusted and left. I lit into Mike and told him he had better keep the room clean or get out.

Ellie came to me and asked me to help her run her motel, because the people who ran it were leaving at the end of August. I helped her at the desk, and I got Kathy and her sister to help as chambermaids. Ellie also had herself and a young guy named Bryan, so we figured between all of us we could handle it for the two months.

George, a longtime resident at the motel, was in his sixties, and he was at the VA in Albany. He wanted Ellie to bring him back to the motel, so we brought him back on September 1.

On August 30, I dreamed that little Jennifer was close to water but that all her things were on the ground. I could not get the dream out of my head. I called Debi and told her to watch Jennifer carefully when they went to camp, for I felt there was significance to my dream. The next day Jennifer went over her handlebars and was placed in the hospital with a concussion. She came out of it, but I thank God, for I prayed for her after this dream.

I worked at the motel and took care of George, who was really sick. He was failing fast and Ellie didn't know what to do. He had a son but the son didn't know him too well because George had abandoned his mother.

Ellie called me and said she was afraid that George might die. I took him to the hospital and found out the tumors from his cancer were cutting off most of his oxygen. I drove him to the VA, and I wanted to go back to the motel, but he pleaded with me to stay. He feared they would not admit him, and he was right. I went to Dr. Fisher and asked him if he wanted another case like Larry Higgins on his hands, and he listened to me. He reluctantly admitted the dying man, and George thanked me from the bottom of his heart. He lived six more days and died on September 18. One of the social workers was so shook up about the way the VA handled George's case that she quit, declaring she could no longer stand their inhumane treatment.

That month I was finally able to wrap up Larry's estate and pay all of his bills after a full year of work and numerous trips to the probate court. Thank God everything was paid and his grave was all taken care of. I looked up to the skies and told Larry he didn't do me any favors. Then I smiled and thanked him for the unexpected annuity.

Dorothy Claydon, Marilyn and Polly's mother, called me on September 18 and pleaded with me to get her because she couldn't stand the confusion at David's parents. Since her kids had asked me to watch over her, I called my sister Aurora, and both of us went to Schroon Lake to fetch Dorothy.

I was now taking four college courses—Biomedical Ethics, Hitler/Nazi Germany, Introduction to Political Science, and Theories of Personality—besides working for Ellie at the motel. On September 22, I paid a deposit on my new home. Meanwhile, Earl was in the process of setting up a date to go to New York Regional Office for my VA case. With the little time I had left, I closely examined every detail of my VA records, with the generous help of Patti, at Congressman Solomon's office.

On September 26, a handful of us attended George's funeral then I went to JB White to pick a purchase order for the mobile home. I also learned that someone else was interested in buying my place, and I prayed it would sell.

Ellie had a large two-bedroom apartment at the motel. She asked me to move into it and keep an eye on the place for the winter. I told her I would pray about it, but it didn't feel right, so I told her no.

On October 1, the man who was going to buy my home backed down because his wife was critically ill. I also discovered that the realtors who were selling my home were asking $40,000. I was infuriated because I told them to ask for $33,000—$3,000 for them and $30,000 for me. I took it out of their hands and gave the job to Bob Noonan, who felt he might be able to sell it for me. He brought a woman down with her daughter, but she couldn't come up with the money. Nevertheless, I became relaxed about the whole thing because I firmly believed if God wanted me to move, then He would provide me with a sale.

Keeping up with my schedule wasn't a piece of cake, especially when combined with my other regular activities. I continued to bowl on Friday nights and worked Bingo for the Ambulance Corps during the Holidays and spring vacation.

In the middle of October I knew I would be staying in my home the whole winter, so I accepted it and went on from there. I was burning a lot of midnight oil. I had a heavy load with the subjects I was taking. I had Dr. Muscari for Biomedical Ethics, and he was just super. The class was very interesting. Ellie was also in this class with me. We went out nearly every night after class and talked for hours. By November 1, I would be finished with working at the motel.

On October 26, I was working at the desk of the motel when I got a call from Ellie's son. He told me Ellie's mother had just committed suicide. She had threatened this for some time, and she belonged to the Hemlock Society. She took an overdose of Valium and then put a plastic bag over her head to make sure no one could revive her. I went to school that night feeling very upset. I had a talk with my teacher, and he told me I should not have come to class that night, and how right he was.

Earl and I wanted a personal hearing for my VA case in New York. The date we were to go there was January 8, 1990.

My sister Marie called from Binghamton. She was devastated because she had been cited for DWI. I asked Ellie to let Marie rent her apartment without security, and she said it would be alright.

It was at this time I got my highest single bowling score in my life—seven strikes in a row with a final score of 253! That was some achievement in my book. I got 150 pins over my average for three games and 100 pins over my average for 1 game, so I got a special award for each.

On November 17, Ellie made me a birthday dinner and gave me a gift. Julia and my family also came over with some gifts. My two sisters gave me cards as well.

Ellie went away for a much-needed ten day break. On Thanksgiving Day, I went to Debi and Alan's and had an argument with them because I had invited a woman who had no place to go. Debi told me to get out, and she said she never wanted to see me again. I picked up the woman and bought her dinner at Spa City Diner. Then I drove her back to her place and went home. Marie and Eugene went to Binghamton for Thanksgiving.

Since Debi was still not speaking to me, Ellie and I planned a Christmas dinner for the people at her motel who had no place to go. On Christmas day, 1989, Ellie, Marie, Eugene, Jeanne, Barry, and Bryan came to my house for dinner. I lit the fireplace, and we gave everybody gifts—for that is the real meaning of Christmas. That night I made homemade turkey soup and invited them all over for the next night, and we all watched "Mississippi Burning."

In this way I pulled the curtain on 1989 with its many adventures and my continuing effort to get justice from the VA after more than three decades of injustice. When I first started to go to college, I had 22 carry-over credits. Now I had 43 credits, with an "A-" in Theories of Personality and an "A-" in Hitler/Nazi Germany, and an "A" in both Introduction to Political Science and Biomedical Ethics. It hasn't been easy—many nights I cried out to God, "Are You sure this is what You want me to do?" In my spirit I knew I was on the right track.

Much happened to me in the decade of the 1980's, but I knew I was a different person. I still had lingering emotional problems, and I dared not look back for fear that I would go back. Yet I was determined to enter the decade of the 1990's to see what the years ahead hold for me. With the Lord carrying me, surely I will come to major victories along with some things that might appear to be defeats. Nevertheless I will hold on to the Scripture that promises, "And we know that all things work together for good to them that love God, to them who are the called according to [His] purpose" (Rom. 8:28).

The 1980's consisted of five hospitalizations for less than approximately 60 days. I experienced two surgeries, no mental problems, some minor health problems, and one moped accident. Praise God for His goodness and mercies. Hallalujah!

Chapter 13

The Nineties

As I entered the decade of the 1990's, I wondered if the old patterns would ever end. Once again, I was accompanying my sister, Marie, to court to face DWI charges. When I told her court-appointed attorney that Marie was indigent, the judge suspended her fine.

On January 8, Earl and I went to my VA hearing at the New York City Regional Office. Of course, we got lost in the city, but the office told us to come anyway. We were allowed one hour to present our case. Earl and I covered all the bases, and at the end of the hearing, I knew the officer had already seen the information invalidating Dr. Eisele's diagnosis in 1961. When I asked her if it would qualify as "new and material evidence," she said, "I really cannot answer that question" (when would I ever find someone who could answer it?) Once again we waited for a decision.

Roger, Jr., and Mike were living with me again, but I threw them out because of their drinking and drugs. On January 24, I finally located Dr. Chelnek, but we finally dropped the idea of getting anything substantial from him. By this time, I was really getting hooked on gambling. I wasn't losing or winning much, but I knew that I was hooked. I even called from school to place bets, and I had a bank with the bookie. I began to feel the gentle prompting of the Holy Spirit, but I wasn't ready to stop yet.

My college studies were pushing me to the limit, and I wanted to quit. But I decided to stick it out with God's grace. Many times I took things personally, and I felt I was drowning in the old whirlpool of mental illness, but God brought me through.

On March 31, the VA Regional Office once again stuck to its trusty guns and denied my appeal, claiming that I had merely given them a stack of "cumulative" evidence instead of new evidence proving my nervous condition. Again, we fired back a request for additional time to prepare the case for the Board of Veterans Appeals in Washington D.C. I also wrote, "Your interpretation of that evidence as 'cumulative and not probative' is a cop out. Please do not play semantics with my case, my life, and my livelihood. Please see that I am awarded service-connected disability for the conditions that were caused and aggravated by my military service."

The only one way to prove that Dr. Chelnek was wrong when he diagnosed me with a personality disorder was to demonstrate that I was "problem free" prior to service. I demonstrated a stable work history with psychological and personality normalcy prior to service; my VA representative felt that the new evidence had been ignored.

Aurora, underwent spine surgery at the Glens Falls Hospital because she had been falling without warning and in continual pain. On August 3, my brother Billy, and his wife Jackie had to leave the motel where they lived, and they couldn't find a place to stay. Freddy kept Jackie and Aimee, and Billy came to stay with me.

Before Billy left, Jackie told me he had said that he would never see us or Saratoga again. She asked Billy if he wanted to stay in Saratoga while she settled things in Texas, but he chose to leave because Texas was his home. Then Jackie called me aside to say Billy would have a hard time saying good-bye and asked me not to stay up late with him. It was hard to leave Billy after we had "found each other" after many years of alienation. The day after he left, I had a spirit of heaviness for him.

Earl and I learned we would get a chance sometime in October and November to present our VA case to a traveling Board of Appeals operating directly out of the New York. I spent Thanksgiving at Debi's, Christmas Eve with my family, and New Year's Eve with Julia, Kathy, and Ron. It was a hectic year with a great deal of academic accomplishment, and "to God be the Glory," for He truly has renewed my mind.

I spent the first day of 1991 in bed with some kind of virus, and the weather raged. On January 23, I started school again, looking forward to graduation and a degree in May! I found out I was no longer eligible for student aid because I had withdrawn from a class, but I talked with the dean and financial aid was again restored to me. I was also shocked to learn that I'd been selected for *Who's Who Among Students in American Junior Colleges,* and my state senator sent me a letter congratulating me on the selection! I began to spend a lot of time with Marie and Aurora. Since they were usually broke by the middle of the month, I would help them with food when their money was spent.

I graduated *summa cum laude* in May with a 3.82 average, and I received my degree in front of nearly all of my family and friends. Who would ever believe that a messed-up person like me could go back to college and graduate with honors in her sixties? To God be the glory for what He has done. I had a write-up in the local paper, and Debi and Alan gave me a graduation party on May 18 attended by 86 people! That was also the night I found out my sister Aurora was spitting up blood.

Aurora had a shadow on her lung that had been there a long time, according to Dr. Ying. On May 29, he confirmed that Aurora had cancer and scheduled an operation for June 10. She came out of it all right. We had to wait about a week for to see if they had removed all the cancer.

I spent quality time every day with Aurora, and on June 14, I found out that the cancer was in her lymph nodes, but I felt this was not the time to tell her. On June 19, I took Aurora to my home to recuperate, and the next day I had to rush her to the emergency room.

After another scare on the twenty-third, Aurora began to improve and returned to her apartment. On July 12, Aurora and Marie called to tell me there was a bad odor in their apartment and asked to come to my home for the night.

Aurora asked me to help her straighten out her medicine, so on July 16, she came to stay with me for a while. I finally stopped betting with the bookie, for that "still small voice" got to me. I went to my bookie and told him I was not going to wager anymore because it was not of God. He really didn't appreciate me quitting, but I could have cared less. Since that time, the only betting I do is with my grandson on the World Series, the NBA Finals, and football.

I learned that my appeal to a Travel Section of the Board of Veteran's Appeals was scheduled for October 7, so I knew we had our work cut out for us. On August 31, I had an ambulance take Aurora to the Emergency Room. The next night was a repeat performance. On September 2, I found out my sister's cancer had spread to her spinal area, and her doctor wanted to give her radiation. When he told her what was wrong with her, she didn't accept it well. By now, I really did not want to go to the hospital anymore because it was hard to see her in such pain. By September 11, Aurora was back home in Marie's care.

On the eighteenth, Marie and I took Aurora for the last of her radiation treatments. The staff abandoned Aurora for long periods of time—even while she was suffering from severe nausea, I told Marie to wheel Aurora out to the car. Then I went to the desk and told them that they did not give a damn. I contacted Dr. Litts and I told him I was not about to let Aurora be subjected to this kind of treatment, especially if the treatments would never help her, and he agreed with me.

On September 26, Aurora told me she couldn't be buried because she had no money. She wanted me to promise to always care for Marie, but I couldn't do it. I could hardly tolerate Marie, how could I care for her?

On October 7, 1991, my brother, Roger, drove Dorrene, Earl, and I to the New York Regional Office for my hearing before the

Traveling Review Board from Washington, D.C. Roger really knew New York City and he got us there in plenty of time. There was one female and one male doctor on the Board in addition to another man and woman, and for the first time, I really got a chance to tell my story. It was difficult because I had to relive everything again, but it was now all in God's hands. After lunch, we went back to our homes, and I found out my childhood friend, Polly, had died on October 2. That night, Kay and Joan told me that Julia was on a respirator in I.C.U. after emergency surgery. I cried, "God, how many more shocks do you have for me""

On October 15, Aurora asked to stay at my house, so I prepared a room for her. Nine days later, Julia died, and I cried silently. Her daughters asked me to speak at her memorial service, which I did. I took care of Aurora for five weeks, and God gave me a new love for her. The cancer had gone into her bones, and they were breaking. Aurora begged me not to let her go to the hospital, so with God's grace, I kept her in my home. She had to be changed often to prevenet bed sores. She had nightmares and screamed that animals were everywhere. I just put my arms around her and assured her she was safe (although her nightmares were doing a number on me). Her priest gave her the last rites, but I still managed to give her a surprise birthday party.

By November 20, Aurora was unable to talk, and she was again given the last rites. The last thing I told her was: "It's been a pleasure taking care of you," as tears streamed from her eyes. This bothered me more than anything. Marie and I were with her when she died on the November 22. I loved her so much by then that I took her passing very hard.

I went to Debi's for Thanksgiving dinner, and I spent a lot of time organizing my VA papers. On December 21, I wrote, "I am feeling depressed today. I pray God will help me, for my faith and courage are waning." On Christmas night, we went out to dinner, and I stayed at Debi's. I was so disheartened and dejected that by New Year's Eve, I didn't want to go anywhere. I just wanted to be alone with God.

In January 1992, I was depressed and having trouble sleeping. I didn't want to associate with anyone. I stayed home and buried myself in sports and movies. I read my Bible every day and did my meditations, but something was wrong. I just couldn't put my finger on it. I was stuttering, and I suffered from terrible tremors. Dr. Litts sent me to a neurologist who said I had an "Anxiety Neurosis," and sent me to the Mental Health Clinic. He said I was not dealing with my grief over the loss of my friends and sister. The one thing I did know was that I wasn't "running on high." Everything was cloaked with darkness and despair.

When I called Claire, she told me it would pass, but that I had to deal with it. I didn't want to go to the Mental Health Clinic again, but everything kept getting worse. My only anchor was that He would keep me "in perfect peace" if my mind was stayed on Him (Is. 26:3).

A violent storm hit on the day I was to see the psychiatrist at the Mental Health Clinic. As I waited for the doctor, the veil of oppression was weighty and I perceived no hope. I was returning to the whirlpool of lunacy because I had nothing to live for. I seemed to operate like a normal human being, but I felt far from human. I was becoming a vegetable and a child of fear. I asked the doctor with tears in my eyes, "Do you think I will ever get better?"

On February 15, I got a loan to buy a van for Debi and Alan (their bankruptcy made it impossible for them to get a loan). I still read the Bible, but I got nothing from it. Had God left the book? I continued grief therapy, where I was told that my physical manifestations and depression stemmed from my inability to deal with the deaths of my sister and friends. Meanwhile, I took my Valium when I started to shake or stutter, and I wondered where it would all end.

On March 18, the Hospice organization held a memorial service for all the patients who had died within a one-year span. As they called out the names and handed flowers to the next of kin, I realized that I had not really accepted Aurora's death. I had become a mother to her during the last five weeks of her life, and somehow, I felt I should have been able to extricate her from the angel of death. For the first time I freely admitted that I loved my sister.

As I reluctantly probed my memory, I saw Nanny beating Aurora and hitting her over the head with a chair. I saw her doing all the work inside of the house, and for the first time, I felt her pain. I saw her inability to learn, and at the same time I realized she was far from stupid. I saw her seeking her identity and getting into dysfunctional marriages, yet loving her kids beyond my comprehension. I saw the alcohol and drug road she traveled, and then the healthy love she finally found with Bob.

I saw all this in a matter of minutes, and I silently screamed inside because I realized that she was never really loved or accepted. I wanted to get one more chance to hold her and take all the pain away, but I was powerless. God showed me the shell she had put around herself as a buffer against the pain of existence. God had given me a vision of what my sister would have been like had she been nurtured and loved. She was a little girl crying out for someone to care for her. In awe, I also saw the Good Shepherd, the Lily of the Valley, the Rose of Sharon, wiping the tears from Aurora's eyes as she entered the portals of Heaven.

This precious preview let me see these things clearly, and I knew it was all right for me to hurt because she was gone. When I got home, the tears flowed freely. It was then that I recognized I was in a state of anger and disbelief because Aurora had gone just when I found out who she really was. I also started to deal with my own mortality.

I then focused on Julia and the good times we had shared in college, on the golf course, and laughing in the saunas and whirlpools. Then I saw Polly, our childhood, and the poverty we had shared. The love in her home had nourished me spiritually, and sometimes physically. I remembered the many round-table discussions, and I realized that it was good to remember. Now it was time for me to recognize that God had taken her home for a reason, which I would know only when I met Him face to face.

I was ready now to deal with my pain through the grace of God. I finally bid good-bye to the three of them, looking forward to the day we would walk the streets of gold together. I was at last out of the denial stage and advancing to the stage of acceptance.

In April I received a copy of the letter that the Board of Veterans Appeals sent to the New York Regional Office in New York City. It said in part, "...it is the decision of the Board that the preponderance of the evidence demonstrates that new and material evidence sufficient to reopen the claim of entitlement to service connection for a chronic acquired psychiatric disorder has been submitted." The letter ordered that new psychiatric examinations be conducted by two VA physicians to determine the nature of my disability. My appointment for the examinations was scheduled for May 18, 1991, and to me, this was a favorable letter.

On April 10 I got word that Ricky was back in jail—so what else was new? I got into a confrontation with Debi over Ryan's disobedience, and we didn't talk for some time. I also received a call from the VA. The representative said that my appointment had been cancelled because they were having difficulty getting another psychiatrist. This really aggravated me because I had waited a long time, but there was nothing I could do about it.

I told Debi I wanted my credit cards returned to me because I did not want her to continue charging on them, so she tore them up and sent them back in spite. On May 28, the VA notified me that my psychiatric exam would be held on June 15, 1992. Earl, Dorrene, and I went to the Albany VA Hospital, where I was examined by Dr. Andrus and Dr. Yonkers. They asked me a host of questions, which I answered honestly. The woman doctor knew Dr. Knoblauch, and I felt comfortable during the examination.

Debi and Alan wanted another baby, so she had a reversal of her tubal ligation. She got pregnant, but she lost the baby on June 30, and it devastated her. On July 2, Ricky got out of jail and came to stay with me for a while. That month I got fed up with Alan and Debi getting mad at me and using me, so I told them I wanted the van back. (This was just my old nature trying to get even. I was even thinking of petitioning the family court for visitation rights to my granddaughter.) Then God made it clear to me that I was wrong to ask them for the van when they were paying for it. When Alan brought it to me, I told him I was wrong, and I vowed before God that I would never do this again and told him so.

On July 31, Earl called me and told me the New York Regional Office had again denied my appeal—even though the two VA psychiatrists had vindicated me and diagnosed me as having an "Anxiety Neurosis" and no personality disorder. The regional office still held that I had manifested a personality disorder while in the service.

The Board of Veterans Appeals could not do anything until my folder was sent back to Washington, so I wrote, "Please be advised that I have sent my claim for appeal directly to Washington, D.C., as you seemingly refuse to look into my records and see that I do indeed have service-connected disabilities for a nervous condition. Please send my files to Washington D.C. Thank you for your prompt attention to this matter."

Earl managed to get this information to them with amazing speed. Just before he sent the material, he left an inspiring message for me on my message machine: "Just sit tight. Trust God! We got this thing licked. It's just a matter of time. I know you don't feel time is on your side. It's not really on any of our sides. But for some reason God uses time the way He does. And we trust that all things work together for good!"

Ricky was staying with Marie, and on August 13, he was in the car with her when she had an accident and was arrested for DWI. The same day, Ricky was picked up by the police. I also received a letter in the fall from the Internal Revenue telling me I owed income tax on the annuity Larry set up for me. I phoned them right away and told them I could not pay them and received a waiver for a year. I told them I would pay as soon as I could.

I spent Thanksgiving at Debi's, and despite having some horrid pains on my left side, we had a nice time. On December 4, a medical test showed that my left kidney was scarred and shrunken, but at least it was working.

I had very little money for Christmas, so for the first time, I borrowed $300 from my brother Freddy. I promised to start paying him back in April of 1993 at $50 a month. Then, wonder of wonders, I found out on December 16 that I would be getting a monthly increase from Social Security!

I decided to check on three of the four doctors who had signed the alleged 10-hour examination in 1954, and discovered that none of them were licensed neuro-psychiatrists in 1954!

On Christmas Eve, we all went to the Ash Grove Inn for dinner, and after seeing the Christmas lights, we went back to Debi's for the night. On New Year's Eve, Ryan and Shawn spent the night with me, and we saw the New Year in together with noise makers.

I was still seeing the therapist occasionally, but the pain of my loss was diminishing. I could see some light at the end of the tunnel. But the constant lies of the Veteran's Administration turned my stomach into knots. I wanted to shout from the housetops, "Look what they have done!" Is this America? If so, then there is no way that God can bless it. Earl was putting up a valiant fight. We believed that the Board of Veteran's Appeals would give me the justice I had long-awaited. In the meantime I had to trust God more and get closer to Him in 1993.

It was a joy to launch 1993 with my grandsons, Shawn and Ryan. January 2 was Shawn's birthday, so we all went to Debi's to celebrate, and the boys again returned home with me. My appetite for reading was insatiable. (Before the year ended I would have read a total of 97 books.)

I still saw Julia's daughter, Kay, occasionally, and I was still volunteering at Schenectady to help Earl, but he was being promoted within the administration, so I planned to leave there when he left.

On January 16, I invited Dorrene to go to the Malta Ambulance Banquet, but when we got there, I was shocked to receive the "President's Award" for my volunteer work with the corps. I wrote to Ricky, and I watched a lot of college basketball without betting a dime! I was winding down with therapy, for with God's help, the pain had lessened. Of course, I was still waiting impatiently for the Board of Veterans Appeals' decision on my case.

Around this time Congressman Solomon's office sent me a copy of a letter they received from the Board of Veteran's Appeals, which basically reassured him they would "carefully review" my entire case. I don't know if he believed it, but I had my doubts!

On February 6, I went to meet Phil and his wife, Elmire. I had agreed to stay at their home with Phil's 85-year-old mother, Marie, while they traveled to Florida. They made dinner, then went out so Marie and I could get acquainted. She was agoraphobic, and had tremendous anxiety. She didn't go out, except to see her doctor or buy shoes. She worried about everything, but I liked her. My job was to get her meals. She slept downstairs, and I slept upstairs. When I got up in the morning, I could leave until it was time to get her dinner.

Ricky called me several times in February, and Ryan stayed over a few nights. I started my job with Marie on the thirteenth, and everything went just fine except for the weather. I brought Marie the movie about the Great Carouso, and she really enjoyed it. By the nineteenth, my job was over.

On March 1, I took the money I'd made and paid a full year's worth of taxes to the Internal Revenue Service. When we weren't being snowed in that winter, I did a lot of walking outside whenever possible. On April 8, I called Washington, D.C., about my VA case. It was a waste of money. I felt depressed about it all, but by faith I turned it all over to God. I kept busy reading, and watching the Net games and professional bowling, so I didn't dwell on my problems too much. I was really consistent with my daily Bible study, and I know that is what kept me on an even keel, for His Word is truly a lamp unto my feet.

Ricky was now staying at the Northwood Motel in town, and I found an exercise and weight lifting outfit for him at a garage sale because he likes to keep himself in good physical shape. Ricky gathered cans and bottles to make money, so when I went walking I picked them up too, to help him.

On Mother's Day that year, both Debi and Ricky came by to see me. In May, the Social Security Administration sent me a letter claiming it overpaid me $335. Earl wrote a letter protesting their efforts to collect something when it was their error. He also noted that I had actually called their representative to verify that the payment was mine at the time. I received no more letters from the Social Security about my alleged debt after that.

I continued my daily Bible study and meditation, but now I sensed that the Lord had spoken to me through the Scripture that says, "the year of My redeemed has come" (Is. 63:4 NKJ).

I asked Ricky to clean my porch, for it was one big mess. He did an excellent job for me. He was a good worker and very meticulous, so I talked to someone I knew about giving Ricky a job working outside. I told the man the truth, but he was willing to give him a chance.

While working bingo, I met a woman who was looking for someone to help with her 92-year-old mother who was coming in June to stay with her for six months. I was interested because I could definitely use the extra income.

By the end of May, Ricky was going to Alcoholic Anonymous and also working full time for AJ. He could no longer say he couldn't get a job because of his record. He was getting Medicaid, and he would eventually get his much-needed teeth if he stayed on the straight and narrow.

The first weekend in June, Elmire asked me to stay with Marie again, so I did. They had a boat, so they tried to spend as many weekends on it as they could, and I began working weekends at Marie's. Ricky was doing fine working up front for AJ, and they were very pleased with his work. Ricky had a room in a motel with the help of welfare, but he stayed at my home a lot. He faithfully attended an Alcoholic program and worked regularly. I wondered, *Is this too good to be true?*

On Wednesday June 23, I started a new job in Clifton Park caring for Blanche, Joan's mother. I just thanked Jesus for this much-needed employment. I woke up the next morning with a semi-mild attack of Melkerrsdon's Syndrome, but I still went to work at Joan's. I worked at Marie's on Friday and Saturday night, and at Joan's on Wednesday, Thursday, and Sunday. My only full day off was Monday.

Joan's mother owned a camp in the Lake George area that had been built in 1947. On July 15, Joan picked me up with her mother, and I went with them to the camp. I was able to spend some time looking over the lake, meditating while listening to music. I thanked God for the privilege of being there. The next afternoon we stopped at Joan's father's grave then proceeded home.

Debi and her family took a trip and asked me to watch the house for them. I asked my friends, Jo and Tom, to go by it when I wasn't going to be in town, and they agreed. On Tuesday, July 20, Jo called to tell me that Debi's front door was open! I called the police, but when we searched the place, we knew no one had broken in. Debi and Alan must have neglected to lock their door. I then drove Ricky to his motel, and he told me he was going to an alcoholic meeting.

The next morning I found out that Ricky had gone to his cousin's house. She had a problem with alcohol and with the man she lived with. A fight ensued, and Ricky had to be taken to the hospital for stitches. His cousin got a DWI. I told him that if he had gone where he was supposed to go, that being the alcohol program, that would not have happened. He was so devastated that I felt sorry for him and tried to encourage him. Would he ever learn?

On July 24, Chuck, Dorrene's husband, lost three fingers on his right hand in a lawnmower accident. Four days after that, Kay and I visited him at the Albany Medical Center. On August 15, I went to camp with the Thulls, and their family. I picked up Blanche for the ride up there, but she suddenly changed like a chameleon when we got there (I'd been warned about this). She wanted to let everyone know that it was her camp and to make everyone miserable. I had it out with her and told her she was the worst patient I'd ever had. By the time I left four days later, I was totally strung out. I began to see this family with a new perspective. They were no different from any other family with a few dollars and a camp, but my mistake was in thinking they were.

On August 23, I found out that the Board of Veterans' Appeals had made their decision, but I did not know what it was. I also found out that Ricky had to get out of his motel at the end of August. He was drinking and taking drugs, and his head was all screwed up. Meanwhile, there was such tension in Joan's house that you could have cut it with a knife. Something was going on, but whatever it was, I knew God would direct me. I knew I no longer felt comfortable with these people.

Two days later, I had it out with Joan. I called Dorrene to pray for me because Joan had done a complete "about face" with me. After her husband George made some snide remarks about me and God's will, I told Joan I was going to leave as soon as she could get someone else. When George found out I was leaving, he got downright nasty with me. He told me I could go right away.

Before I left, I took Blanche for a walk and prepared her for bed. As I left, I prayed: "Dear Holy Spirit, I don't want to labor over what happened. I want to do what Dorrene told me to do—'to shake the dust off my feet.' I want to cast it all on You, my God, and let You do the convicting in their lives."

That same day, I found out that the decision was in the mail, and that it was good news. On August 30, Marie called to tell me that Ricky was in trouble. He had robbed a store. He claimed he really wanted help so I drove him to Alcoholic Services. Between Debi and I and Alcoholic Services, we were able to get him into Conifer Park for rehabilitation. I hoped he meant business, for the taxpayers were paying a lot of money for this. It was all up to him.

On the thirtieth, I also received a letter from Congressman Solomon's office that said the Board of Veteran Appeals had reversed the decisions and diagnosis of the Regional Office and granted me service connection compensation for my anxiety disorder! I was elated!

The decision of the Board read: "...following review and consideration of all evidence and material of record in the veteran's claims file, and for the following reasons and bases, it is the decision of the Board that service connection is warranted for an acquired psychiatric disorder, namely chronic anxiety disorder." In another section, it said, "As a preliminary matter, we find the veteran's claim to be well grounded; that is, it is a claim which is plausible and capable of substantiation."

Early in September, the VA again contacted me to say that even though I had won the case, they were only giving me 70 percent of the service-connected compensation owed for January 1971 to the present! Earl and I immediately filed an appeal, stating, "In light of the BVA Ruling, it seems arbitrary, and inconsistent for my disability rating to be lowered from 100% during any part of the 1970's. During the decade of the 1970's, I had not been able to work, and was treated frequently at Saratoga Hospital's Mental Health Clinic. I was incoherent, anxious, fearful, and deeply depressed. Medical evidence submitted to and cited by the BVA verified this.

In September and October of 1993, I received two separate checks from the VA. The VA deducted all the non-service connected pension monies I'd received since 1971. I asked for an audit, but I only received one from 1981 to the present. The other one has not been sent to me to this day. I have received well over $100,000 in retroactive benefits.

On September 4, Ricky was going to leave Conifer Park because he was upset, but I told him he would regret it. This was his chance to get his act together, so he decided to stay. I stayed with Marie for the Labor Day weekend. Elmire proofread some of my book and made corrections. I have decided to work for them as long as I can because they have treated me regally.

Once I won my VA case, my school friend, "Kathy T." became very interested in writing my book. Unfortunately, she also wanted money up front and the rights to the book. I really felt I needed counsel before I agreed to anything like that, and I told her so. To this day, she wants no part of me. I still like her, but I would have had to pay her while she was writing the book and then pay her royalties if it was published! I felt she was, in essence, "hedging her bet."

On September 12, I visited Ricky and took him some new sneakers and some other things. He looked good, and once again, I told him I would help him if he meant business. Six days later, I received my first big VA check, and I made plans to pay my bills. After I gave my tithe, the first person I wanted to pay back was my friend Jo Lucas, who had signed notes for me and had ended up paying them when I couldn't. I also owed her son $500. With pleasure, I paid her every dime I owed her. Then I looked at her husband, Tom, and said: "You did not believe me when I told you God would someday make it possible for me to pay you back." Of course I could not blame him, but now he knew.

On September 19, I found out that Ricky was in Schenectady county jail, and he was also wanted in Louisiana. He had left the rehabilitation center, so I had to "wash my hands of him" for my own survival. Meanwhile, when I prayed about what I should do for my daughter Debi and her family, I felt I was to pay off her van. I also put $1,000 into a savings account for each grandchild. They could use it for things they wanted, but not foolishly. Later on, I also cleared up all of my daughter's credit cards and my own.

I did some things to my home and decided to buy a computer so I could write my life story for the glory of God. I knew nothing about the monsters, so Earl ordered one for me. On October 15, I got my new computer along with a laser printer, and faithful Earl put it up for me. At first, I really feared that I couldn't write this book myself. I was afraid of the computer, and just felt totally inadequate. Finally, Chuck told me I was the only one who could initially write this book. I listened to him, and God has proven him to be right.

My foot doctor came down to the mobile home a few times to help me get used to my new computer, but he was too advanced for me to comprehend much of what he was saying and doing. I appreciated his trying anyway. It was mind-boggling, but I managed to write down the first 23 years of my life, along with the "Army" section. These were in fairly good shape, and the rest of the book was also written in extremely rough form.

By the end of October, I was mixed up and confused about everything. Too many people wanted to get in the act with my testimony, and I was going nowhere fast. I had received my second check, and I put away a substantial sum where I would not have ready access to it. (I soon learned that money was not my god, but it could easily become anyone's god—given the opportunity.) God eventually gave me some wisdom, and although I do not love money, per se, there is a certain accountability that must go with it. I know I did a lot of good with most of my money.

In the hectic month of November, I decided one particular person, who was an excellent writer, should be the one to write my book with me. However, very little was accomplished. I at least managed to sort out a lot of my papers and tried to get everything organized.

On November 27, I spoke at a "Friends Fellowship," and Earl brought his music ministry along too. I did not know what I was going to say, so I left it all to the Holy Spirit. My daughter and grandchildren came to see me that night too. The Lord really gave me everything that He wanted me to say. He also wanted me to publicly apologize to my daughter for not being the mother I should have been. She needed to hear it, and ever since, we have enjoyed a much better relationship as a result of it.

I was able to bless many people that Christmas, and it was a great joy to me. I had asked God if He wanted me to do anything special for someone, and I got an unexpected call from Ellie, my friend with the motel. She was having a Christmas gathering for a lot of people who had nothing. I stopped by and gave her some money to buy the kids presents. I also dropped by there on Christmas Eve for a couple of hours. Through God, I was able to bless the parents as well.

Debi, Alan, the children, and I went to the Canterbury for Christmas dinner. Then we went to look at the lights afterward. I really felt cold that night, so I went straight to bed. By 1:00 a.m., I fell asleep, only to wake up around 5:30 a.m., feeling deathly sick and shaking with terrible chills. I slept most of the day, and that evening, I felt a little better.

I figured I had the flu, so I stayed in bed. The next night, Debi came down and cleaned the place for me. She left Ryan to stay with me. The last thing I remember was going to the bathroom around 10:00 p.m. on Sunday December 26. As I was going back to bed, I fell on the floor and tried to get up, but couldn't. The next conscious memory I had was on December 28, when I woke up in Intensive Care at Albany Medical Center.

Ryan had found me at 12:30 p.m., and when Debi talked to me, I was not lucid. Kathy's daughter, a nursing student, took my temperature with my mouth open because I would not close it, and it was 103 degrees! They called an ambulance on the spot. At first, the doctors thought I might have had a stroke, or even spinal meningitis. Later on they discovered that I had a massive infection of the urinary tract. My blood was sepsis (poisoned by germs), and I had gone into kidney failure.

Needless to say, I made it. Pastor Jay Frances visited me often. He told me I would not die and read Psalm 91 to me. I ended 1993 at Albany Medical Center in the Intensive Care Unit, but God was there all the time. My friends were praying and visiting me, while my blood sugar went up to nearly 600. I was insulin-dependent for days. My whole system was shutting down, but God had other plans for me.

Even though I had failed many times, it was my sincere desire to tell through my life story what God can do with broken pieces. "All the king's horses and all the king's men could not put Humpty Dumpty back together again"—well, I am a form of Humpty Dumpty. Somehow, God managed to put my mind back together again after it went through the whirlpool of insanity and pain. If there was hope for me, there is hope for others!

I spent New Year's Day in 1994 on an oncology ward at the Albany Medical Center because they had to find someplace to put me until I was well enough to go home. When my kidneys had failed, a catheter was inserted through my neck into my heart to measure the fluids in my body. The measurement of fluids proved that I needed more, and when this was initiated, my kidneys kicked in again.

I talked to a doctor the last night I was in I.C.U. I told him that I saw nurses laughing and leaving when they felt like it to go on break—while I was nearly dying. I was alert enough to notice that one nurse left me to answer a personal phone call while a blood-soaked gauze bandage was dripping blood down on my neck! I pulled it off, so when she returned, she berated me. The bottom line was that she should never have gone to the phone while she was taking this catheter from my neck. The doctor told me that it was very rare for anyone to perceive what I had because I.C.U. patients are usually so ill that they are unaware of the pettiness that takes place.

It was going to be sometime before I would regain my strength. I was as weak as a baby kitten, and a hospital isn't exactly the best place to get rest. My doctor was very kind and appeared to have a genuine interest in my well being. We shared some about the game, "Tetris," and he was interested in the book I was writing.

Doctors decided that when my blood sugar stayed under 200, I would be placed on diabetic pills. This led to a unique experience. One morning a nurse wakened me, and another nurse stood behind her with milk, orange juice, and crackers. They said my blood sugar was at 38, and I had to drink and eat right away! Later on, I told my doctor that if I stayed on those pills after I got home and went to sleep that I could slip right into eternity—I wouldn't have any nurses there to wake me up! That's why I am on nothing for diabetes today. I do not tempt fate, though. I monitor closely the sweets I eat and try to exercise as much as possible.

Two nights before I went home, my roommate received a visitor who worked at the hospital. The visit wasn't a problem, but the hours were. When I complained about the visit stretching out so late into the night, I was told by the charge nurse that visitors to the oncology section could stay as long as they wanted. I said, "You mean I have no rights. I am not to be considered?" If I'd had clothes, I would have taken a taxi home right then! The next morning I called the Patient's Rights Department and lodged my complaint. After 95 hospitalizations, this was a first for me.

On the last day. Dr. M. handed me his card and said, "Theresa, will you please send me a copy of your book?" He was so sincere, that I knew he believed in me, and I assure you he will get a copy.

When I got home, I was weak at first, and I didn't do much of anything for around a week. Then I started concentrating on the book. Dr. M's sincerity and belief in my book encouraged me, and I began to organize papers. It was a massive job, complicated by the fact that I was having a lot of problems with WordPerfect 6.0. (Eventually I received an update and a lot of my problems were solved.)

Meanwhile, I believed that my records were again at the Board of Veteran's Appeals in Washington, D.C., but Congressman Solomon's office called me on January 13, and told me that my file had been mailed to the BVA in Washington, so I wrote a letter to the chairman of the Board and asked him to advance my case on the docket. I was getting tired of waiting. I wrote, "Mr Chairman, forty years is a long time to wait. I am 66 years old. I feel my request is a valid one to justify the moving up of my case on the docket."

At the end of January, I also received a statement from the New York Regional VA Office that basically said I should not have gotten compensation from 1953 because there was nothing wrong with the decision of 1955 that took away my service connection via Dr. Chelnek and three other unlicensed psychiatrists. Despite the overwhelming preponderance of evidence, they were saying, "We will give you 100 percent from 1988 to the present. In essence, we should not have given you the money, but since it was our error, we don't want it back. But you are a basket case now, and have been one since you reopened the claim in October 1988." It was interesting to see that there was no signature on the decision of January 1994. Sure, they gave me more money, but that was not justice. I was determined to pursue it until the end.

Earl mailed a rebuttal in March of 1994, and did another masterful job of showing them their incongruities along with their dishonesty and duplicity. But we never got the courtesy of an answer. Since Earl had been promoted, he could no longer work on my case.

On January 20, I took the plunge and drove my car to the store and went for Chinese food with Debi. Dr. Litts saw me, and he actually got up and hugged me! He hadn't been too sure I would make it, for he had been in contact with the doctors in Albany.

On January 24, I went to the Albany VA with Dorrene to see about getting my medicine. I talked to the Assistant Director and he told me I had to "turn all my records over to the VA and could not have an outside doctor." I told him thanks but no thanks—I would keep Dr. Litts and that was that.

By January 28, I had the first 23 years and the Army section completely finished and printed out. I started the "Chicago" section and finished it by February 5.

On March 2, I received a check from the VA and proceeded to give God His share. Then I decided to give away my car to someone who needed one, and update mine. I bought a 1993 Dodge Dynasty in a very conservative color, same as my Buick. The Holy Spirit also brought to my mind the alleged debt Empire State College said I owed. I called the college and was told I owed $364, so I mailed them the full amount. My promise to the college had now been fulfilled

I worked diligently on the book, but I also let my grandkids take over the computer periodically. I went to several good movies like

Schindler's List, and I ended up loosing my cat, Dusty, in March. I felt terrible because my feline bed partner was now gone. I was so accustomed to having him around that I never knew how much I would miss him until he was gone.

In April, I lost 150 pages, and I had to retype every one of them. I was disgusted and discouraged, but I never once entertained the thought of quitting. I had promised God that by faith I would write my testimony, and then He would direct me. I made countless calls to the computer software people to keep the process going.

At the end of April, I found out that my oldest brother, Billy, was critically ill. He had been on dialysis for about three years. We kept in touch by phone, and he had written me several times. We were believing that he would be able to come visit in 1994 because a dialysis unit was being installed in Saratoga. I called nearly every hour the last night of his life. Early on May 1, I was told that Billy had expired at 8:00 a.m. He had been able to understand, but was unable to communicate.

Freddy, Roger, Marie, and I sent a blanket of flowers, and in my solitude I cried for what might have been. At least, we had gotten to know each other, and I knew he had a special love for me. He had expressed his caring to me and that was very important. He knew I loved him, but to this day, I find it hard to conceive of his passing for so many miles had separated us between each reunion. Now I must wait for the grand celestial reunion when we will all come together. Then there will be no more pain and suffering and we shall be like Him.

In May, the Albany Medical Center contacted me about my complaint. They sent me a draft of their revised "Patient's Visitor Guidelines," into which they had carefully incorporated my suggestions. I was glad I could make life a little easier for someone who followed after me.

On June 8, I had a gathering of friends on my new Florida porch, and we all surprised Jeanne Conway with a birthday cake. My beloved granddaughter was going to turn 16 that month, so I schemed with her parents to throw her a special party with a live DJ. Was she ever surprised! I invited my brother, Freddy, and his wife; along with Jo and Tom, Dorrene and Chuck, Kathy and Ron, Sally Cogan, and Joe and Jeanne Powers, and Jeanne Conway. Debi asked me if I was going to invite Phil and Elmire, but at first I felt that they really didn't know me that well. Elmire had worked on my book and never judged me. I respected and admired them, but basically, I wondered if it was ethical to ask them to come? I finally decided it wouldn't hurt, since Elmire was "real people," and she would not be bashful if she felt she and Phil could not come. Praise God, they came, and they made an elegant couple.

In July I became a prayer partner via phone for a Christian TV station in Scotia. I also met Joan Allen who orchestrated the telethon and prayer ministries there. She is a "go-getter." On July 13, Elmire came to visit me, and I had an enjoyable time playing "Jeopardy" and "Wheel of Fortune" on the computer. After she showed me a few other things on the computer, we went out to dinner. I really liked her. I also had a great deal of respect for her. She called home, and when she found that her husband was home, she went right home. I appreciate her priorities. I would have loved her to stay the whole evening, but she did what every woman who wants to solidify their marriage has to do. They have to always consider their husbands, and husbands have to do the same for their wives.

On July 21, I was in bed reading when a bat suddenly came flying out from the corner of the room! I was terrified. I chased the thing with a fly swatter, and I sprayed a half a can of "Raid" bug spray on him (I almost choked to death from the smell, but the bat did just fine.) I called the Sheriff's office, and they gave me another number to call. The man I called lived in the park, so he showed up quickly. He poked around for the bat, but it was fruitless. I suggested that we sit with a dim light and listen. When we did, he heard a noise coming from my fire place. The bat was up in my chimney, so the man taped up the mouth of the fireplace and said he'd return the next day to flush it out. After I paid him $50, he told me, "Where one bat is, there are others." Good news!

I went to bed believing the bat was taped up in the chimney, but when I woke up at 8:45 a.m., to my amazement, I saw a bat sound asleep on my wall near my clothes tree! I called another man, a "bat specialist" who gave me a three-year guarantee, and he removed the unwelcome intruder.

My sister Marie had been nagging me to let her stay for a while in my home, and I reluctantly agreed. Well, after the "bat man" removed the bat, he told me to put blankets by my bedroom and bathroom door. When Marie came, she asked why I had the blankets out, so I told her about the bats. When she heard that she would have to sleep in the living room, she abruptly decided to go to her niece's home. (You see, Romans 8:28 says, "All things work together for good!") I was fully "bat-sealed" on July 24. There were a half dozen that were evicted. At $100 dollars each, it was a very expensive eviction!

Although Elmire has a very full life with her marriage and profession, she said she wanted to devote a summer to reviewing my manuscript for grammar and flow, and she did it. Now it's in God's ballpark.

At the end of August, my VA representative asked the VA for a status report on my two stalled appeals. He also asked to combine them into one action essentially seeking a full 100 percent reimbursement rating. To this date we have received nothing in writing from them since January 1994.

On September 6, I was interviewed for one-half hour by Joan Allen on a local TV show. Again, no preparation was needed. Everything I said was from God. The very next day, I found out that my beloved friend, Jo Lucas, had died suddenly. We were to go out to lunch that week, and I found the news difficult to believe and digest. Even though I had been busy, we had kept in contact. Jo often sent me clippings from the paper because she knew I didn't get the *Saratogian*. Whenever I had asked her and her husband to do anything, they were always willing. I still think she will answer the phone when I call her husband, Tom. I was asked to pick a Scripture to read at her memorial service. I picked Proverbs 31.

On October 1, 1994, the first draft of the book was done. On September 21, I felt that God told me to publish the book myself. At one time, I thought I would title the book *Child of Fear* but I decided, with Elmire's help, to call the book *Pearl at a Great Price*. Jesus said, "Again, the kingdom of heaven is like unto a merchant seeking goodly pearls: who, when he had found one pearl of great price, went and sold all that he had, and bought it" (Mt. 13:45-46). The Book of Revelation says, "And the twelve gates were twelve pearls, every several gate was of one pearl..." (Rev. 21:21). Pearls are real special to God; for God knew me in my mother's womb. He had my mother name me Pearl Theresa, and even though no one ever called me Pearl, God was making me into one all the time.

When a bit of foreign matter enters an oyster shell—material such as a grain of sand, a parasite, or an undeveloped egg—the pearl isolates the "irritant" by gradually coating it with layers of a lustrous material called *nacre*, or mother-of-pearl. The pearl is one of the few gems created by an organic process. The process is slow; it may take three years or more for a mature oyster to produce a pearl large enough to be commercially valuable. The most prized pearls come out of saltwater, and they have a high degree of luster and iridescence.

With me, the foreign matter entering the shell was the louse of mental illness, the sand flea of hatred and unforgiveness, the dog flea of gambling, the cat flea of infirmity, the roach of alcohol, the leech of drug addiction, the tick of depression, and the mite of suicide. Through the years, all of the irritants entered into the heart of my "oyster" with their abrasiveness, gnawing, erosion, grinding, rasping, chaffing, and galling. But the Holy Spirit gently and faithfully coated my inner shell with His nacre. He knew when and how to place His mother-of-pearl to protect this massive pearl in the making.

After all, a quality pearl takes a lot of time and effort to create. God said: "She is the work of My hands, and the more the parasites try to destroy her, the more *nacre* she will have. And some day, she will come forth as 'A Pearl at a Great Price!' "

The long, difficult road I have traveled has been strewn with agony and pain. Much of the time, it was difficult, if not impossible, for most people who knew me to believe there was ever a chance I would come out of my twilight-zone existence. But our God is an awesome God, and His arm is not shortened! Is there anything too hard for Him?

When you have finished reading this book won't you bow your head and ask Jesus into your heart. Just tell Him that you acknowledge that you are a sinner, ask forgiveness from Him, then invite Him into your life. You will never be the same. He loves you so much that He would have made that trip to Calvary if you had been the only person on earth—Thank you for letting me share with you what He can do.

Epilogue

When I signed the contract for my book in November 1994 there was no epilogue included, yet because of the magnificent thing God did for me in 1995 I know I must, with my publisher's consent, insert one now.

In February 1979, I stopped seeing doctors and gave up all prescription drugs, including aspirin. In December 1981, I was led to again enter the field of medical care. I had one doctor whose intructions God told me to follow. I knew by doing so I would never become addicted again. Nevertheless, I found myself psychologically dependent on a certain pain medication, as well as Zanax and Valium. It was never a question of overindulgence.

I questioned God many times as to the purpose of the whole situation. I felt He had told me it was necessary for me to return to the very profession wherein I was bound by. I even had therapy for grief. I returned to the VA hospital as well as other hospitals and doctors. Thus, I felt I had gone full circle.

On Christmas night of 1994 my right knee gave in. I was unable to walk. My grandchildren took care of me. The orthopedist injected the knee with Cortisone and told me I needed a complete knee replacement. I had bone upon bone—no cartilage. The pain was excruciating, yet I felt that God was going to intervene and that I would not have to be operated on. I felt it become bone-upon-faith. As of this day, I am not only walking without any aid, but God has also led me back to not taking any more prescription medicines. The most difficult for me to surrender was my pain medication. A few weeks ago I said to God, "Show me Thy glory," and that is exactly what He did.

Does this mean I am pain free all the time and that there won't be tests and trials in this area? By no means, but, according to my faith, it will be done. What He told me in 1978 would be done if I would believe it, has again been reestablished. It was so easy for me to become psychologically dependent on certain drugs because I was physically and psychologically dependent on them for years.

This choice is for me, and I am not advocating it for anyone else. Although His grace is for all of us, the precious Holy Spirit is the one who must lead and guide you. Never give up your medication or medical care on impulse as a result of reading another's testimony. Remember, He is your personal Savior, and He will lead and guide you in all truth. He knows your frame, and He is able to accomplish anything in you when you allow Him to work and do His good pleasure. My great desire was to be medication free again and to once again rely solely on God. He said: "Delight in Me and I will give you the desires of your heart" (see Ps. 37:4), and that is exactly what He did for His *"Pearl at a Great Price."*

The year of 1995 has also brought tragedy: On Mother's day, May 14, 1995, I received a call from my only son Ricky, who was in Louisiana. Two days later, on May 16, 1995, he was killed in a fall from a roof. His body was brought back to Saratoga Springs, New York, so he might be buried at the place of his birth.

After I laid my son to rest, the Lord gave me Isaiah 50:7:

For the Lord God will help me; therefore shall I not be confounded: therefore have I set my face like a flint, and I know that I shall not be ashamed.